THE CORRUPTION OF
REALITY

A Unified Theory
of Religion, Hypnosis,
and Psychopathology

JOHN F. SCHUMAKER

 **Prometheus Books**

59 John Glenn Drive
Amherst, New York 14228-2197

Published 1995 by Prometheus Books

99 98 97 96 95   5 4 3 2 1

Library of Congress Cataloging-in-Publication Data

Schumaker, John F.
    The corruption of reality : a unified theory of religion, hypnosis, and
psychopathology / John F. Schumaker.
        p.   cm.
    Includes bibliographical references and index.
    ISBN 0-87975-935-6 (hard)
    1. Reality. 2. Reality principle (Psychology) 3. Psychotherapy.
I. Title.
BD331.S414   1995
110—dc20   94-41812
                                                                 CIP

Printed in the United States of America on acid-free paper.

To my wife, Cheryl, without whom this book would not be possible. And to my brother, Tom, who taught me more than he knows.

Contents

Preface

The peculiar course of my career, as well as my life, determined to a large extent the contents of this book. It is one that deals simultaneously with the topics of religion, hypnosis, and psychopathology. A background in clinical psychology explains my interest in psychopathology, or what is also termed abnormal behavior or mental illness. My interest in hypnosis dates back to my early adolescent years which saw me experimenting with self-hypnosis in various ways. Much later, as an academic, I became intrigued by the ways in which autohypnotic processes are involved in the construction of psychological symptoms. Then, shortly after taking up a teaching position in Africa nearly twenty years ago, I developed an interest in the powerful therapeutic techniques of traditional healers. It became apparent that most of these could be understood as superior versions of what we in the West call hypnosis. Moreover, I learned that traditional "hypnotic" healing practices are typically a part of the religious or spiritual practices of these non-Western societies.

The workings of religion have captured my imagination for many years. About ten years ago, I began researching the relationship between religion and mental health, an activity that culminated in my recent book *Religion and Mental Health*. Once I began to study the dynamics of religion in global perspective, I discovered that, with the partial exception of Western society, the religions of the world have an unmistakably hypnotic component. With all the above similarities in mind, it did not seem unreasonable to entertain the prospect that religion, hypnosis, and psychopathology were overlapping manifestations of a single general human faculty. As I looked further into this possibility, the pieces of the theoretical puzzle fell into place with remarkable ease. But this happened only after I realized the unifying factor, or common denominator, in these three categories of behavior.

In some respects, this book is an extension and elaboration of some of the ideas that I introduced in my earlier book *Wings of Illusion* (1990). The core thesis of this work was that greatly amplified intelligence, as an evolutionary strategy, forces the human being to seek psychological sanctuary in the form of illusion and self-deception. While writing *Wings of Illusion*, I was influenced strongly by the works of Ernest Becker and Otto Rank, both of whom realized that the most important question to be answered is, "On what level of illusion were we meant to live?" That question is also a main feature of this book as it explores our remarkable ability to dismantle and reconstruct reality in strategic ways.

In *Wings of Illusion*, I focused in a somewhat philosophical way on the disaster that awaits us as we continue to *transcend* reality at a time when we must be facing and accepting reality. I blamed our unique type and degree of destructiveness (including ecological destruction) on our capacity to deceive ourselves about the world in which we live. Organized religion was singled out as a primary means whereby cultures foster illusions that serve us in one way, but threaten us in another. One critic of *Wings of Illusion* went on radio, and also published a book review, describing it as the most "immoral" book he had ever encountered. This was based on the critic's sentiment that the book's theory was plausible to a degree that belief (and even hope) could be undermined. While this book is less existential in flavor, and less pessimistic in tone, I suspect it will attract similar sorts of criticism.

Following the publication of *Wings of Illusion*, I was nagged by the feeling that I had tried to do too much in the span of one book. Additionally, I feared that some of the book's theoretical content was overshadowed by its emotive and controversial elements. In particular, there was one important theme that I felt compelled to explore further. This had to do with the essential *sameness* of three broad categories of human behavior, namely religion, hypnosis, and psychopathology. In retrospect, this particular theme was not developed sufficiently in *Wings of Illusion*. Moreover, my thinking at the time was that human *suggestibility* was the principal factor that united religion, hypnosis, and psychopathology. While suggestibility certainly plays an indispensable role in these three categories of behavior, I came to understand that an even more fundamental ability was at work. This ability, known as *dissociation*, threads together the various topics of this book. Dissociation, although not a new idea, is one of the most exciting concepts in psychology, one that stands to reshape large parts of the discipline, and several related disciplines.

As with my other writings, the theoretical picture I paint here is done with a large brush and broad brushstrokes. This I feel can be a fruitful alternative, or supplement, to highly focused research that asks small questions and provides answers with little scope for reformulating our understanding of ourselves. My goal was to give some shape to the bigger picture, and to fill in details wherever I felt able and sufficiently knowledgeable. However, many more details remain to be added, and hopefully this work will stimulate theorists and researchers to improve the overall picture with needed detail. If this is done, we may begin to take seriously the idea of a *unified* theory, possibly even a unified theory that explains far more than the three subject areas of this book.

I was advised by a sociologist colleague of mine not to use the word "unified theory" in the title of this book. He said that sociologists would be immediately turned off to it since any talk of a unified theory is currently very much out of favor in the field of sociology. My colleague added that the notion of unification entails the sort of reductionism that is also not fashionable, especially in sociology. My cowardly first reaction was to replace the term "unified theory" with "integrated understanding." But soon I came to accept that I had, in fact, sought to develop a theory that could *unite* religion, hypnosis, and psychopathology to the extent that these three can be regarded as essentially the *same*. The fact that they look different and are acted out in different contexts does not negate their essential sameness. Thus I decided to retain "unified theory" in the book's subtitle, even though the theory is by no means complete and even though this breaks with popular academic trends.

As for the matter of reductionism, I did *reduce* the topics in question—so much so, in fact, that each was stripped bare of misleading disguises. Only this made it possible to reach deeper understandings and to create a new foundation on which to expand our knowledge. Regrettably, some religious people are bound to take offense at the way in which religion is "reduced" to a type of dissociative responding. Like *Wings of Illusion*, this book might be labeled "immoral," since religion is exposed as a form of strategic reality corruption designed to serve the individual and society. In defense of my approach, however, I believe that an elemental knowledge of ourselves, which includes our religious natures, puts us in a much better position to promote the type of change that is required at this point in time. This change can come in the form of new and far more effective psychotherapeutic methods to deal with the current epidemic of mental disturbance. The theoretical model presented here also opens the way for new revolutionary treatments of our sickly culture, including its pathological values that are pushing us toward extinction.

I would like to thank Paul Kurtz and Prometheus Books for their continuing support. I am also grateful to Eugene O'Connor for his thoughtful and painstaking editorial assistance.

1 The Problem of Reality

Thinkers continue to be puzzled by what will be the central topics of this book, namely religion, hypnosis, and so-called abnormal behavior. The fundamental nature of each remains a mystery despite a long history of debate and scientific investigation. While all three phenomena are highly complex in their own right, the reason for our persistent ignorance is quite simple. Our general approach has been to attempt understandings of these aspects of behavior *within* their own confines. To do so is to limit one's knowledge to the vocabulary and concepts indigenous to these different areas of study. Over time, these take on a life of their own, one that is self-sustaining and largely immune to competing propositions. However, each comes into a new focus when examined in the broader framework of over-lapping manifestations of behavior. As we explore religion, hypnosis, and psychopathology in each other's light, it becomes clear that they are part of a single story, namely, the *regulation of reality*.

Our quest for a broad-based understanding must also take us beyond the body of knowledge that is available to us within our own culture. To this end, I will examine these topics as they present themselves in different cultural settings. In so doing, it will become apparent that, despite many superficial differences, the same general picture emerges in virtually all cultures of the world. It has been the tradition in the social sciences to direct their attention to the *differences* that exist between cultures. Without question, much has been learned from such investigations. Yet we have done this to the point almost of excluding from our studies those aspects and elements of culture that are *constant*. Radical cultural relativists sometimes deny the existence of universal explanatory mechanisms. This precludes the development of any unified theory of human behavior, and limits our knowledge to the differences that exist across cultures. My approach will be to continue to explore variations in behavior while attempting to show that *common* forces exist in all human cultures.

Our journey will also take us across the unfortunate lines that separate academic disciplines. While I was schooled in psychology, and in particular clinical psychology, I would be the first to concede that there is a need to draw on knowledge from other related fields. These include sociology, anthropology, philosophy, and the biological sciences. All these fields have an important place in the theoretical formulation to follow.

At the heart of my thesis is the firm conviction that the theoretical and conceptual boundaries between religion, hypnosis, and psychopathology are largely artificial. I also believe that recent advances in all three fields have paved the way for an *integrated* model. In showing that all three are variations on the same theme, I will give special attention to a fascinating cognitive process that represents the key *common denominator* in all three behavioral categories. This is the dissociation-suggestion mechanism that has itself been shrouded in mystery, myth, and errant assumptions. When these are swept aside, this unique *ability* reveals itself as the pivotal process enabling humankind to *regulate* what is here being called "reality." Since reality is also a controversial construct, let us begin with a discussion of this slippery term.

WHAT IS REALITY?

In their much-heralded book *The Social Construction of Reality*, Peter Berger and Thomas Luckmann maintain that human reality is an artifact of the *culture* in which individuals find themselves.[1] In stating their case, they describe the ways in which language, institutions, and socialization practices function to construct, or "legitimize," the structure and content of reality. While Berger and Luckmann draw a distinction between objective and subjective reality, they claim that both these realities are constructed at the level of culture. They are quite unequivocal in asserting that "society exists as both objective and subjective reality."[2] Similarly, David Heise discusses reality within a social constructionist framework, while stating that truth cannot be used as a criterion by which to define reality.[3] He argues this position on the basis that "truth" varies across different social groups, and that what is "true" in one society may be "false" in another.

Certainly, one cannot deny that there is some substance to such a view. The reality of a Tibetan monk is certainly different from that of an Oklahoma used car dealer, which is again different from the reality of a Kung bushperson living in Botswana's Kalahari desert. Culture is almost certain to be an influential agency in the shaping of subjective reality; indeed, it even seems reasonable to speak of objective reality in terms of culture. Throughout human history, cultures have served as conveyors of "knowledge" or "facts" that became the building blocks of people's *impressions* of objective reality. Growing up in my own culture and subculture, I acquired among many other things the "knowledge" that poison ivy is noxious, that the earth is round, and that Lutherans can never go to heaven. Another person, in another culture or at a different point in history, might have assimilated the cultural "knowledge" that ringed snakes are deadly, that the earth is flat, and that the gods can only be appeased by sacrificing virgins.

Since some cultural "knowledge" is true and some false, it is highly misleading to speak of objective reality in terms of the information that derives from cultural sources. It is true that culture tends to *homogenize* people's conceptions of reality. But objective reality implies a reality that has a consistency beyond the purely relativistic one espoused by some cultural relativists. In their view, objective and subjective reality are basically the same thing, since no account is taken of reality as it exists in a *truly* objective way. Their entire formulation is thus limited to the human *perception* of reality.

David Heise acknowledges that social constructionist formulations of reality are sometimes unremittingly relativistic to the point of being nihilistic. He also admits that, even within the nihilistically inclined field of sociology, many people find such a stance to be extreme. And there is good reason for dissension, since one must do more than depict reality as an ever elusive figment of cultural imagination. The earth, for example, has a certain shape at any one point in time. That shape remains what it is, despite the culturally transmitted shape entertained by individuals. I suppose that some cultural relativists would disagree, saying that the earth *is* flat if that is a feature of an individual's socially constructed reality. Likewise, they would say that the earth *is also* round if that is an element of the reality of another person from a different cultural setting. But unless one abandons oneself completely to nihilism, simple logic should tell one that the earth cannot be *both* round *and* flat.

In his book *The New Skepticism*, Paul Kurtz refers to a reality that remains constant despite the endless number of ways that we interact with the world via our activities, and the different ways that reality can be interpreted:

> . . . there is a real world out there, but we interact, modify, or interpret it in different ways in terms of our contexts or fields of behavior. But the world does not evaporate into, nor is it totally assimilated by, a person's action. Reality is not equivalent to activity; activity presupposes a real world independent of oneself. It is that which exists and causally interacts with other things, separate and distinct from an intersubjective community of observers. And it is that which endures and functions in some sense independent of my activities. . . . The real is that which exists or would exist if I were not around, but I could say little about it if I did not observe, study, probe, manipulate, or use it.[4]

In my opinion, it is inappropriate to use the term "objective" reality as Berger and Luckmann used it earlier. According to *truly* objective reality, the earth is round in shape. The objective reality of which Berger and Luckmann spoke should be again understood as the culturally influenced *perception* or interpretation of objective reality. It is hardly more stable than the subjective reality to which they also made reference. As Kurtz also realizes, there is an important difference between knowledge and impressions, and between knowledge and belief. It is not sufficient to equate belief with knowledge. Instead, in Kurtz's view, there are objective "anchors" in the real world that exist independently of beliefs, imagination, dreams, fantasies, and so forth.[5] It is even possible to judge the veracity of these mental constructions in terms of their alignment or misalignment with the objective "anchors" to which Kurtz refers.

In contrast with some prevailing schools of thought in sociology and anthropology, the fields of psychology and psychiatry have long histories of recognizing a stable reality that can be used as a touchstone by which to assess the personal reality of individuals. There would be no hesitation in saying that someone deviated from "real" reality if, for instance, that person claimed that he/she was Napoleon. Conversely, I know of no sane mental health professional who would take the position that such a person *was* Napoleon because this particular belief was an aspect of the personal reality of that person.

The phrases "real reality" and "unreal reality" are redundant and conceptually perplexing. The situation is little better for the words "objective" and "subjective" as they relate to reality, since they have attracted so many contradictory meanings. For my purposes, I would like to select, not the usual two, but rather three different terms in order to describe human reality. Although the addition of an extra category adds a certain amount of complexity, it does serve to clarify the confusion that has arisen regarding *socially* constructed reality, while permitting us to speak more confidently about *individual* constructions of reality. Brief mention will now be given to each of the three ways in which the concept of reality must be understood.

Primary Reality

Primary reality is reality as it would present itself if *only* that information or data available to the person were used as the building blocks of reality. This does not, however, mean that primary reality would necessarily be the result of rational modes of mental activity, such as critical and analytical thinking, reasoning, and so forth. Nor does it refer to "ultimate" reality in the sense that everything is known about an event or object. Instead, primary reality is *uncorrupted* and unbiased because the creature does not modify, translate, or otherwise distort incoming information. This category of reality is reserved for nonhuman animals, due to the human being's natural tendency to rely on *non*rational, as well as rational, modes of cognition in the formation of its unique *blended* reality.

Virtually all nonhuman animals operate within primary reality. Consider the squirrel. With no added bias from higher-order distortive mechanisms, the reality of a squirrel is a comparatively stable primary one wherein *things are as they are*. An acorn always remains something to eat or to stick into the hole of a tree. In the absence of the cerebral apparatus to *misinterpret* an acorn, squirrels never have acorn gods, nor do they ever develop acorn phobias. When another squirrel dies, decomposes, and disappears, the remaining squirrels have no ability to alter the empirical data about the squirrel's death. When the dead squirrel is gone, it is gone. The primary reality of a squirrel does not permit a squirrel heaven or a happy acorn ground in an afterlife. Quite simply, there are no data to indicate, either to a squirrel or to ourselves, that there exists an afterlife. Because of its brain design, the squirrel is prevented from reinterpreting empirical data, which gives it exclusive access to primary reality.

On the other hand, human beings have only one cerebral foot on the ground. They possess a talent that automatically banishes them from primary reality, at the same time offering endless other possibilities over the squirrel and all other nonhuman creatures. Berger and Luckmann gave the "dog-world" and the "horse-world" as examples of comparatively stable realities that differ from our own, proposing that the difference can be understood by degree of *instinctual determination*. That is, nonhuman animals "live in closed worlds whose structures are predetermined by the biological equipment of the several animal species."[6] This, according to Berger and Luckmann, contrasts with the "man-world," which has "no species-specific environment, no environment firmly structured by [its] own instinctual organization."[7]

But a point of clarification is essential here. While I agree that nonhuman animals have a generally stable reality by comparison with human reality, Berger and Luckmann ignore an important fact in arriving at their conclusion. It is that a large proportion of non-human animal behavior is acquired through social learning, in much the same way that it is done for human beings. Even the humble squirrel must learn that it is to eat acorns, and that a certain squeal from its mother means to scamper up the tree to safety. Furthermore, the Berger and Luckmann model discounts the ways in which some dimensions of human behavior are locked into biologically determined patterns. These may not be as obvious as those appearing in other species, but they do exist.

We might even go to the heart of the matter about reality and ask why it is that human beings, in all cultures, construct for themselves a reality that is not strictly empirical in nature. Why, all throughout our history, have we harbored irrational and often wildly false notions about the empirical world and our place in it? It is said that Socrates frequently began his speeches by imploring his listeners not to be angry with him if he tells them the truth. One gets the sense that Socrates definitely knew that falsehoods and errors held a central place in the human mind.

From the perspective of human beliefs, Paul Kurtz writes about our astonishing capacity to tolerate beliefs that mock our own awesome intellectual capabilities:

> The surprising fact about human beings is that *a belief does not have to be true in order to be believed by them.* Indeed, most of the belief systems that generations of humans have heralded, lived by, and died for are in fact patently false. Yet they were held with deep conviction and fervor. . . . The fads and fallacies, delusions and fantasies that people have believed in are so numerous in human history that they constitute, as it were, the very fabric of our cultural existence. The list of erroneous belief systems is endless. . . . Human culture is comprised of the castles in the sand that we have constructed. . . . These are the products of our fertile imaginations and especially our yearnings for other worlds. The web of human civilization contains both the ingenious ways that humans have developed for understanding and dealing with the world with clarity and precision and the extraordinary palliatives and smoke screens that they have laid down for themselves.[8]

The universality of the distortion of primary reality requires us to consider that this phenomenon is not simply the result of society acting upon an otherwise structureless human being. Instead, as Kurtz argues, "there are powerful drives in the human species that often lead human beings to subvert their senses and reason and to accept popular delusions. These tendencies are rather general, and they may be invariant in all cultures."[9] Yet human beings are also capable of arriving at what Kurtz terms *reliable knowledge*. It is well within our abilities to process incoming information in order that our mental constructions correspond to primary reality. The fact that we so often miss the mark in this regard is owing to our tandem ability to regulate reality to suit our ends. This contradiction will sort itself out as we explore the peculiar workings of dissociation and *divided* methods of consciousness and unconsciousness. We will come to see that, as a consequence of our unique brain design, there is a highly fluid quality to human reality. This requires that any social constructionist theory of human behavior must take into account the physiological processes that are responsible for the *consistent* patterns that exist alongside the differences in behavior.

Personal Reality

Personal reality refers to the reality of the *individual* organism. For the nonhuman realm of the animal world, the reality of the individual animal overlaps exactly with primary reality. They are one and the same. Again this is because nonhuman animals do not have the sophisticated brain faculties required to *translate* and then retranslate incoming empirical information in such a way that reality can become virtually anything at the level of the individual.

To the human being, acorns can be little bombs planted by aliens from outer space (an aspect of the reality of a paranoid person). Or they can be the source of powerful magic, capable of ensuring the immortality of a dead person if the corpse is dusted with burnt acorn powder prior to burial (an aspect of the reality of certain former religious beliefs). Or an acorn can be merely an acorn. Many options are open to members of our species, and we naturally try to avail ourselves of them for purposes of social, psychological, and physical survival.

Culture usually specifies the alternatives to a strictly empirically based reality. But, in our species, the reality of the *person* never overlaps completely with reality as it would be constructed with empirical or factual data only. This is true in "normal" as well as "abnormal" individuals. Also not exempt are the existential pathfinders who consider themselves to be at the front lines of the truth. Their personal reality is also skewed and biased, albeit with superficial differences in the appearance of that bias. Human reality is destined to contain large amounts of error. In saying this, I am using primary reality as the criterion by which to gauge the world as it *really* is.

It must be conceded, however, that primary reality could also be false as it reveals itself to us. Take the acorn once more. It may be that acorns *are* little bombs, or that their burnt dust *is* the bestower of everlasting life. But in using empirical data to define *real* reality, one is proceeding on the basis of available data and probabilities and/or improbabilities. Therefore, it is highly improbable, in light of empirical data, that an acorn is an alien's bomb or that burnt acorn dust defeats the problem of mortality.

Religion cannot be given special consideration if we are to understand the principles of reality regulation. So, similarly, it must be said that, *in all likelihood*, religious beliefs are examples of adaptive cognitive errors. They are *probably* false because they are constructed in defiance and ignorance (in the sense of "ignore") of available empirical data. Thus they are deviations from primary reality.

We *know* that this is largely the case, since the thousands of religions in the world contain beliefs that directly *contradict* one another, thereby canceling out their credibility. For example, it cannot *both* be true that a bird-god gave birth to this planet four million years ago in the form of an egg, and also that the planet was born six thousand years ago when, over the course of six days, a different god created the earth one step at a time. Even so, there is no way of knowing that *all* religious beliefs are inaccurate, since their premises are not circumscribed by empirical evidence. Yet, with the aid of simple logic, we can safely say that most religious beliefs are *probably* false. They are certainly useful, however, as will be seen.

It is interesting to speculate about the birth of personal reality. That is, when did human beings develop the cerebral skills required in order to construct a reality that was deviant from primary reality? In my earlier book *Wings of Illusion*, I proposed that this occurred when the human brain reached a critical developmental threshold wherein we became conscious to a potentially debilitating degree.[10] It was then that a tandem brain capacity was needed to *absorb*, so to speak, the collision between amplified consciousness and many emotionally terrifying and confusing facets of this-world existence. New irreconcilable conflicts needed resolution, and new unanswerable questions demanded pacifying answers. The future viability of nature's experiment with the big brain depended on an evolutionary move that would preserve the many advantages of elevated consciousness, while simultaneously reducing the emotional impact of that same adaptation.

This evolutionary strategy came in the form of the capacity of the brain to *dissociate itself from its own data.* More specifically, the human brain gained the ability to (a) selectively perceive its environment, (b) selectively process information, (c) selectively store memories, (d) selectively disengage from already stored memories, and (e) selectively replace dissociated data with more "user-friendly" data.

Ultimately, this empowered human beings, like no animal before us, to *regulate* their own reality. One might compare this capacity to an automatic thermostat that regulates the temperature of a room, except that our ability to regulate is infinitely more sophisticated. The following chapter will attempt to isolate the actual brain-level processes involved in this astonishing evolutionary feat, in order to show that it is the cognitive basis for religion, hypnosis, and most forms of mental disturbance.

In short, personal reality defines itself by its deviation from primary reality, even though personal reality partially overlaps with primary reality. For most people, then, personal reality amounts to empirical reality *plus* or *minus* whatever *empirically unjustified* modifications or biases are made to empirical reality.

One can only speculate about the *degree* of bias that features in personal reality. Ernest Rossi, an Ericksonian hypnotherapist, estimated that at least 80 percent of the information contained in the human mind is *false.*[11] What makes this estimate more remarkable is that Rossi was referring to the vast quantity of error that is entertained, not as a result of formal hypnosis, but during the normal waking state. And here we are not talking about an animal with insufficient brain power to get things right. Instead, we are dealing with the creature with the most highly developed cerebral cortex. Yet, despite our cerebral talents, it seems that the mental world of the human being is often at odds with the true nature of things. Not only that, we will fight to preserve what is false. We do this while also, paradoxically, apprehending the world with astonishing precision. As a result, any useful theory about human behavior must explain the fundamental contradiction which is our capacity simultaneously to construe and misconstrue the world about us.

Whatever the actual extent of our cognitive error, it should be remembered that the generation of this error is the consequence of intricate cerebral processes that safeguard the integrity of the entire nervous system. Also, attempts to estimate the proportion of error in personal reality ignore the fact of individual differences. We should expect a substantial amount of variation regarding the distortive component of personal reality. These are reflective of situational, constitutional, and sociocultural factors that weigh differentially upon people. The actual *content* and *emotional valence* of the error contained in personal reality determines whether we describe that error as religion, psychopathology, or something else.

Cultural Reality

The inclusion of a category with the label "cultural reality" reinforces what was said previously about the "social construction" of reality. The reality of the individual is *to some extent* the result of constructions that are fabricated and propagated by culture. We are all tattooed from birth with indelible beliefs and understandings as they are served up to us by the culture into which we are born. However, this does not necessarily imply that all people rally around a single culture which manufactures a single set of messages, or suggestions. Granted, in many instances, the vast majority of those born within a specific culture will endorse the dominant core of that culture. For example, most adult people in contemporary Western culture would not feel threatened at the prospect of allowing their children to receive an education. Indeed, the majority would probably see it as a positive and worthwhile undertaking. But certain individuals are also subject to the influence of any number of subcultures which, together, make up the composite culture. Even with regard to the matter of the desirability of education, one could point to significant Western subcultures wherein education is viewed with fear and suspicion (e.g., the Amish and Mennonites). Therefore, our approach to the concept of culture must be flexible enough to include the shaping forces of subcultures, as well as those of the mainstream culture. As a result, we need to define cultural reality broadly as the *constellation of externally delivered suggestions that are normalized on the basis of group endorsement*. The term "normalized" as it is used here means normal both in the sense that a suggestion has achieved *normative* status, and that it is *experienced* as normal by the person.

The above definition allows for the possibility that a suggestion can be normalized by a subculture, sometimes even if it lacks majority endorsement in that society as a whole. One question that immediately arises is this: How *large* and/or cohesive must a group be for it to be capable of normalizing a suggestion? There is no simple answer that will apply to all individuals across all cultural contexts. While not trying to beg the question, it can only be said that a cultural suggestion becomes an element of the reality of a person when the group is, in fact, sufficiently large and/or cohesive for the person to perceive that suggestion as normal, or normative.

We see, therefore, that cultural reality refers to reality that is *shared*, or agreed upon, at the group level, even if that group is only one portion of the total population. Of course, conflicts can arise between the reality of the dominant culture and that of a subculture. For instance, some Amish children are quite literally presented with two opposing cultural realities on the issue of education, progress, technology, and so forth. As a result, conflict situations can arise later when educational and lifestyle decisions become necessary.

We saw that personal reality overlaps only partially with empirical reality, and that the capacity to err is an inevitable feature of personal reality. The same is true of cultural reality. In fact, one central function of any workable culture is to offer mental constructions of reality that are erroneous in relation to empirical reality. In a sense, culture is the central bank of cognitive distortions that provide individual members the means by which to translate empirical reality into a more acceptable form. The mass biasing of empirical reality often carries the label "religion," even though this process spills over into other terminological categories.

There may be some truth to the adage that the job of the old is to lie to the young. Likewise, Ernest Becker may have been justified in describing culture as a "macro-lie."[12] In addition to normalizing errors, culture also transmits a great deal of vital data that is in close accord with primary or empirical reality. This has the obvious advantage of delivering information that is essential for survival. But cognitive error is also a requisite for survival; therefore, cultural reality must be viewed as an intentional and necessary blend of information and misinformation.

Since both cultural reality and personal reality overlap partially with empirical reality, we must next consider the overlap between personal and cultural reality. In the same way that the individual can *self*-control empirical reality, the individual can take *self*-initiative in modifying cultural reality. Under hypothetically ideal social and situational conditions, individuals would have little need to deviate much from culturally constructed reality. In most instances, alterations to cultural reality are made only when situational and/or intra-psychic factors deem this to be necessary. However, the general breakdown of traditional systems of religion, such as we have seen over the past three centuries, can also lead to widespread individual modifications to cultural reality.

In the pages to follow, the concept of reality will be discussed from many angles. For practical purposes, the word "reality" will be used without making reference to one of the above categories. When this is done, the reader can assume that I am referring to primary reality. In most instances where I am referring to other than primary reality, the context should make clear which of the other possible definitions I am referring to.

I have been using the term "regulation" as it relates to reality since the word connotes four qualities that are unique to the human experience of reality. The first of these is that *reality is not a fixed thing* for human beings. The contours of one person's particular reality may differ quite dramatically at various points in time. Second, the word "regulation" implies that *personal reality is potentially inaccurate* in the sense of being out of alignment with an "anchored" primary reality that is not subject to these shifts. Third, "regulation" implies an *ongoing adjustment process that is purposeful*. Fourth, the word suggests that *some intelligence is at work*, providing the information which, in turn, determines the degree and direction of the adjustments. Since we are accustomed to equating normality with degree of contact with a reality that we imagine to be stable, the prospect of a reality regulation process casts doubt over our usual methods for defining what is normal and abnormal.

REALITY AND NORMALITY

In this section I will argue that abnormality in the sense of "out-of-touchness" with reality is a very normal thing. Moreover, total sanity, in the sense of being closely aligned to primary reality, will be depicted as a highly undesirable prescription for emotional and psychological well-being. Such peculiar and potentially offensive assertions require a few words of explanation.

As stated earlier, most psychologists and psychiatrists still assume that mental health is reflected by a person's ability to perceive reality accurately. The reverse of this reasoning has also been a popular method by which to diagnose abnormal behavior. That is, people who misperceive or misconstrue reality are mentally disturbed, or at least highly prone toward the development of psychological maladies. This typical viewpoint is voiced by Marie Jahoda in the book *Current Concepts of Positive Mental Health*: "The perception of reality is called mentally healthy when what the individual sees corresponds to *what is actually there*."[13] Yet available research paints a radically different picture of the relationship between psychological health and the mental construction of reality. In actuality, a considerable amount of insanity, in the sense of being out of touch with reality, is requisite to optimal mental health.

In line with this position, many scholars throughout the ages have described aspects of reality as so potentially noxious that people must somehow defend themselves from it. Furthermore, this seems to be a universal characteristic of our species, common to virtually all cultures of the world. Speculative wisdom about humankind's distaste for factual reality and truth dates back to the earliest writings by members of our species. Even before we mastered the art of putting pen to paper, or chisel to stone, I can imagine that certain individuals stood back for the moment, scratched their heads, and marveled at our incredible knack for entertaining the false and the unreal.

Over the past decade, increasing numbers of quantitative researchers have tested the hypothesis that people do indeed generate transformations or distortions of reality that act as prophylactics for mental health. The results of these studies are remarkably consistent, with nearly all findings indicative of a natural human inclination toward self-deception, illusion, and other health-giving biases about reality. One of the first experimental studies in this area was conducted by Harold Sackeim and Ruben Gur.[14] They employed a variety of devices aimed at giving an index of a person's ability to engage successfully in *self-deception*. In addition, they gathered information about the mental health of their subjects by determining how many symptoms of psychopathology they experienced. A subsequent statistical analysis of these data revealed a strong *negative* correlation between self-deception and psychopathology. In other words, it appears that people are less likely to suffer from psychological disorders as they become more adept at self-deception.

Harold Sackeim has written at length about the *adaptive value of lying to oneself*. According to Sackeim, "self-deceptive practices may be efficient strategies by which to promote psychological health and, at least in some circumstances, their use may lead to higher levels of functioning than their absence."[15] His overall summation coincides with that of Freud, who felt that reality was too strong for individuals to operate without the advantage of reality-distorting measures. Sackeim is also one of the first investigators to extend this line of reasoning to the area of dissociation theory, writing that dissociation may allow one part of the cognitive system to remove itself in an adaptive way from certain taxing representations of reality. In fact, dissociation is the crucial mental procedure that responds to our motivations for self-deception and other modes of reality transformation.

The best summary of other work on the relationship between reality distortion and psychological health can be found in Shelley Taylor's *Positive Illusions*.[16] For purposes of illustration, I will mention a small number of the studies that are included in her book. In all instances, they demonstrate that maximal psychological integrity should be understood in terms of our ability not only to function within reality, but also to reject and modify reality in purposeful directions. They also confirm the emerging view that illusions are the result of an *active* process by which skewed mental constructions are manufactured for the long-term and ongoing psychological benefit of the individual.

Numerous studies support a model of mental health incorporating reality distortion and self-deception as integral factors. Some of these deal with the *illusion of self-control*; that is, the illusion that individuals possess environmental or situational control that they do not have in actuality. For example, several experiments have shown that the illusion of control is inversely related to depression. That is, depressed people are less adept than nondepressed people at generating such illusions. Stated otherwise, this particular category of illusion appears to insulate people from the experience of emotional depression. Reality, it seems, is depressing. However, we can reduce the depressing effects of reality by imposing upon it the alterations that are here being called illusions.

The importance of reality distortion and self-deception in the establishment and preservation of mental health is further revealed by some interesting studies on self-consciousness and, in particular, *private self-consciousness*. This term refers to the extent to which an individual's attention is self-focused. As such, private self-consciousness is considered to be a measure of degree of *self*-insight and *self*-awareness. Theoretically, those with a high degree of private self-consciousness would be more "in touch" with themselves, including their thoughts and emotions, and to be less inclined to resort to denial, self-deception, and other related defense mechanisms. Allan Fenigstein and his associates were among those to spearhead research on this topic, using their measurement device known as the *Self-Consciousness Scale*.[17] Several studies using this scale show that people with high private self-consciousness have more accurate *self-knowledge* than those who are less self-aware. That is, self-consciousness is related to more *realistic*, and less biased, perceptions of oneself.

In terms of what was said earlier about the psychological advantages of self-deception, we would predict that self-consciousness, or self-awareness, would correlate with *negative* emotional states. Again, the reasoning would be that a failure to achieve cognitive bias results in *too much reality*, which in turn impinges deleteriously upon the person's emotional integrity. A series of recent social psychological studies demonstrates a strong positive correlation between private self-consciousness and levels of depression. These are also presented in Taylor's book *Positive Illusions*. Together, they reveal that the more people are able to favorably bias their perceptions of themselves, the less likely they are to be depressed. One might argue that the actual state of depression is causing the individual to be less effective in distorting certain realities about himself, but this does not appear to be the case. For in one study that is summarized by Taylor, mood was measured before and after subjects were made to focus attention on themselves. Under such conditions, increasing self-awareness actually *precipitated* negative emotional responses. I suspect that the same is true regarding the above-mentioned relationship between depression and the illusion of control. A failure to impose adequate amounts of distortive cognitive bias concerning the control one has over life events *causes* the depression, rather than the reverse.

So far, we have seen that we fare better emotionally if we can generate unrealistic conceptions of ourselves, including the extent to which we can control our surroundings. Another set of experimental data shows that we are also at a mental health advantage if we are adept at deceiving ourselves about our *emotions*. Some research in this area has made use of the Self-Deception Questionnaire.[18] This test measures how inclined a person is to deny, or otherwise distort, unpleasant or threatening feelings which one would expect to experience in the course of living (e.g., guilt, sorrow, anxiety, and sadness). Using this instrument, one team of researchers found that self-deception was *inversely* related to depression.[19] Thus, being able to distance oneself from certain negative emotions insulates one from the debilitating consequences of depression. Further support for this thesis comes from Frederick Gibbons, who reported that the misery of already depressed people improved when they were exposed to communications fostering *self-enhancing illusion* (i.e., the adoption of an inaccurate view that they are better off than others).[20]

In *Positive Illusions*, Taylor cites still other findings in support of a modified view of mental health, with illusion and self-deception as key mechanisms. It is demonstrated that illusions: (a) increase one's capacity for productive and creative work; (b) facilitate certain aspects of intellectual functioning; (c) improve memory relating to *focused* tasks, while inhibiting disturbing memories that could interfere with performance; (d) increase one's level of motivation and aspiration, as well as one's ability to persist toward specific goals; (e) improve quality of performance and increase likelihood of success; (f) allow us to cope more effectively with tragedy; and (g) promote physical health.

Illusions, according to Taylor and her colleagues, predictably distort reality in *positive* directions that are aggrandizing to the self as well as to the perceived world in which we live. In drawing general conclusions from the large corpus of research dealing with the psychology of illusion, Taylor writes:

> Traditional concepts of mental health promote the idea that an accurate or correct view of the self is critical to the healthy self-concept. But decades of empirical research suggest that a quite different conclusion is merited. Increasingly, we must view the psychologically healthy person not as someone who sees things as they are but as someone who sees things as he or she would like them to be. Effective functioning in everyday life appears to depend upon interrelated positive illusions . . . that make things appear better than they are.[21]

In the conclusion of her book, Taylor qualifies the overall thrust of her work by stating that "most people do not distort reality to a very substantial degree."[22] While I do not agree in general with that view, Taylor is correct in the limited context of her review of the research. In generating the illusion that we have more personal control over life events, for example, we do not usually become filled with Napoleonic delusions of grandeur and omnipotence. Self-serving cognitive biases, as they are called, tend to have roughly predictable limits that are self-constrained by the perpetrators of illusion. Taylor's comment is also accurate in the sense that human beings do not embark on a total rejection of reality as they engage in their illusions. In fact, illusions about reality are a direct consequence of the nature of reality, thus implying that the one who misreads reality is simultaneously aware of its nature. This, as will be seen, remains the case even *after* the illusion has been manufactured.

But Taylor's overall treatment of the topic of illusion fails to take into account the massive distortions of reality that are fostered and sanctioned at the level of culture. While many of these would be labeled as "religion," huge cultural alterations of reality are not necessarily limited to religion. Some political ideologies, for instance, involve an extremely high degree of active reality defiance. The same is true of the many facets of what might be termed secular fanaticism, some of which are sustainable at the subcultural level.

Many people steer away from a scientific study of religion since it is a sensitive, emotional issue. However, my own view is that religion, defined in the broadest manner possible, holds the key to a much deeper understanding of human behavior, especially in the area of abnormal behavior. This is because of the very fine line separating religion from many classes of psychopathology, with that line being culture itself. That is, without cultural sanction, most or all of our religious beliefs and rituals would fall into the domain of mental disturbance. Religion is *abnormal* in the literal sense of the word. By this I mean that, in the course of adopting religion, one is required to construe (or misconstrue) the world in terms of principles that contradict or supersede naturalistic modes of understanding.

It could even be said that, strictly speaking, religion is *abnormal* because its fundamental tenets and propositions are never *norm*-al or normative when examined across the full range of human cultures. Taylor points out that people in *all* cultures exhibit the full range of small-scale positive illusions, even though a certain degree of cross-cultural variation is bound to exist. Similarly, it is the case that all cultures possess group-enacted religion that, along with their related rituals, involve *large-scale* distortions of reality. The fact that reality distortion appears to take place at all levels makes it impossible to speak meaningfully about the "normality" or the "mental health" of human beings. Instead, if one equates mental health with reality contact, we see that it is more appropriate to speak of the different types of insanity, or psychopathologies, that characterize the mental operations of the human being. On the surface, such a statement sounds rather extreme. It is somewhat reminiscent of cynics who, throughout the ages, have made sweeping claims to the effect that everyone is insane. Yet this is exactly the case if we adhere to a strict definition of mental health as a reflection of reality contact. As we have seen, our bearings on reality are skewed and erroneous in both small and large ways.

Matters become more complicated if we consider the popular *statistical* model by which to define mental health. Accordingly, one is psychologically healthy if one is among the *majority* in relation to one's perception, understandings, and patterns of behavior. Using this reasoning, someone who is out of touch with reality would be regarded as normal if most other people were similarly removed from reality. Then, by superimposing our two differing definitions of mental health, we end up with a confounded situation in which we can begin talking about *normal abnormality*. This, in fact, is the best psychological depiction of the human being. We are well-distanced from reality and therefore abnormal in one sense. Yet we are also *norm*-al because most other people are also in retreat from reality. Again we see that human beings, unlike any other animal, have a unique system of brain capacities that enables them to convert empirical reality into any number of alternative forms. It is very human to do this, and very human to be insane according to a true reality-based definition of mental health.

At this point, we might ask if large-scale reality distortions such as those seen in group-sanctioned religion are psychologically beneficial to us in the same way as the smaller-scale "positive illusions." In light of the universality of religion, common sense would lead most people to speculate that religion somehow functions on behalf of those who partake of it. Conversely, religion's ubiquitous nature would make it difficult to argue that vast numbers of our species would take part in a form of behavior that was counterproductive or disadvantageous. Mary Maxwell deals with the subject of religion in the context of evolutionary biology, suggesting quite logically that religion evolved for reasons of survival and enhanced coping.[23] Exactly the same sentiment is offered by E. O. Wilson, who writes in *On Human Nature* that "religions are like other human institutions in that they evolve in directions that enhance the welfare of the participants."[24] For the most part, this is what we find as we explore the potential psychological and social merits of religious belief and ritual.

A great deal of recent research has examined the interaction of religion and mental health. These are summarized in my recent work, *Religion and Mental Health*.[25] In it, the value of religion is appraised in relation to such variables as depression, anxiety, sexual adjustment, self-esteem, guilt levels, psychoticism, suicide potential, well-being, self-actualization, rationality, drug use, marital adjustment, and so forth. When all evidence is viewed as a whole, it becomes apparent that religion has a *positive sum effect* on mental health.

This does not mean that religion is favorable to all dimensions of mental health, nor does it mean that all types and expressions of religion have similar positive effects. Furthermore, it cannot be said that all people experience favorable consequences by way of exposure to religion. Without question, some individuals must be seen as religious casualties. Also, not all modes or categories of religion are equally effective. But, without elaborating here on this complex subject, it is now clear that, with all considered, religion in general tends to be advantageous to psychological health. This fact also emerges from a survey of the research that compares the mental health of religious and irreligious people.[26] When traditional definitions of mental health are employed, irreligious individuals are seen to have more symptoms of psychological disturbance than their religious counterparts.

We have, therefore, a situation in which the human being appears to derive a range of benefits in the course of misreading reality. Some of these are small in magnitude and the result of adjustments made at the level of the individual. Others, such as the dramatic reality transformations of traditional religion, are achieved by way of the normalizing force of culture. Whatever their source, it is quite clear that out-of-touchness with reality is purposeful and intended to better equip us for survival. In this light, there is probably considerable truth to the observation of George Santayana, who, in *Interpretations of Poetry and Religion*, writes that "sanity is madness put to good uses; waking life is a dream controlled."[27]

Reality is something that we were meant to live in, not something that we were meant to recognize or accept. Such a conclusion seems unwarranted when we consider the heightened levels of intelligence that are the hallmark of our species. Yet one could say that it is very "intelligent" to keep reality at bay. Furthermore, our remarkably developed brains appear able to generate any quantity of cognitive error, especially if that error is affordable and enhancing from the perspective of survival. Yes, that is very intelligent indeed.

In his poem "Meru," William Butler Yeats writes that "civilization is hooped together . . . by manifold illusion."[28] Yet he also alludes to the rare person who, despite feelings of terror, pursues the truth until that person is thrown into the desolation of reality. I would not disagree that some people are less able, or even less willing, to abandon themselves to illusion in its various forms. We are reminded in this regard of the highly gifted but psychologically tormented literary figure of Eugene O'Neill. His equally gifted biographer, Louis Sheaffer, mentions the poet Richard Lebherz who saw in the dreadful eyes of O'Neill a man who was "in hell looking out at the world." Lebherz believed that O'Neill's inner hell was "the result of a man who had stripped away every illusion from his mind only to find there was nothing in the end."[29]

Historical events have made it exceedingly difficult for large segments of the population to avail themselves of the "manifold illusion" to which Yeats referred. As cultural sources of reality distortion have dried up in modern times, many people have been forced to improvise and construct personal pathways to reality transcendence, some of which carry the label of psychopathology. That aside, our composite perceptions of the world and ourselves tend to be a translated version of reality, a hybrid of truth that represents a workable (and sometimes unworkable) compromise between fact and fiction. The end result is usually, but not always, an improvement on primary reality.

It must be reemphasized that it is perfectly *norm*-al to be removed from the reality of the world and the truth of ourselves. As we replace reality with bias and distortion, we buffer the nervous system and safeguard psychological intactness. Oppositely, there are distinct psychological repercussions that stem from an overexposure to ourselves and the world in which we live. Consequently, as we proceed with our discussion of the regulation of reality, we should bear in mind that this regulatory function is a vital aspect of our peculiar method of coping. If this means that we were destined to be insane in the purest sense of the word, this should not blind us to the highly adaptive nature of our ability to manipulate reality to our own ends.

As our story unfolds, we will see that seemingly diverse classes of human behavior are actually intimately related as mechanisms by which to regulate reality. At one stage, our reformulation of these behaviors will enable us to speak of the psychopathology of religion, and the religion of psychopathology, while revealing the essential sameness of these strategies in the management of reality and emotion. First, however, it is necessary to explore the cerebral anomaly that makes possible both religion and psychopathology. In the course of outlining the dissociation-suggestion process, other uniquely human behaviors, including "hypnosis," will be cast in a new light.

2 The Mechanics of Dissociation and Suggestion

CONSCIOUSNESS AND ORDER

Many contradictory theories exist regarding the fundamental nature of conscious and unconscious functioning. The terms themselves, while very much a part of our vocabulary, can be highly misleading since they imply a duality that may not exist. Lancelot Law Whyte is one scholar who attempted to dispel the widespread view that there are two distinctly separate realms, one of which is characterized by consciousness and the other not.[1] He stated that such a model, which can be traced to Descartes, is one of the greatest theoretical blunders in human history. Beyond that, the persistence of this particular idea remains an enormous obstacle to a more accurate comprehension of our mental operations. Of this, Whyte writes that "a unified theory is possible, and lies ahead, in which 'material' and 'mental,' 'conscious' and 'unconscious,' aspects will be derivable as related components of one primary system of ideas."[2]

In my opinion, the great strength of Whyte's work lies in his assertion that *order* is the primary goal of human mental activity. Our mental processes involve themselves in an inherent *ordering tendency* that serves individual, social, and biological ends. Much of the ordering we do involves the recognition and acknowledgment of order where patterns of order exist in actuality, or *actual* reality. Order exists, for example, in the changing of the seasons. As the planet rotates on its axis, certain information reaches our senses in relation to the resultant changes in our environment. These are readily ordered by us based on our scientific knowledge of the physical world. We might call this justified order since the ordering tendency is satisfied in this case by data that correspond with primary reality.

Some might question the reliability of science and other related methods in arriving at certain conclusions, and the scientific method certainly has its limitations. Even so, some knowledge can be viewed as reliable in nature. This is what I am calling here *justifiable* order. Where I come from, for example, the seasons *do* change. Trees *do* lose their leaves and it *does* become colder in winter.

A different ordering situation presents itself if we consider the same matter of the changing seasons, but first transport ourselves to an earlier time in human history when we had no explanation for this phenomenon. According to Whyte, human beings remain in a state of "tension" until order is established. This means that tension continues to motivate the person until a time when order is achieved, even if that order must be contrived. In terms of the changing seasons, we must ask what happens when a need for order coincides with an *inability* to provide such order based on the workings of primary reality.

The solution requires the individual to establish and maintain unjustified or *artificial* order of the type described by Michael Gazzaniga in his book *The Social Brain*.[3] In his explanation of the inevitability of religious beliefs, Gazzaniga argues that the human brain evolved in such a way that it became capable of arriving at *greater order than it perceives*. Stated otherwise, the human brain can, when required, lower dramatically its own criteria for accurate reality testing, the goal of which is to arrive at order that would otherwise be rejected on the basis of available information. Even though we might be at a total loss to make orderly sense of disorder, we will nonetheless forge ahead and concoct order where there is none. This is a predictable species-specific form of behavior that reduces the "tension" accompanying the experience of disorder.

Artificial order, while essential to the integrity of our psychic systems, is more complicated and energy-intensive than justified order. It requires an additional set of mental operations whereby *contraindicative* information is eliminated. This is essential before unjustified mental constructions are entertained with any degree of confidence. Only by *eliminating* competing data from consciousness can artificial order be achieved, and "tension" reduced. It is exactly here that one must propose a process whereby artificial order becomes possible by way of *dis-association* from knowledge or cognitive capabilities that would otherwise preclude this type of order. This will be done as we understand religion and psychopathology (and, indirectly, hypnosis) as systems of artificial order that are dependent upon an active dissociation process. But first we should attempt to put our need for artificial order in its rightful perspective.

Viewed in its widest context, the remarkable way in which the human being creates artificial order is a direct consequence of its unique evolutionary history. At one stage, our brains reached what Whyte termed a "historical discontinuity," a developmental threshold wherein we became capable of recognizing, and being negatively affected by, disorder.[4] Until that time, we were confined to primary reality, finding order only where order existed in the actual world. No gods or angels existed prior to this cerebral "historical discontinuity." Just as religion was impossible, then so too were the types of psychopathology that have come to carry the somewhat misleading label of "neurosis." Quite simply, neither religion nor madness was necessary since order, or the lack thereof, was not yet a problem.

At one crucial stage in the development of our brains, however, we were exposed to new types of information that either defied order or could not be ordered without negative emotional repercussions. A solution came in the form of two *abilities* that would be unique to our species, namely religion and psychopathology. These two abilities emerged *simultaneously* in our evolutionary past and both remain very closely related in the roles they play in establishing patterns of artificial order. Religion and psychopathology, as they would come to be known, became the two major mental strategies to regulate reality and thereby safeguard us from the expanding powers of our brains.

In my earlier book *Wings of Illusion*, I have written a more detailed account of our passage across the "cerebral Rubicon," an evolutionary milestone that ushered us into the realm of the irrational. Once we fell victim to the "collision of amplified consciousness and reality," we found ourselves in a hybrid reality that rested on error, self-deception, and bias.[5] But here I wish to take this line of reasoning one step further by examining dissociation as the brain mechanism that makes it possible for us to create artificial order, and thereby regulate reality in meaningful, albeit nonsensical, ways. At that point, it will become clear that religion, hypnosis, and psychopathology are explainable according to the same brain mechanism and the same underlying patterns of motivation.

THE FACULTY OF DISSOCIATION

In general, the error pervading the human mind in the form of illusion and artificial order is not the result of passive ignorance. On the contrary, it is a complex mental operation that has two essential components. The first of these deals with the means by which the brain can *disengage* itself in such a way that information will be processed in contravention of its own capacity for accurate higher order information processing. In the course of this, the person essentially prevents or blocks a conclusion that would otherwise present itself in light of available information.

The second step in the operation concerns the manner in which the person is delivered false alternatives that serve as functional surrogates to the rejected portions of reality. This process will be considered in the next section, when we discuss internal and external suggestion in relation to the mechanism of dissociation. Here let us introduce the concept of dissociation by asking how it is that we highly intelligent creatures are able to entertain error that should not exist given our sophisticated brains. A more succinct form of the question would be this: "How do we manage to accept, and act in accordance with, *error that we know to be error*?" Such a question seems to imply that the human mind is multidimensional, with its different dimensions acting independently of one another. This is exactly the case and it is only this situation that makes possible all forms of reality modification, including religion and psycho-pathology.

Most everything we are and do is the end result of *associations* made between two or more elements of our internal and/or external experience. A young girl might make an association between her father and pleasant sensations that derive from him when he throws her in the air and then catches her. Without her being conscious of the association itself, it will be one of many associations that guides the girl's future behavior. In fact, a great deal of our behavior revolves around these and endless other types of associations.

Human beings would not be so difficult to comprehend if we were guided *only* by associations. Our behavior might even be explained and predicted by some of the popular learning theories that see us simplistically as accumulations of learned associations. Unfortunately, we are considerably more complex than that. The human brain is equipped to be *selective* about the associations it makes, with the selection process representing a type of intelligence that has so far eluded our understanding. In addition, the brain has the means by which to sense, without conscious intervention, any "toxic" associations that need to be *dissociated* in order to maintain psychic equilibrium. Very often, dissociations have only minimal and un-observable effects on the person. At other times, they have a dramatic impact on behavior, as in the case of religion or bizarre forms of psychopathology.

In their book *The Unconscious Reconsidered*, Kenneth Bowers and

Donald Meichenbaum adduce some of the puzzling phenomena demanding that a mechanism such as dissociation be at the center of any theory of human behavior.[6] These include pathological syndromes such as fugue, multiple personality disorder, depersonalization and other anomalies of memory, sleepwalking and sleeptalking, dreams, and hypnosis. To this list I would add religion since it involves cognitive, perceptual, and affective distortions that are completely dependent upon dissociation. Also, a growing number of mental health professionals are coming to realize that dissociation is the common basis by which to understand nearly the full range of mental disturbances. Research supports this position and, as we will discuss in a later chapter on psychopathology, dissociation has been implicated in many disorders, including obsessive-compulsive disorder, phobia, paranoia, eating disorders, post-traumatic stress disorder, multiple personality disorder, psychogenic amnesia, and others. It has also been proposed that dissociation is the faculty enabling all types of trance states, possession, faith healing, shamanism, visionary experiences, age regression, glossolalia, and automatic writing.

John Kihlstrom and Irene Hoyt emphasize the splitting or dividing of consciousness that dissociation makes possible:

> Dissociation involves two cognitive states of affairs. First, there must be a division of consciousness into multiple, simultaneous streams of mental activity influencing experience, thought, and action. In addition, one of these streams must influence mental life outside of phenomenal awareness and voluntary control. The first is compatible with contemporary views of attention, which hold that attention can be allocated among several activities as long as the total requirements of the tasks do not exceed the total amount of available resources.[7]

Dissociation is defined by Yvonne Dolan as "the mental process of splitting off information or systems of ideas in such a way that this information or system of ideas can exist and exert influence independently of the person's conscious awareness."[8] A somewhat similar definition is given in the *Psychiatric Dictionary*, where dissociation is defined as:

> the segregation of any group of mental processes from the rest of the psychic apparatus. Dissociation generally means a loss of the usual interrelationships between various groups of mental processes with resultant almost independent functioning of the one group that has been separated from the rest.[9]

In order to appreciate the far-reaching effects of the dissociative mechanism, we might consider the slightly more technical definition offered by Louis West. Like the others, it stresses the role of the *compartmentalization* of information that is made possible by this feature of cognition. Dissociation is "a psycho-physiological process whereby information—incoming, stored, or outgoing—is *actively deflected from integration with its usual or expected associations.*" West goes on to say that dissociation allows "a discernible *alteration in a person's thoughts, feelings, or actions . . . an experience that may or may not be considered psychopathological.*"[10] Of key importance here is the idea that dissociation provides a means by which incoming information can be *deflected* from the course of its usual associations. Similarly, West's definition draws attention to the intellectual, emotional, and behavioral *alterations* that are made possible through the mechanism of dissociation, regardless of whether or not they are experienced and deemed as psychopathological in nature.

Fred Frankel wrote that "at the heart of dissociation is a disconnectedness or lack of integration of knowledge, identity, memory, and control."[11] While many thinkers on the subject would agree with that general observation, there has been a variety of viewpoints regarding the specific mechanisms underlying this process. Some scholars have pointed to the relative absence of critical and analytic thought that can be observed during states of dissociation. Since critical and analytical thought are generally considered to be left brain functions, there has been speculation that dissociative behavior could be the result of *cerebral hemispheric lateralization.* This refers to the different functions that are performed by the left and right hemispheres of the brain. It is often claimed that, by contrast with the "logical" left hemisphere, the right hemisphere is largely responsible for irrational modes of behavior, including religion and all types of "automatic" behavior. In addition, it seems to be the part of the brain that determines musical ability, a sense of rhythm, imagination, intuition, emotionality, and spatial ability.

Supporters of a hemispheric lateralization explanation of dissociation frequently cite the substantial body of research showing a shift of brain activity from the left to right hemisphere during states of dissociation. Lynn Frumkin and her colleagues summarize some of these studies and illustrate this phenomenon by describing the effects of the drug sodium amytal.[12] By itself, this particular drug produces a state of dissociation as well as the characteristic hypersuggestibility that follows. It is also known as "truth serum," since it is sometimes given in the course of police interviews and other types of questioning that seek to bypass people's ability to critically analyze their responses. Because of its action, some people have concluded that the *dichotomies of awareness* produced by such drugs are basically the same as those deriving from nonchemical dissociation techniques, such as formal hypnosis. This implies that the changes occurring during chemical dissociations (e.g., via sodium amytal) involve the same brain mechanisms and changes.

On the basis of such assumptions, Frumkin describes research in which sodium amytal was *unilaterally* administered to only the left brain of the subject. Then an object was placed in the person's hand. After the sodium amytal effects wore off, it was found that the person did not *verbally* know what had been in the hand. However, the person had no difficulty pointing out the object when it was presented along with a series of other objects. Since verbal ability is largely a left hemisphere function, this provided evidence that the left hemisphere had been suppressed (or dissociated) as a result of that "hypnotic" drug. Of this, Frumkin and Ripley write:

> The split in consciousness evidenced by the contrasting verbal/nonverbal reports from the amytal patients clearly resulted from a change in cerebral lateralization, namely, temporary suppression of left hemisphere dominance. The finding that hypnosis temporarily reduces left hemisphere dominance strongly suggests a possible cerebral lateralization explanation for the hypnotically induced split in consciousness.[13]

In an intriguing way, the lateralization model of dissociation fits into the broader picture of dissociation as the principle cerebral method by which to deal with the problem of reality. For example, Arnold Mandell's exciting work on the psychobiology of transcendence demonstrates that the brain's left hemisphere is prone to pessimism, depression, and emotional "tarnishing."[14] Mandell also shows, conversely, that the brain's right hemisphere has a distinct tendency to perceive the world in a "polished" fashion, with optimism and elation as emotional accompaniments. Of course, this would make perfect sense, since we would expect the critical and analytical left brain faculties to expose people to reality. We know that reality is depressing, based on research wherein reality contact is predictive of depression. On the other hand, we also know that those who are good at self-deception tend to be less depressed, or less "tarnished." If the right brain is home to self-deception and the dissociative faculties that remove people from depressing reality, it follows that the right brain would be biased toward a "rosy" outlook. Thus Mandell's findings support the theory that dissociative behavior is achieved when the right brain suppresses certain left brain capabilities.

In actuality, it is probably oversimplistic to limit one's understanding of dissociation to cortical shifts that occur between the brain's two hemispheres. This may be part of a much more complex process that operates in relation to the faculty of dissociation. Other theories about the actual mechanics of all forms of dissociative behavior, including hypnosis, have been ventured. We will consider some of these while tracing the evolution of the concept of dissociation. Many of the insights that we achieve will also be directly applicable to the topics of religion and psychopathology. For that reason, some of the examples that I will use relate to religion and psychopathology even though later chapters are devoted exclusively to those topics.

A BRIEF HISTORY OF DISSOCIATION

The concept of dissociation is often attributed to the pioneering work of Pierre Janet (1859-1947).[15] Although involved in the study and practice of hypnosis, Janet attempted to construct a general unifying theory concerning the organization of human consciousness. Dissociation was a prominent component of this grand scheme. Janet was struck by the *discontinuous* nature of consciousness, and the ways in which awareness could be sectioned off into dual or multiple parts, or even different "subpersonalities."

Janet was especially intrigued by the fact that people could *selectively forget* material and events that were dissociated from consciousness. Earlier, Mesmer had marveled at the same "amnesic barrier" that was present in some of his "mesmerized," or hypnotized patients.[16] Specifically, Mesmer realized that information available during hypnosis was sometimes unavailable once the person was in a fully awake state. However, it was not forgotten in any true sense, since that information was again accessible when the person was rehypnotized. Janet made the important discovery that *selective forgetting* could be spontaneous in certain people who had experienced various types of trauma.

Janet illustrated this in the case of Irene, a patient of his who had successfully removed herself from all memories of the death of her mother.[17] Apparently Irene had witnessed the death and had been severely traumatized by the experience. Later, if questioned about the whereabouts of her mother, Irene conceded that she must be dead because the mother was no longer around, and also because many people had informed her of her mother's death. But that intellectual supposition had no grounding in terms of the memories to which she had access. In fact, Irene insisted that she could remember absolutely nothing of any of the events which supposedly surrounded her mother's death. Even so, Janet was fully aware that such memory traces existed, since Irene would repeatedly reveal those memories in detail while she was in a "somnambulistic" (i.e., hypnotic) state.

Janet was rightly curious about the *location* of Irene's unpleasant memories when she was able to eliminate them from conscious awareness. He was dissatisfied with the crude distinction between consciousness and unconsciousness which was gaining wide acceptance at the time. As an alternative, Janet devised an extended version of the principle of association, also an accepted theoretical construct in the late nineteenth and early twentieth centuries. According to this principle, memories gain access to conscious awareness via an *association* of ideas. Janet then reasoned that those memories that were somehow prevented from association, and therefore from conscious perception, were *dis-associated*. From this logic emerged the term *désagrégation*, or dissociation. But Janet's thinking about dissociation did not develop into a fully elaborated theoretical system. In fact, he wrote in 1926 that "it is only an idea that I express. It is an hypothesis for your research."[18]

Freud and his colleague, Josef Breuer, developed a concept similar to that of Janet.[19] They proposed that the human nervous system employs *associative* thought in the course of constructing what they labeled "impressions." However, they felt that certain "hysterically" inclined individuals were somehow able to prevent traumatic "impressions" from being dealt with at the level of associative thought. In their words, "the content of consciousness becomes temporarily dissociated and certain complexes of ideas which are not associatively connected easily fly apart."[20] Freud and Breuer felt that the memory of the traumatic "impression" became dissociated and located in a separate level of consciousness, where it could exert only secondary influence by way of hysterical symptoms.

In some respects, this paralleled Janet's dissociation theory to the extent that several modes of consciousness were seen to operate simultaneously, and possibly even with some degree of independence. It now seems clear in retrospect that Freud misdiagnosed many of the psychiatric patients whose symptoms and treatment were influential in the development of psychoanalytic theory. Had Freud realized that they suffered from multiple personality disorder, and not "hysteria" as he thought, it is probable that he would have persisted with dissociation as the foundation for his theory.

As it turned out, psychoanalytic theory came to rest on the now familiar assertion that psychic integrity depends upon the maintenance of a line of defense against unacceptable thought, desires, and instinctual demands. This caused the thinking of Freud and his early associates to gravitate toward the Cartesian dualism of conscious/unconscious. In this "vertical" model of the mind, Freud postulated the existence of a repression barrier that served to prevent *unacceptable* information from reaching consciousness. This also meant that the person was *unaware*, as well as unconscious, of mentations or "impressions" that were excessively toxic.

Dissociation was largely abandoned as the mechanism by which threatening material was effectively isolated from mainstream consciousness. Instead, Freud developed the concept of repression as "a system whereby the ego accomplishes the exclusion from consciousness of the idea which was the carrier of the unwelcome impulse."[21] Consequently, dissociation disappeared as the method by which psychoanalytic theorists explained the defensive control and regulation of cognitions that were somehow diagnosed to be the source of intrapsychic conflict. Toward the time of his death, however, Freud apparently realized the flaw inherent in the notion that unconsciousness could be equated with unawareness. In a return to some of his earliest insights and intuitions, he seemed finally to comprehend that unconscious streams of thought were also "aware," even if not at the conscious level.

According to Kenneth Bowers, Freud's notion of repression can be explained largely in terms of *inattention to information*, or what he also calls *thought avoidance*.[22] Once again, Freud maintained that the essential function of repression involves the ejection from consciousness of certain cognitions. Additionally, the repression process was thought to play an *ongoing* role in depriving those cognitions of direct access to awareness. By contrast, dissociation theory involves a "horizontal" model of mind that does not equate consciousness with awareness. As such, and unlike Freud, it leaves open the possibility that there is such a thing as *unconscious awareness*, a prospect that requires us to reconsider the traditional view of the human mind as singular and unified.

It is possible to add to our knowledge of conscious and unconscious information processing by taking a critical look at the theoretical model put forth by Charles Tart. This can then be compared to the alternative model that rests on dissociation theory.[23] Tart breaks down consciousness into a set of subsystems. These include, but are not limited to: (a) *exteroception* (i.e., the sensory systems of sight, hearing, smell, taste, and touch); (b) *interoception* (sensory receptors for judging body position, pain, and so forth); (c) *input processing* (inputs involved in converting information into abstract percepts of generalized reality); (d) *memory*; (e) *identity*; (f) *evaluation* (the functions involved in decision making); (g) *emotions*; (h) *space-time sense*; and (i) *motor input*. Tart notes that all these subsystems are subject to alterations, something we know to be true from our broader understanding of various distortive procedures. Hypnosis comes to mind here since it can be employed to alter any or all of the above subsystems mentioned by Tart. Yet religious and psychopathological processes act similarly to alter the workings of these subsystems.

Tart criticizes the loose and imprecise usages that have been made of the term *consciousness*, as well as the term *altered state of consciousness*. He prefers instead to frame his discussion in relation to two slightly different concepts, namely, *discrete state of consciousness* (d-SoC) and *discrete altered state of consciousness* (d-ASC).[24] The d-SoC is defined as a system or configuration which is unique *for any given individual*, and characterized by a relatively *stable* pattern of awareness. Tart adds that this system (i.e., the d-SoC) is able to maintain an intact and recognizable identity despite the ever changing nature of environmental inputs. In terms of the d-SoC, Tart states that "our experience of our mental functioning remains within a familiar experiential space that we call our 'ordinary' state."[25] He also asserts that the processes that function to stabilize the d-SoC are highly adaptive in terms of our ability to cope with the environment and the *consensus reality* in which we live.

Tart originally viewed altered states of consciousness as the end result of a transition from d-SoC into any number of possible d-ASCs. According to that model, an individual in an "altered" state of consciousness would abandon the more stable d-SoC, at least for the duration of the altered state. In my opinion, this largely "vertical" view of consciousness does not entirely explain the way in which people are able to switch themselves from a d-ASC to the baseline d-SoC if they so "choose." That is, such a model does not specify the process that allows a person who is in an "altered" state to recognize the need to return to "generalized reality," and then to initiate such a return. We know, for example, that people in even the deepest hypnotic trance have the capacity to detect imminent danger and return to a reality-based orientation. In the same way, people in the throes of a faith-healing episode, or a deep trance séance, or a deeply altered state that allows one to drive large needles or hooks into one's body—they and others in similar altered states can *deinduce* themselves if conditions dictate a return to an "unaltered" mode of cognition. Likewise, the deeply entranced firewalker, however far removed from his/her d-SoC, will *know* when the fire is too hot (i.e., when the coals do not have sufficient ash on top of them to prevent burning).

According to Tart's earlier formulation, "deinduction" is possible because the d-SoC is "tremendously overlearned," and therefore it is the baseline mode of consciousness.[26] As a consequence, any significant disrupting stimulus will break down the integrity of the d-ASC and result in a return to the baseline mode of consciousness. This, Tart says, usually involves a transitional period during which a person's "mind" can reorganize itself in order to process information with a stable reality orientation.

The weakness with this latter proposition is that very sudden returns to an unaltered reality orientation are possible. These are potentially so quick that we must entertain the seemingly illogical prospect that the person's consciousness was somehow altered and not altered *at the same time*. Herein lies the greatest strength of dissociation theory. Its fundamental premise of multiple parallel channels of information processing opens up the possibility that the human being is capable *simultaneously* of being both "in touch" and "out of touch" with reality. Stated differently, dissociation theory permits us to consider that the composite of conscious and unconscious processes can lead to states of mind that are *both* altered and unaltered at the same point in time. The evolutionary adaptiveness of such a form of cerebral organization is obvious, since we are allowed to indulge our inherent need for cognitive dissociation (which manifests as "altered" states), while concurrently being able to safeguard ourselves from the hazards of being removed from reality.

Some of these points are highly relevant to our present discussion of the human being as a creature of *self-deception*. In the book *A Study of Self-Deception*, M. R. Haight writes that psychoanalytic theory is faulty because of its "vertical" view that unconscious material is completely cut off from the person's awareness. According to Haight, it is much more appropriate, and in accord with empirical findings, to replace the concept of unconscious with that of *conscious (i.e., aware) but dissociated*. This implies that *consciousness is a nonessential property of thought*.[27] The adaptive value of this cognitive design becomes even more apparent when one explores the dynamics of self-deception.

But first let us look again at Freud's theory of unconsciousness and consider its inadequacy as a model for self-deception. Freud saw the human being as a creature with a single consciousness and, consequently, a single narrow window of awareness. From a practical standpoint, self-deception would be virtually impossible since material ejected from consciousness would have no source of awareness that could: (a) assess that the material is still toxic and unacceptable for entry into conscious awareness; and (b) make "decisions" that energy should continue to be spent in an effort to retain a *barrier* against consciousness for that material. Freud should have realized the theoretical need for *unconscious awareness* from his own clinical work which brought him into contact with his patients' *resistances* as he sought to bring toxic unconscious material to the level of conscious awareness.

In *Being and Nothingness*, Sartre saw the shortcoming in Freud's model when he asked what it was that did the resisting during resistance.[28] If the unconscious were also unaware, there would be no theoretical provision for a censor or a monitor that could sense the danger and then generate the resistance based on an awareness of the overall situation. One could not attribute this to consciousness since, in Freud's model, consciousness no longer *knows* about that which has been ejected from consciousness once it is gone. By contrast, Sartre might say that, in order to lie to (i.e., deceive) oneself, one must always know and remember the lie at some level. Therefore, even when something is "repressed" from consciousness, there is a requisite awareness of what is being repressed. In a paradoxical way, this means that there must be *awareness that exists outside of consciousness* before it becomes possible to regulate the degree to which we are aware or unaware.

Consciousness is thus capable, on an ongoing basis, of regulating itself, but only by means of awareness that exists outside of consciousness. Again in terms of self-deception, we the deceiver must be aware of the entire self-deception process (including what it is that we must become unaware of) before we can remain deceived. This type of unconscious awareness, as Sartre recognized, is indispensable if we are to achieve unawareness of certain targeted toxic material. Ultimately, this theoretical stance leads us to the conclusion that we are never unaware of unconscious material. That being the case, we see the problem with the traditional Freudian view of so-called unconsciousness. In terms of dissociation theory, this also means that dissociated material remains at the level of awareness, although not conscious awareness.

Haight further illustrates the existence of unconscious awareness by using the example of functional fainting. It is well known that some people faint when exposed to acutely stressful situations. Freud himself fainted on two occasions, both times apparently as the result of an intense emotional crisis during his professional and personal break with Carl Jung. Yet fainting is by no means a conscious decision. For this reason, fainting is typically regarded as an involuntary response that enables a person to escape from whatever event, situation, or memory is generating the stress.

However, an important question remains concerning the *source* of the decision to faint. Undoubtedly, such a decision is based on "knowledge" about the potentially damaging effects of excessively high degrees of emotional arousal. If this is not a conscious decision, one is forced to concede that there must be some pattern of unconscious awareness and knowledge that is acting on behalf of the person when it detects the need to faint and initiates its action. In fact, functional fainting can be understood as one of the most dramatic forms of dissociation, one in which all of consciousness is eliminated in order to protect the individual.

NEODISSOCIATION THEORY AND BEYOND

Recently, Ernest Hilgard presented a revised *neodissociation* theory which has sparked a strong renewal of interest in this subject area.[29] At the heart of neodissociation theory is the view that the mind operates along *multiple and largely independent systems of cognitive control*. With special reference to *amnesic barriers*, Hilgard diagrammed the differences between his theory of dissociation and that of the traditional views explaining information that is somehow denied entry into conscious awareness.[30] With dissociation by way of *amnesia*, there is a *split* among usually available memories. Hilgard circumvents the need for the counterpart of a "preconscious" since, in his view, the unavailable memories do not need to be of a painful or unacceptable nature. In this regard, it is self-obvious that, at any one time, we need to be dissociated from the vast majority of our memories. Again, if this were not the case, consciousness would be flooded with information inputs, and order could not prevail. But Hilgard also speaks of *targets of amnesia* wherein certain specific memories are selected out for isolation from conscious awareness, a matter that will be a central theme as we discuss psychopathological and religious patterns of dissociation. But, very importantly, the targets of amnesia, although pushed out of conscious awareness, remain in awareness at the unconscious level. Thus, current dissociation theory views the mind as continually aware across the conscious-unconscious barrier, even though we might be consciously *unaware of being aware* at the unconscious level.

Hilgard illustrates dissociated systems of cognitive control by describing a situation in which a person was required to perform two tasks at once, with only one of those tasks given access to consciousness. Hypnosis was used in order to prevent the second task from entering conscious awareness. In this demonstration, Hilgard instructed the person to name colors from a chart, a rather simple task performed with conscious awareness. At the same time, one of the person's hands was concealed from view and blocked from conscious awareness with hypnotic suggestions. The person was then instructed to use the hand to perform some simple arithmetic tasks. One of those was to start with a given number and then successively to add 7's to it. Hilgard found that selected hypnotic subjects were able simultaneously to perform the two competing tasks, one of which was accomplished without any conscious awareness. A number of such experiments enabled Hilgard and his associates to show that the human brain is able to process information along parallel and potentially independent pathways. The implications are enormous since this stands to rewrite our usual models of the mind, as well as the therapeutic strategies employed to treat psychological aberrations, including the maladaptive manifestations of religion.

Somewhat parenthetically, Hilgard also makes reference to automatic writing when noting that it has been one of the most widespread methods used by mediums to convince their clients that they have made contact with the dead.[31] This was especially popular among nineteenth-century mediums who let it be known that the "spirit" was delivering a message from another world, using the medium's hand as a method of communication. Then, while the medium was engaged in various verbalizations, the hand was usually able to produce sensible messages that were seemingly independent of other activities taking place. When outright fraud is not at play, this practice is best understood as *autodissociation* whereby a person processes information on parallel pathways, and allows those two groups of information to reveal themselves by way of two different physical expressions (e.g., talking and writing). It may be as Hilgard implies, that such a dissociative exercise enables the individual to tap new levels of memory or imagination that are beyond the awareness of most of us during the ordinary waking state. Yet there is nothing magical about these and related techniques. With training, most people could improve their ability to exploit more effectively their natural capacity for dissociation. We can only hope that this exercise would not be used by unscrupulous people to exploit those who naively yearn to be reconnected with lost loved ones.

John Beahrs uses the term *co-consciousness* to describe "the existence of more than one consciously experiencing psychological entity, each with some sense of its own identity or selfhood, relatively separate and discrete from other similar entities, and with separate conscious experiences occurring simultaneously with one another."[32] Beahrs compares the human mind to a symphony orchestra since, like an orchestra, it constitutes a complex whole made up of many "part-selves." Each of these part-selves has a large degree of autonomy and each is capable of personal experience. Yet each is also operating under the organizational control of some *executive* leader (or conductor, to continue the symphonic comparison). Very importantly, Beahrs argues that *functional co-consciousness* operates in "normalcy" as well as in a variety of psychopathological disorders. He makes special reference to multiple personality disorder, but qualifies his analysis by adding that every personality is *multiple* in that "any human individual is both a unity and a multiplicity at once."[33] Furthermore, "normal" people are only to be distinguished from clinical cases of multiple personality by the *degree* of multiplicity. This, in turn, is determined by the *amnesia* separating the different systems of cognitive control, or the different "ego states," as Beahrs prefers to call them. Such a hypothesis resembles that of Hilgard who also explained the entire range of dissociative behaviors (including hypnosis) in terms of amnesic barriers between the various control systems.

This takes us back to the great unanswered question concerning the phenomenon of dissociation: What mental ability is responsible for making decisions about the actual *content* of consciousness? In Janet's case of Irene, was there an unconscious process that "knew" it was specifically her "death of mother" memories that threatened Irene's psychic integrity? As we saw earlier in the case of fainting, Irene's decision was certainly not a conscious one.

We could also take the example of a person with a conversion disorder in which that person goes blind, not because of any organic factor but as the result of witnessing a horrifying event. While again acknowledging that this is not done at the level of experienced consciousness, one could ask what set of mental or physical events led to the final decision that "blindness" would somehow serve this individual. Beahrs concludes his discussion of co-consciousness without a definitive answer regarding the executive organizing force that governs and regulates the content of consciousness. He merely speculates that the temporal lobe and certain limbic structures might be involved since they are crucial to both memory and attention. But Beahrs does ask a highly challenging question: "What process presides over these others, giving us not only our sense of selfhood, but coherence and direction to our life course?"[34] If there is an executive controller, Beahrs reasons, it would be "all knowing" and relatively autonomous in its mode of operation.

Dissociation theory has yet to come to terms with the "brain self-regulation paradox," as Gary Schwartz labels it.[35] Yet there can be no doubt that an active cerebral process, operating outside of conscious awareness, makes assessments on an ongoing basis in the course of *deciding* how and when the dissociative mechanism should distort reality by modifying the information available to us. Quite literally, this assessing function makes decisions about the ways in which reality reaches us and the ways we establish in ourselves a semblance of order. A solution to this paradox must take account of the fact that many of our mental constructions are grossly inaccurate and in complete defiance of the actual information reaching our senses. Something very significant takes place as information gets transformed in a manner that eventually serves to misinform us in any number of ways.

In our attempt to broaden our understanding of dissociation, it becomes apparent that we are dealing with a *censoring* system that is capable of attaching positive or negative valences to new information, as well as information already stored within the brain. Then, astonishingly, this capability allows us to receive only selected information, or information that has been predistorted in a meaningful way. This is similar to the process of *reification* as described by Charles Lumsden and E. O. Wilson, two eminent Harvard sociobiologists. In accordance with what has been said up to this point, their work suggests the existence of "a diagnostic activity of human consciousness."[36] The word "reification" implies *purification*, something the brain seems able to do to the information it receives.

Among other things, reification theory proposes that the human brain *filters* vast amounts of information in order to diagnose data sets that are potentially *noxious* to the individual. As this is done, the person is also able to greatly reduce the complexity of incoming and stored information in such a way that a sense of order is more likely. To facilitate the maintenance of artificial order, the individual generates "mentifacts," fictitious categorizations or understandings of the world and the self. The power of reification theory is evident when Lumsden and Wilson place it within the context of culture while arguing that culture tends to *co-evolve* with the reification process. They theorize that culture is *actively* involved in producing and sustaining our mentifacts, and thus the illusory order that works on our behalf.

Reification is certainly one aspect of dissociation, although it is not correct to call this a diagnostic activity of *consciousness* as it relates to dissociation. The diagnoses, or decisions, about what should be dissociated and distorted take place at an unconscious level. What reaches consciousness is *already* treated, based on the diagnoses made outside of awareness. A brief example might illustrate this and lead us back toward the symptoms of religion and psychopathology, as well as the manner in which those symptoms are formed. From this, it will eventually become clear how hypnosis fits into the larger picture.

Earlier, while discussing the topic of associations, I gave the example of a young girl who made associations between her father and the pleasure stemming from his innocent play with her. But now let us consider a much different case: that of a teenage girl who entered psychotherapy following an unsuccessful suicide attempt. Let us call her Jane. Initially, the severe depression that caused Jane to become self-destructive remained a mystery. Only after an extended period of intensive therapy did it become apparent that she had been a victim of sexual abuse by her father when she was between the ages of seven and twelve. Until the breakthrough in therapy, however, Jane had no memories whatsoever of the traumatic and painful sexual encounters. This was not the result of false memories that had been implanted during therapy since corroborating evidence and later developments with the father confirmed that the incidents were real.

Jane's memories of the highly noxious sexual abuse posed an ongoing threat to Jane's emotional world. They not only caused her to relive disturbing occurrences, but they engendered powerful feelings of guilt and shame. Moreover, since Jane loved her father and needed the sense of security she found in him, the memories placed her in an *irreconcilable conflict*, making it impossible for her to carry on with him in such a way that she could meet her love and security needs. By *dissociating* herself from the sexual abuse memories, however, Jane solved this dilemma, albeit in a temporary and less than ideal way. But, as in the other examples, Jane's decision to prevent the sexual abuse memories from reaching consciousness was not made at the level of consciousness.

Bowers and Meichenbaum attempt a synthesis of dissociation and cognitive theory in their speculation about the nature of dissociative "decisions." In *The Unconscious Reconsidered*, they write that "the principal problem for a neodissociation theory of divided consciousness is to indicate how such mental activities can proceed involuntarily, and outside of phenomenal awareness."[37] One possible resolution of this problem has to do with the relationship between memory and attention, as originally described by Ernest Hilgard in relation to the Deutsch-Normal model of cognition. As such, it may be that the storage of memory is preceded by an "automatic semantic analysis and attention positioned late rather than early in the sequence of cognitive operations.[38]

In essence, this postulates that there is a certain amount of lag or delay that takes place while memories are being stored. This is what is meant by the phrase "attention positioned late." Before we are able to retrieve those memories, the material to be stored is given *active* attention at the unconscious level, thereby allowing for certain decisions to be made "in accordance with both short-term and long-term personal goals and situational demands."[39] This means that the potential for *reification* might be realized in relation to memory and in particular the manner in which memories are stored. It is also possible that, following an unconscious "diagnosis," associations are broken, either partially or completely, and recon-structed so that the memory is stored in modified form. Or, in extreme cases, a "decision" can be made that a memory is so noxious that it needs to be dissociated altogether and made unavailable to consciousness, as in the case of Jane's sexual abuse memories.

Complicating matters even more is the fact that *dissociated memories are not forgotten.* Jane had no conscious recollection of abuse, yet those memories were stored in vivid fashion in her brain. This was seen clearly when the dissociative barrier was finally broken. Therefore, dissociation and the way it acts over the course of *preconscious* memory storage must be understood as taking place along multiple pathways that have a high degree of separation from one another. Ernest Hilgard's notion of *amnesic barriers* seems appropriate as a means by which to describe the gulf existing between our different parallel streams of mental activity. It follows that all forms of dissociation-based reality distortion and self-deception are limited to the window of consciousness. At the level of unconscious awareness, reality remains undistorted and the person remains undeceived. This is why someone like Jane continued to suffer at the emotional level even though she had dissociated herself from the abuse memories. Likewise, many dissociation-based religious beliefs that are aimed at anxiety control rely on dissociation (e.g., "I will go to a blissful heaven when I die"). Yet such beliefs, while partially effective, do an incomplete job of alleviating anxiety since the person is unconsciously aware that the belief is reality distortion.

Conversely, evidence of unconscious awareness may be seen in certain dissociative disorders involving symptoms that would be expected to generate great anxiety, but do not. In conversion blindness, for example, the person dissociates in such a way that all eyesight is lost, even though nothing is physically wrong with the person's eyes. Feelings of panic and devastation would overcome anyone who was suddenly faced with the actual fact of complete blindness. In this regard, it should be noted that this type of conversion blindness is "real" in the sense that the person cannot see. It is also the case that the person is completely convinced *at the conscious level* that he or she no longer possesses any eyesight. Yet it is also clear that the person knows that the blindness is not real. This is revealed when, quite predictably, the "blind" person shows remarkably few signs of distress, worry, or concern about being blind. This characteristic pattern associated with most conversion symptoms is termed *la belle indifférence*. It represents a compelling clue that, at an *unconscious* level, the person is fully aware that the blindness is not real and that vision could be restored at any time by the unconscious diagnostic and decision-making process.

Dissociation is the cognitive faculty that allows us to alternate in purposeful ways, and in varying degrees, between reality orientedness and a lack of reality orientation, while never actually abandoning an awareness of reality at the unconscious level. But if decisions to dissociate are not made consciously, how does the person "know" when to dissociate? Also, once dissociation is achieved and the reality orientation is suppressed, what enables the individual to reshape reality in meaningful ways? The answer to both these questions lies in the relationship between patterns of dissociations as the *learned cues* that trigger those dissociations. We might speak of a *brain-level encoding process* whereby it becomes possible for the person to establish automatic links between certain cues and certain *specific* dissociative configurations. These lie dormant, so to speak, until the cue is encountered. In the absence of a triggering cue, the dissociative configuration might be compared to a computer program that exists in coded form, but is not activated. Psychologists sometimes use the term *cognitive map* in referring to coded information that determines cognitive behavior once instructions have been received to follow that particular map.

The maps under discussion here are ones that, when activated, will cause the person to dissociate from a specific set of information, the end result being a distortion of reality that usually has personal and social meaning. It might be useful to speak of *dissociative maps* that become conditioned, through paired associations, to relevant cues. As a result of participating in numerous church "services," for example, a wide range of cues would become paired with the dissociative trance that emanates from the service. In turn, certain dissociative maps (in the form of reality-distorting data sets) are planted (i.e., suggested) while people are in a dissociated state. The situation is similar to that of a person who, during hypnosis, is given a word (i.e., cue) that will enable the person to enter hypnosis immediately when that word is repeated on subsequent occasions. In this way, a *learned* connection is established between a cue and a dissociative trance state. This connection can go further in the case of church services, since the cues are also associated with additional *content maps* that manifest themselves in order to structure the trance state in predefined and practiced ways.

In the context of religion, these maps would be called religious beliefs. I once had a guardian angel belief which was the end result of a dissociative map implanted during an official trance procedure (i.e., church service) involving ritual and music. This is the traditional and age-old method by which to foster dissociation and to subsequently redefine reality for members of society. The situation with Jane, our sexual abuse victim, is somewhat different. Her dissociative map, which allowed her to dissociate from painful memories of her abuse, was paired with various cues related to her father. When Jane encountered any of these cues, her brain was able to respond automatically in such a way that she "forgot" the sexual abuse memories. While those memories were still in storage in Jane's brain, they never reached awareness because they were always *intercepted* by an *adaptive* process in the form of dissociation that was specific to a signaling cue (i.e., her father). Furthermore, we know that this dissociative map was limited to the episodes of sexual abuse, since Jane had no similar memory gaps in relation to other aspects of her father's behavior or to other areas of her life.

Jane's symptom differs from such a symptom as my religious belief in the same way that heterohypnosis (i.e., group-based dissociation) differs from autohypnosis (i.e., autodissociation). She did not enjoy an official trance-inducing technique, such as a formal religious service, in order to promote dissociation and establish the cues that would subsequently trigger dissociative trance and reality reconstruction. Instead, Jane and people like her find themselves in a position of acting *independently* in order to foster a dissociative trance that can satisfy their need for self-deception, very similar to the person utilizing so-called self-hypnosis. But before describing the essentially "hypnotic" nature of both religion and psychopathology, it is worthwhile to analyze further the paradox of dissociation and see how this requires us to reconsider our current theories of the mind.

TRANCE LOGIC

The ability to accept, at the same time, two completely contradictory sets of information is called *trance logic*. While hypnotists sometimes claim that trance logic is achievable only following hypnotic induction, trance logic can be seen to varying degrees across the entire spectrum of human behavior. Nevertheless, hypnotized subjects do provide us with some of the most dramatic displays of trance logic. After a man has been hypnotized it is possible to illustrate this remarkable ability by suggesting to him, for example, that he will "see" (i.e., hallucinate) his wife sitting next to him in an empty chair. If the man is a good hypnotic subject, he will be completely convinced that his wife is there with him in the room. With relevant suggestions, it would be quite easy to get the man to have a detailed conversation with his wife, or even to give her an affectionate hug and a kiss.

But what happens if we then take another empty chair and suggest that the man "sees" his wife in that chair as well? Logic would tell us that the impossibility of having two identical wives in front of him would destroy his ability to see the second wife. Or we might expect the man to relinquish the first fictitious wife in order to regard the second wife as real. On the contrary, he is readily able *simultaneously* to maintain the belief that both wives are real. If asked if Wife A is his *real* wife, the man will answer affirmatively. When asked the same question about Wife B, he will respond in the same way. Of particular interest is the fact that such a person shows no surprise or bewilderment at the prospect of having two wives instead of one. To illustrate even further the phenomenon of trance logic, we could next bring the man's *real* wife into the room and sit her in a third chair. He will claim that she, too, is his real wife, thus giving him a total of three.

In a state of trance logic, people can delude themselves about a matter while also knowing the truth about it. They can be in touch and out of touch with reality at the same time. This may be seen with our hypnotized man if we ask him which of the three wives he would like to take home with him if he could choose only one of the three. Predictably, he will pick Wife C, the one who is not an illusion. He will not be disturbed at the prospect of leaving his other two wives behind because, even though they are real to him, they are also *not* real to him. Some executive cognitive process, working outside of awareness, maintains a grasp of the overall situation, even though conscious awareness flits from one illusion to another.

The reason that we do not label as crazy the man who is so

deluded about his wives is that he has undergone a formal induction of hypnosis. Specifically, the dissociation acting to enable the trance logic is viewed as a direct result of hypnotic procedure. If hypnosis were not available as an *excuse*, kissing and conversing with a nonexistent wife would be interpreted as signs of mental disturbance. By contrast, trance logic is easily seen in many types of psychopathology that do not escape being branded somehow "pathological." The person who has an intense phobia about the color red and who goes to all lengths to avoid that color also knows that there is nothing to be feared in the color red. If asked, that person, even while trembling and turning away from someone's red shirt, will readily acknowledge that the color red is totally harmless. Yet the person also "knows" that the color red is so potentially harmful that any amount of effort is justified in avoiding that color.

In the above examples, as well as that of Jane who both knew (i.e., remembered) and did not know that she had been raped by her father, the person is able simultaneously to hold two beliefs in absolute defiance of one another. The conditions were different in each of these cases, but the mental mechanics were the same. Dissociation was activated in all instances, thus affording the person a means by which to *divide* information along separate and independent systems of information processing. Once this division takes place, the person is empowered with a method by which to alter consciousness toward psychologically beneficial ends.

The reality distortions that are achieved via the dissociative process are sometimes made possible by way of dissociations of memory. This was obvious in the case of Jane, since it was precisely her sexual abuse memories that were dissociated. But let us shift the context and say that someone suggests to me, in the absence of a single shred of verifying evidence, that something called a guardian angel exists and follows me around continuously, looking after my welfare. I accept that proposition, believe in it wholeheartedly, and act in such a way that it is true beyond reproach. I even talk to the guardian angel from time to time, and sometimes I get the unmistakable impression that it is speaking back to me. Is it possible that this is still another form of trance logic and that dissociation is again at work, making it possible to know and not know? And if so, can we speculate about the exact way in which this is accomplished?

We have within our brains a highly sensitive *monitoring authority* that allows us to determine with great accuracy what constitutes *reasonable evidence* in support of the propositions offered to us. When this is operational, we are able to maintain what Ronald Shor labeled the *generalized reality orientation*. This he defines as "a structured frame of reference in the background of attention which supports, interprets and gives meaning to all experiences."[40] Like a critical member of a jury in court, we are capable of rejecting information if there is *reasonable* doubt. Or we can accept something as probably true if sufficient evidence exists that it is. When our monitoring authority is engaged fully and when we are operating with the general reality orientation, our mental scales are quite finely balanced. At these times, we would not find someone guilty of murdering her/his boss simply because it was shown that the accused person worked for that individual. That evidence would be analyzed critically and deemed inadequate to *justify* the charge.

If a critical jury were gathered to decide about the existence of guardian angels, the verdict would be an emphatic *guilty* since it would be judged that they do not exist based on insufficient evidence. In fact, there would be *no* evidence at all. We excuse belief in guardian angels on the basis of faith, but this does not help us comprehend the dynamics of religious beliefs or other beliefs that defy reality. It is more fruitful to view this faith in guardian angels as still another demonstration of dissociation, one that makes possible the acceptance of otherwise completely unacceptable propositions by interrupting the workings of the monitoring authority. In so doing, we are no longer compelled to reject propositions that *should* be rejected given the cognitive skills at our disposal when the monitoring authority is fully operational. Dissociation, then, needs to be seen as the brain level process that lets us *disengage* the monitoring authority and consequently our orientation to general reality, thus paving the way for the incorporation of irrational and erroneous propositions. These coexist with rational or accurate propositions. Again, this is what is meant by trance logic, or what might be more aptly termed *dissociative logic*. Therefore, just as dissociation is necessary in enabling a person to distort information that has already reached that person via certain experiences (e.g., Jane's sexual abuse), it is also essential if a person is to accept as true information that lacks all evidential support.

In the instance of my guardian angel belief, I would need to dissociate myself from memories relating to my experience with the natural world, which would emphatically contraindicate the existence of entities fitting the description of guardian angels. Dissociation theory is consistent with the fact that believers in guardian angels can also hold beliefs (and memories) about the natural order that would eliminate the possibility of guardian angels. In accordance with this theory, the existence of multiple channels of information processing permits the person to divert to an unconscious channel those chunks of information that must be eliminated for purposes of reality distortion at the level of consciousness. This means that believers in guardian angels do so only during those times when they dissociate competing bits of data. Moreover, this temporary belief is usually short-lived and no longer in duration than, say, a church service or a personal plea to the angel. At other times, when the monitoring authority is reactivated with regard to the workings of nature, these people do not possess such beliefs. Beyond that, even when they are dissociating appropriately and believing in angels, they simultaneously do *not* believe in those angels. This is because their dissociated knowledge is still alive and well at the unconscious level. That is, these people are still aware *unconsciously* that guardian angels are thoroughly impossible in light of the totality of experience with, and memory of, the real world. Of course, the implications for this are enormous, and they warrant that we consider new theoretical pathways for understanding religion and the closely related phenomenon of dissociative psychopathology.

Returning to the central goal of mental activity, namely *order*, we should keep in mind that dissociation is usually triggered by a disturbing lack of order. Stated somewhat technically, disorder creates tension which leads to a demand for reality alteration. A guardian angel belief, for instance, can be traced to the existential tension that stems from our inability to make sense of, and to adequately order, the world in which we find ourselves. But only more disorder would be generated if we had to suspend permanently a reality-based set of information in order to hold one that is reality-defying but order-rich. This is the great advantage of dissociation as a cerebral faculty since we can temporarily shift certain elements of reality while reassuring ourselves at the conscious level about the factuality of a biased reality.

SUGGESTION, DISSOCIATION, AND REALITY DISTORTION

We still need to elucidate the specific process whereby otherwise contentless dissociative states are filled, or structured, in such a way that order is restored by means of reality distortion. This could be posed as a question: What are the cognitive *building blocks* of the new reality that is assembled after dissociation has enabled a person to relinquish his or her hold on actual reality as it otherwise reaches that person when in a state of general reality orientation? A potential answer takes us into a discussion of *suggestion* as a process that operates in conjunction with dissociation.

Some of the commonly accepted definitions of suggestion reveal the reality distortion that is a dominant feature of suggestive responding. William Edmonston goes to the heart of the matter in defining suggestion as the *central distortive mechanism*.[41] His astuteness about suggestion as a vehicle for distortion is reminiscent of the view of William James, who wrote that "suggestion is a directive which informs the senses to *distort or change* the interpretation of the sensed stimuli."[42] This then allows the person to create illusions or what William James called *facsimiles of the real world*. These are constructions of an alternative reality, manufactured outside of conscious awareness but able to enter consciousness later in their altered form.

At the turn of the century, psychologist William McDougall offered a definition of suggestion that is still widely accepted. He wrote that suggestion is a type of communication "resulting in the acceptance with conviction of the communicated proposition *in the absence of logically adequate grounds for its acceptance*."[43] A somewhat similar definition is put forward by Hans Eysenck and his colleagues who define suggestion as "a process of communication during which one or more persons cause one or more individuals to change *without critical response* their judgments, opinions, attitudes, or patterns of behavior."[44] Gordon Allport also drew special attention to the marked *absence of rational and critical thought* when people were responding to suggestions. These, he said, are conspicuously *disengaged* when people achieve a state of readiness for suggestion.[45]

From each of these definitions, we see that suggestive responding is a type of behavior that is performed when the general reality orientation of the person is circumvented. In giving added emphasis to this crucial point, we can say that suggestive behavior is possible *only* when someone has been successfully removed from his or her capacity to process information in a reality-based manner. This is where a discussion of suggestion must blend with our knowledge of dissociation. Otherwise, we would be forced to conclude that suggestion *itself* is also the means by which people arrive at a state that makes them *prepared* to act on suggestions. If, with no prior preparation, I suggest to you on a freezing winter day that it is becoming extremely hot, it is unlikely that you will accept and experience this proposition as true *without critical response*. The mere suggestion does not possess what is necessary to make you ready to respond to that suggestion. Despite the suggestion, you are still in a state of general reality orientation with an engaged, conscious monitoring authority. So you know consciously that it is actually cold and you are able to reject that suggestion as nonsense. Therefore, the suggestion alone had little or no impact on your appraisal of reality or your behavior.

But we also know that this very same suggestion can cause people to believe and feel that they are burning up, even if they are sitting on a block of ice. They might even peel off some of their clothes and fan themselves in hope of obtaining some relief from what they perceive as suffocating heat. The difference between the two situations again has to do with readiness. People who do respond to a distortive suggestion are in a state of *dissociative preparedness*, which entails a neutralization of the critical faculties that would detect the distortion and render the suggestion ineffective.

Dissociation and suggestion need to be understood as separate but tandem processes that work in close conjunction with one another. Dissociation must *precede* suggestion before we can expect suggestions to succeed. However, it is crucial to realize that dissociation is basically a blank and directionless state. A person's reality orientation is diminished and the possibility exists for suggestive responding. But, at this stage, it is only a possibility. Dissociation remains directionless and unproductive without suggestion. In a sense, dissociation is given life by suggestions.

To highlight the important distinction between dissociation and suggestion, we might imagine a person who undergoes hypnotic induction but then is left to sit alone without any further participation by the hypnotist. In all likelihood, nothing happens. We recognize hypnotic induction procedures as one of many methods by which to promote a state of dissociation. But if no suggestions follow the actual induction procedure, very little of interest takes place. After a time, the person will slip out of the dissociative state. If anything, the person will be a bit agitated or confused as a result of a structureless period of externally induced dissociation.

Religion, hypnosis, and psychopathology are three *contents* in which dissociation is fostered by various techniques. In each of these areas, however, suggestions are indispensable *antecedents* of the dissociations achieved by these different methods. The dissociative states that are engendered during hypnosis, religion, and psychopathology are essentially the same, with the usual override of critical and analytical brain functions. But the suggestions associated with each of these processes differ greatly. This is why we sometimes fail to realize that they are all variations of the same process by which reality is regulated for strategic purposes.

Arnold Ludwig is one notable scientist who writes of dissociation as a *strategic* capability. He argues very convincingly from a sociobiological perspective that our dissociative faculties evolved so as to empower us in very significant ways.[46] Dissociation, Ludwig maintains, makes possible the following: (a) reality transcendence;

(b) escape from conflict and trauma; (c) social control and social cohesion, and enhancement of the herd sense; and (d) neurological conservation and economy of effort.

The first three of these objects of our dissociative faculties will be treated in detail in the chapters dealing with religion and psychopathology. But we might devote a small amount of space here to the last of these, namely, *neurological conservation and economy of effort*. It represents an exception in that it is a type of dissociation that does not necessarily involve a concomitant suggestion process.

Every minute of every day, we are flooded with information inputs, the accumulated effect of which would be to overwhelm us and place a large drain on our nervous systems. There is a very important need for a means by which to escape, even temporarily, from certain situations that are deemed nonessential. In doing this, we conserve ourselves neurologically and preserve our energies for more demanding efforts. An example of dissociation for purposes of economy of effort might be "highway hypnosis." After driving many miles with no other stimulation than white lines in the road, people fade into a mild dissociative trance. Once they return from this state, people often claim that they have no memory of long stretches of their trip. Some even express a bit of worry that they were not in control during the time of the dissociation. Of course, these people were in control as evidenced by the fact that they arrived safely and without incident, still another example of the simultaneous knowing and not knowing that is an aspect of dissociation.

There are many other times that we use dissociation in order to go into "neutral" or "automatic pilot" and thereby conserve ourselves neurologically. Boring lectures, tedious staff meetings, noisy children—these and countless other circumstances might lead people to employ dissociation in a form that does not involve subsequent suggestions to guide the dissociation in meaningful ways. Meditation is a dissociation technique that is relatively *contentless*. Yet it is used more and more by people for the therapeutic benefits that come when simple dissociation lets them deactivate the processes taxing the nervous system. Beyond that, it is not unreasonable to postulate that these and similar dissociative states have associated curative effects that cannot be explained by current models of body and mind.

The method of induction for these contentless types of dissociative trance states is also very simple. When I used to lecture on statistics, my students displayed the entire range of these techniques. In hopes of dissociating, some students clicked their pens at evenly spaced intervals or tapped them lightly on their desktops. Others preferred to grasp a clump of their hair and to stroke it repeatedly.

A few moustaches proved very handy in this way. Repetitious bouncing of the feet or tapping of the toes was also popular. One student liked to take off his wristwatch and put it to an ear, relying on the regular clicking to help him on his way. In all cases, there was a predictable slowing of the blink rate and a characteristic glossing over of expressions. If any suggestion was involved in these faraway people, it came in the form of self-suggested fantasies that offered an alternative to the boredom of statistics. Always remarkable to me was the fact that, if called upon in the midst of their dissociative trance, many students could answer questions concerning the lecture material. They were simultaneously there and not there, adding still more support to the theory that two or more streams of information can be processed at the same time in the same brain.

Entry into meditative dissociation is also achieved by way of *repetition*. This sometimes involves the repeated drawn-out utterance of a single word resembling the sound of the English word "ohm." Repetition plays a key role in all sorts of dissociative trance induction. Some of these are of the variety that simply punctuate a person's day in the course of neurological conservation efforts. Some people use jogging, a highly repetitive activity that is associated with a dissociative reaction. Marathon runners frequently place themselves into a dissociative trance, which functions to reduce boredom as well as the pain stemming from the extreme demands put on the body.[47] I have my own version of meditation which I practice while fishing. For long periods of time, I cast a spinner over and over again into the water of a rushing river. All sense of time disappears and the act loses all connection to the actual catching of fish. The endless identical repetitions, like the meditative "ohm," assist my passage into a dissociative trance and I disconnect myself from my generalized reality orientation. Even in the absence of suggestions that structure this empty dissociative state, the exercise is most therapeutic. In fact, on more than one occasion, I felt disappointed when a fish actually took the lure and interrupted my therapeutic contentless dissociation

But to repeat, suggestion is a *requisite* component of the other objects of dissociation outlined by Ludwig. Except in its simples forms, dissociation must be regarded not as an end in itself, bu rather as a pathway that can be entered upon if suggestions ar made available. Only then do states of dissociation have a sens of direction that can prove potentially fruitful for the individua This brings us to a combination of dissociation and suggestion tha has captivated us for more than a century.

3 Hypnosis in Global Perspective

John Kihlstrom offers a useful definition of hypnosis since it proceeds on the basis that hypnosis is a mechanism whereby elements of reality become distorted in such a way that reality contact is still retained at some level. Kihlstrom's definition also suggests that "hypnotic" processes may be involved in the reality distortion that characterizes altered states of the psychopathological variety. According to Kihlstrom:

> Hypnosis may be defined as a social interaction in which one person (designated the subject) responds to suggestions offered by another person (the hypnotist) for experiences which involve alterations in perception and memory. In the classic case, these experiences are accompanied by feelings of involuntariness bordering on compulsion, and subjective conviction bordering on delusion. Even the most highly responsive subjects, however, appear to retain some degree of veridical awareness and voluntary control, so that their behavior and experience represents a curious blending of illusion and reality.[1]

Such a definition captures the essential paradox of hypnosis. We see that, while in a so-called hypnotic state, a person can create a fusion of reality and illusion so convincing that he or she will act in total accord with that hybrid of reality. Yet it is also the case that the subject does not relinquish his or her ultimate hold on reality. Hilgard is certainly on the right track in proposing the existence of some sort of "hidden observer" that retains a solid foothold in reality, even to the extent that the "observer" could force the person back to *real* reality if that was deemed necessary.[2]

From the above, it should be apparent that hypnosis must be understood in terms of dissociation and a new model of the unconscious. In fact, Kihlstrom's definition of hypnosis is couched in a wider discussion of the dissociation of memory that becomes possible during hypnosis. This includes hypnotic hypermnesia (heightened recollection), hypnotic age regression, hypnotic agnosia (loss of sensory ability), and posthypnotic amnesia. While the etiology of these phenomena is not without controversy, Kihlstrom nevertheless concludes that they seem to involve "an alteration in consciousness, in the sense that the executive functions which monitor and control memory functions are disrupted. In all these cases, the alteration in consciousness may be described as a dissociation."[3]

Several investigators of hypnosis have noted the fundamental *distortive* nature of this phenomenon. Specifically, it is a procedure that allows reality to become distorted in any number of ways. On this topic, Ronald Shor describes the good hypnotic subject as "a person who has the ability to give up his usual reality orientation to a considerable extent, and who can concurrently build up a new, special orientation to reality which temporarily becomes the only possible reality for him in his phenomenal awareness."[4] Eugene Bliss depicts hypnosis as a "non-Newtonian" world of "realistic fantasy," where aberrations of all sorts can be perceived and experienced with a sense of total reality."[5] In fact, Ernest Hilgard has argued the case that hypnosis should be viewed as an expression of dissociation. He writes quite simply that "dissociation is the secret of hypnosis."[6]

As it turns out, dissociation is the cornerstone of reality distortion which can manifest itself in many different ways. Robert Shor was sensitive to this and described hypnosis as only one of many methods by which people can become disengaged from the *general reality orientation*. He places this insight within the rightful context of culture by arguing that "hypnosis is a special form of trance developed in Western civilization."[7] Shor's observation resembles quite closely that of Fred Frankel, who wrote that "hypnosis is an event developed in the Western world, involving a subject and an operator, and dependent for its occurrence on the trance capabilities of the subject, his or her motivation, the situation, and the relationship between the subject and the operator."[8] This is an extremely important point. Yet books on the history of psychology frequently contain misleading information about the "discovery of hypnosis" without reference to the many similar states whose common denominator is also dissociation.

In truth, it is far more accurate to speak of hypnosis as one of many possible *procedures* for bringing about a state of dissociative trance and dissociative responding. Therefore, what is often celebrated as the "discovery" of hypnosis is actually a very belated

Western discovery of dissociation as it can become more manifest using culture-bound "hypnotic" techniques. The end result is a culture-specific *expression* of dissociative trance. In other cultures, dissociative trance takes on different forms depending on the techniques used, as well as on the cultural conditioning that guides a person's behavior during trance. Furthermore, there is nothing new about such procedures as those used in promoting hypnotic dissociation. For thousands of years, various cultures have been making use of related procedures, many of which *work* much better than the "hypnotic" techniques of Western society. The word hypnosis (from the Greek *hypnos*, meaning "sleep") is a relatively new coinage, but that is all (see below).

Restating this slightly, a state of dissociation is fostered, sometimes very dramatically, as a result of the *procedures* known collectively as hypnosis. In this light, the term *hypnotic dissociation* is more meaningful and less confusing than our usual usage of the word hypnosis. The same type of dissociative state can be achieved by any number of other techniques, something that has been done by members of our species ever since we evolved the capacity to process information along independent pathways, the point at which religion and psychopathology also appeared.

Even though hypnotic dissociation should be considered an invention of Western culture, it is by no means a part of mainstream Western culture. Except for small numbers of people who attempt to draw on its supposed usefulness, hypnosis falls well outside the usual cultural contexts of dissociative trance induction. Most often, these contexts are religious. But there is hardly anything "religious" about hypnosis, or at least not as we generally think of religion. As a mode for amplifying one's dissociative capabilities, hypnosis can be traced to the thinking of certain people in the late eighteenth century when it was called artificial somnambulism or magnetic sleep. In 1843, James Braid introduced the term hypnosis. Among the many other figures influential in shaping our understanding of hypnosis were Jacques Puységur, the physician Franz Mesmer, Louis Charpignon, J. P. Deleuze, psychologist Pierre Janet, Hippolyte Bernheim, and neurologist Jean-Martin Charcot.

Early workers in this area were intrigued by the way in which some people seemed prone to *spontaneous* somnambulism which was typically followed in the waking state by amnesia. From the outset, therefore, it was apparent that hypnosis is a very natural and easily entered state, especially in certain individuals who seemed highly predisposed. It was also obvious that memory inhibition was somehow involved in the phenomenon under investigation.

Some of the first observers of so-called hypnosis also noticed that hypnosis could be either of a *natural* or *artificial* type. People who spontaneously entered a somnambulistic state were often unaware of the *purpose* of that state. As a result, the state lacked the content and structure that we generally associate with hypnosis. It was as if the subject were *waiting* for something. Researchers also recognized another dimension which concerned the relationship between the subject and the hypnotist and, in particular, the method by which suggestions were delivered to the readied subject. This then reinforces what was said earlier, namely that, without hypnotic suggestion, all one has as a result of the hypnotic induction process is a *contentless* state of dissociation. As Hilgard aptly notes, hypnosis is a state of dissociation characterized by a *readiness to respond.*[9]

The person, once dissociated, must be steered or guided by suggestions, something that is done by the hypnotist following successful induction of a dissociative state. In religious settings, as will be shown shortly, the suggestions that follow on the heels of dissociative trance are proffered by "hypnotists" known as priests, shamans, ministers, and so forth. But once again suggestions should be viewed as essential, and complementary, to the process of dissociation. After a person has reached a state of dissociation, he or she must be assisted in order to know what to do or experience during that state. Even though we tend to speak of the "state" of dissociation, it is basically a nonstate in the sense of being vacuous and contentless. In this regard, it is not yet an *altered* state until suggestions are provided, thus giving the person the material needed to *alter* reality in one direction or another.

Kihlstrom's definition of hypnosis also described it as a *social interaction* between two people. It is true that hypnotic induction procedures are usually actively directed by an "authority" known as the hypnotist. On the surface, the role of the subject appears to be a passive and mindless one characterized by obedience to the dictates of the hypnotist. The subject follows not only the instructions used to promote dissociative trance, but also the suggestions that follow. Yet we know that people can enter into a state of hypnotic dissociation without the aid of an external agent. This is the case even if the individual has no prior experience with heterohypnosis, i.e., being hypnotized by someone else. In view of our knowledge of self-hypnosis, Ernest Hilgard wisely concludes that traditional heterohypnosis amounts to *aided self-hypnosis*. On this he writes that, in heterohypnosis, "the person accepts the hypnotist as an aid to hypnotizing himself."[10] Consistent with that claim, Hilgard asserts that the hypnotic subject plays a very *active* role, regardless of the mode of induction.

Even though all trance should be viewed as essentially *self-induced*, the distinction between assisted and unassisted methods of induction will be crucial as we enter into a discussion of religion and psychopathology. While remembering that the potential for trance evolved in order to facilitate reality distortion, we will see that assisted types of trance induction have more desirable effects than unassisted types. This is especially so when the assistance is provided by a group, in which case the reality distortion is deemed to be religion, and therefore not considered to be a violation of reality. On the other hand, self-induced trance and subsequent self-suggestion entered into in isolation usually yields inferior patterns of reality distortion that are deemed to be pathological because of their *idiosyncratic* (i.e., personal) nature.

Hypnosis is a peculiar invention that falls somewhere between the intended group-assisted and the unassisted methods of trance induction and utilization. Even so, hypnotic induction techniques do overlap somewhat with those that have been used over the ages by most societies of the world, as well as those of lone trance seekers. They are therefore worthy of closer examination, especially since they help us better to comprehend dissociative trance as it is employed in more naturalistic (i.e., religious) settings, and in private alternatives to religion (i.e., psychopathology).

HYPNOTIC INDUCTION

Years ago I was told by a psychology teacher, who also practiced hypnosis, that one can hypnotize someone by placing that person in a room that is completely quiet except for the sound of water drips spaced at equal intervals. She argued that, in the absence of any other distracting stimuli, the individual would have no choice but to focus awareness on the repetitive sound. In her view, the person would in time enter a hypnotic trance and be ready to receive and accept suggestions. Upon hearing this, I found the idea a credible one since it closely resembled the famous Chinese water torture techniques for making people talk against their will. While the water drop technique never found a foothold among hypnotists, it does bear the signature of hypnotic techniques that are commonly used to elicit the necessary dissociation before the subject can be open to suggestions.

Among the first techniques used by hypnotists to foster dissociation was *fascination*, a method dating back to ancient Egypt. With this, the subject was requested to focus on a single point.

Sometimes it was a fixed point while, at other times, it was made to move slightly. Many hypnotic induction techniques were built up around the original fascination, or fixation, approach. Some of those that have been popularized in the media include small crystal balls that swing on a chain, pocket watches on a chain, and circular spirals that spin on a wheel. Much more common is the humble thumbtack that can be stuck into a wall or ceiling. Some present-day hypnotists still employ such methods.

While its psychophysiological workings are not well understood, there is little doubt that a concentrated convergent focusing of attention will pave the way for hypnotic responding. One promising theory by B. J. Baars is based on a theory of cognition wherein multiple levels of cognitive processing are seen to coexist with multiple sources of nonconscious information.[11] According to Baars, the generalized reality orientation is in competition with other information sources for access to conscious "workspace." Consequently, the total focusing of awareness has the effect of lowering the chances that the generalized reality orientation will win a place in conscious awareness. In a sense, the person becomes *absorbed* to the extent that the general reality orientation (and conscious monitoring authority) is squeezed out of the competition for access to consciousness, leaving the person in a mental state that lacks grounding in reality. It follows that the individual then becomes more potentially receptive to eventual suggestions that are in defiance of reality. In other words, as a result of becoming narrowly focused, or absorbed, the person is conscious, but in a way that does not assess reality in a critical fashion. Beyond that, prolonged periods of concentrated focusing appear to promote a dissociative trance state that, while in place, precludes any additional successful competition by the generalized reality orientation.

In recent years, the concept of *absorption* has attracted increasing interest as it can help to understand hypnosis and many related phenomena. It is defined formally as "a disposition for having episodes of single total attention that fully engages one's representational (i.e., perceptual, imaginative, and ideational) resources."[12] In one of the most complete theoretical models of hypnosis, Etzel Cardeña and David Spiegel put forward the theory that hypnotic responding is the end result of an interaction between absorption, dissociation, and heightened suggestibility.[13] On the matter of absorption, Cardeña and Spiegel make the observation that, throughout the ages, many indigenous cultures have made use of repetitive drumming, chanting, or dancing as a means for people to become absorbed and to enter into trance. This then paved the way for the effective use of shamanistic healing techniques or other traditional practices employing "magic."

Similarly, although less spectacularly, contemporary hypnotists have their own absorption methods, such as the eye-fixation approach mentioned earlier. It has also become common practice to make the hypnotist's voice, in itself, an object of fixation. Slow, monotonous, and repetitive words or phrases, even if presented as instructions, can be an auditory means by which to narrow one's focus and gain entry into a dissociative trance.

In terms of the threefold model of hypnosis combining absorption, dissociation, and suggestibility, we can speculate that absorption promotes the dissociative state or trance. This, in turn, amplifies *suggestibility*, or the likelihood that a person will respond without critical response to a suggestion. Some people are more suggestible than others following dissociation-promoting techniques (e.g., hypnotic induction), a condition that could be due to any number of factors, including dispositional ones. Despite these differences, the ability to respond uncritically to suggestion depends on a certain degree of dissociation that can be achieved via absorption techniques.

The end result of hypnotic induction techniques is an *altered* state of consciousness whereby diminished reality orientation allows the person to construct an alternative reality based on offered suggestions. But this must be understood in terms of the essential paradox that sees the human being as able to disengage from reality even while maintaining contact with it. It helps if we again consider the possibility that an encoding process dictates when and how a person disengages from his or her conscious monitoring authority, thus making possible the acceptance of reality-distorting suggestions. We might do this by offering another example of suggestive responding that follows hypnotic induction.

This time, let us say that a hypnotist goes through a typical procedure for inducing a dissociative state. In all probability, this entails some sort of attention-focusing technique for generating a dissociative trance which involves a suppression of the general reality orientation. Let us also say that, once a trance is in place and the person is no longer oriented in reality, we suggest that ordinary peanuts are extremely heavy. The subject is told that, each time she tries to pick up a peanut, its enormous weight will prevent her from doing so. We might think of this as a posthypnotic suggestion even though the hypnosis is not strictly over, since the subject remains under the influence of the hypnotic suggestion.

A few days later, we could investigate the subject's conscious belief about the weight of peanuts. Without actually presenting her with a peanut, we could ask her whether peanuts are heavy or light. She will say light since she knows them to be light. Then we could produce a peanut and ask the subject to lift it, something she would be unable to do. At that exact point, we could ask her about the weight of peanuts and she would probably reply that they are very heavy indeed. The only explanation for this turnabout in her behavior is that the peanut constituted a *cue* that, when encountered, signaled the subject's generalized reality orientation to retreat once more, thus enabling her to entertain completely nonrational suggestions. A suspension of her memories about the true weight of peanuts may be one aspect of this transition from reality-based to a reality-defying mode of cognition. Backing up a bit, we can also predict that, in the course of giving the subject a posthypnotic suggestion, the hypnotist was setting in place what earlier I called a dissociative map. This map, along with its cognitive "direction," presented itself to the subject when she came into contact with the relevant cue, i.e., the peanut.

The above example is an admittedly trivial one, but no more trivial than much of the behavior that is enacted when people respond to cues of a religious or psychopathological variety. What is of crucial importance is that suggestions, as well as the cognitive mechanisms that make them possible (e.g., memory suspension), can be inscribed in preset programs that unfold when certain cues are specified. Among other things, this shows that altered impressions of reality deriving from distortive suggestions can be quite removed in time from the actual moment of their inception. Some might find peanuts to be impossibly heavy for some time after being given that posthypnotic suggestion. So we see that suggestive responding does not require that a person become "absorbed" and dissociated *each time* one wants that person to override the monitoring authority and respond to suggestions. Instead, if dissociative techniques are combined effectively with suggestions, those suggestions can be self-delivered at later points when the person encounters a triggering cue.

In *The Psychology of Suggestion*, the pioneering psychologist Boris Sidis wrote that the human being is, first and foremost, a creature of suggestion.[14] That being the case, the dissociation-suggestion mechanism would need to operate somewhat along the lines described above. It would be unreasonable to expect that we always go through the different steps of trance induction prior to acting upon a suggestion. Throughout the day and without even realizing it, people respond to suggestions that warp reality. By pairing cues with suggestions, we can abandon our reality orientation whenever those cues are encountered, even as we harbor opposing reality-based positions when those cues are absent. As a result of hypnotic suggestion, I can "know" that a peanut is heavy when I am around peanuts, yet I know that peanuts are not heavy when there are no peanuts around. Hypnotic types of suggestion work that way, with the same being true of religious suggestion and the suggestion process involved in psychopathological symptoms.

VARIETIES OF DISSOCIATIVE TRANCE INDUCTION

Dissociative trance may be much more a part of our lives than we realize. Some psychologists, such as Ernest Rossi, question whether we are ever entirely free of some sort of trance, however subtle that trance might be. Indeed, Rossi debates whether even our normal waking state is somehow *altered*, leading him to introduce the concept of the "common everyday trance." Of this, he writes, "How little does the average consciousness recognize that it is dreaming rather than awake; that it is altered in ways that it does not totally understand by its own past and currently changing experiences and motivation."[15] On the other hand, some types of dissociative trance are dramatic and gripping, especially some of those that still survive in some non-Western societies.

Dissociation remains the common factor in all types of trance. However, the appearance, function, and mode of induction of trance vary enormously. This point is made by Victor Barnouw when he writes about trance in a cross-cultural perspective: "While contrast-ing methods are used in different societies to bring about trance, there are also differences in the utilization of the trance state, once achieved, and here again cultural patterning is at work."[16] The key words in that statement are *cultural patterning*. Virtually all cultures of the world make *official* trance states available to members of that culture. But these states are closely interwoven with the customs, belief systems, and even the methods of survival utilized in that culture. In other words, there is considerable variation in the cultural suggestions that give shape to the dictates found in the different cultures of the world. To the extent that they do differ, the outward expression of the trance states will also vary. Thus one can readily see an almost endless number of ways in which dissociative trance can reveal itself in formalized culturally patterned ways. Often these fall into the category of religion, while at other times they are not so easily categorized as religious in nature. Even though hypnosis, as a method of dissociative trance induction, is unique to Western culture, it is obviously not an aspect of that culture's religious heritage.

Yet there are some similarities as well as some notable differences between hypnotic and religious techniques for utilizing dissociative capabilities.

Regardless of one's method for classifying dissociative trance states, there are some important underlying patterns that exist concerning the techniques for inducing such states. A discussion of these will cast light on dissociative trance as it is promoted by way of "hypnotic" methods. It will also allow us to assess the *quality* of hypnotically induced dissociative trance in terms of its potential *usefulness*. After all, dissociation is an evolutionary adaptation for general survival purposes. It follows that we should be able to comment critically on induction techniques as they succeed or fail to elicit workable amounts of trance. Additionally, such assessments would require that we examine the suggestions that are made available following the actual induction and determine the usefulness of these suggestions. Some techniques are far superior to others as measured by their final value to the individual and/or to society. The form of dissociative trance that derives from clinical hypnotic procedures in our society is less than ideal and its utility is very limited as a result. Other forms, most notably those found in non-Western societies, are much more effective.

By way of introduction, it should be emphasized that some sort of dissociative trance can be found in virtually all cultures of the world.[17] Again, these are characterized by great superficial diversity. Yet the techniques themselves for induction of the dissociative trance share some similarities. Furthermore, most fall into one of two large categories. Barnouw's classification of trance induction supports this generalization. Writing from a global perspective, he describes the two categories of induction that account for most forms of dissociative trance.[18]

Sensory Deprivation Techniques

As the term implies, sensory deprivation involves "a reduction of exteroperceptive stimulation and/or motor activity."[19] Barnouw gives the example of laboratory experiments in which subjects were cut off from all sensory stimulation. In some of these, the subjects' eyes and ears were covered, and their arms and legs were wrapped in cotton wool. Then they were floated in enclosed tanks of water, cut off from all noise or light. The effects of this procedure strongly indicate that sensory deprivation greatly facilitates entry into dissociative trance. However, reports by subjects participating in these studies reveal no predictable *structure* that is given to dissociative states arrived at under these peculiar conditions. This is not surprising in view of what was said previously about the difference between the processes of dissociation and suggestion.

These experimental subjects had entered a dissociative trance by way of sensory deprivation. But at no stage were suggestions provided about how they were to give content to their contentless states of dissociation. Some subjects claimed that the experience eventually caused them to hallucinate in inexplicable ways. But such reports have been questioned by researchers who maintain that these were actually dreams that occurred once the unguided dissociative trance simply gave way to sleep. Yet available evidence shows that sensory deprivation can be very instrumental in fostering a dissociative trance.

Structure and content are not issues as sensory deprivation is used in naturalistic cultural settings to bring about and utilize dissociative trance. These are provided by the suggestions that direct the dissociative trance in predetermined ways, culminating in beneficial distortions that improve upon actual reality and offer the illusion of order and harmony. Barnouw cites a sensory deprivation method of dissociative trance induction that was found among Canada's Ojibwa Indians. I will mention it here as an illustration of this type of approach even though this spills over into a discussion of religious dissociation and suggestion, the topic of the next chapter.

From time to time, Ojibwa boys were sent out, without food, and made to fast in hopes of being visited by a guardian spirit. If such a visit was made to a boy prior to puberty, he then had the right to become a shaman, a position of great status and power. The "logic" was that shamanistic magic and healing were forthcoming from the guardian spirit and, therefore, that the shaman must be someone who had forged a relationship with that spirit. Very often, simple fasting did not prove effective in eliciting the appearance of the guardian spirit. If puberty approached and the boy was intent upon a future as shaman, more drastic measures were sometimes taken. Boys sometimes built platforms for themselves high in trees, away from everybody. There they would lie by themselves, with no food for up to two weeks. This prolonged period of sensory and nutritional deprivation undoubtedly helped some boys to enter a dissociative trance and to relinquish their generalized reality orientation. Unlike the sensory deprivation subjects in clinical studies, however, these Ojibwa boys were able to mold their dissociative states into highly meaningful experiences. They were thoroughly prepared to interpret any dissociated state in terms of their previous knowledge of the guardian spirit.

Barnouw draws our attention to the remarkable consistency between the various reported encounters with the guardian spirit. Accounts of the visits remained largely unchanged from one generation to the next. The reason for this, according to Barnouw, is due to a process of *autosuggestion*. On several public occasions throughout the year, Ojibwa shamans recounted their own past encounters with the guardian spirit. The boys would have had ample opportunity to hear of these stories and to learn what constituted a socially acceptable visionary experience. They were easily translated into suggestions that could be self-administered once they became receptive by way of the dissociative trance stemming from lengthy sensory deprivation.

The Shakers of St. Vincent in the Caribbean give us another example of dissociative trance that is accomplished by using a less extreme form of sensory deprivation. In this religious group, anyone wanting to be elevated to the status of an elder must go through a process of "mourning" for one's sins. This brand of mourning requires the person to be blindfolded and to lie in isolation on pallets. During this period, the person again fasts. However, unlike the Ojibwa youths who had no contact at all with another person during this period of isolation, the Shaker has periodic contact with a high-ranking member of the community. It is the job of this official to hear of the "trips" that the aspirant has taken and to decide if it is time for the mourning to end. As in the Ojibwa situation, a great commonality is found in the reports of these "trips." This is due once more to what Barnouw calls the "culturally patterned ideas" that become the basis for suggestions that can be self-introduced once the dissociative trance state is entered into under conditions of sensory deprivation.[20]

Absorption is certainly one important element of sensory-deprivation types of dissociative trance induction. In both examples above, most sources of external stimulation were removed, making it likely that attention would become focused in a very narrow way. By themselves, extended periods of absorption will facilitate a state of dissociation that makes possible altered states of consciousness. But suggestions must be made available during dissociative trance if reality is to be reshaped for whatever reasons. With the aid of certain suggestion techniques, both the Ojibwa and the Shaker were able to utilize dissociation in order to deactivate their reality-monitoring faculties and to see and experience something that was not part of actual reality. Yet it should become increasingly apparent that there is considerable value that stems from the ability of societies to generate distortions of reality. Social and psychological benefits derived as pathways to the spiritual world are opened up according to traditional methods. Participants become integrated into the group while also experiencing enhanced status, self-worth, and confidence. This is attested to by the large investment of time and energy put into such enterprises, as well as by the fact that it is a drive endemic to all cultures of the world.

Sensory Bombardment Techniques

The second broad class of dissociative trance induction is *sensory bombardment*, which is probably more widespread than the sensory deprivation method. With sensory bombardment, the senses are *flooded* with *repetitive* stimulation until a state of dissociative trance is elicited in the target person. Of all the many possible instruments available for purposes of sensory bombardment, drumming is unquestionably the most common. From the dawn of the too-big brain, the human being has been drumming itself out of reality, so to speak. There is even laboratory research demonstrating that continual drumming has very noticeable effects on central nervous system functioning. Moreover, this research shows that continuous rhythmic drumming can lead to hallucination, a warped sense of time, and involuntary muscle movements.[21]

In many religious ceremonies throughout the world, a deep dissociative trance is achieved when the drumming begins in a slow and monotonous way, but gradually builds to an extremely fast tempo. Unrestrained dancing at these times will further facilitate entry into dissociative trance. As has been observed in many societies employing this combination, people very often fall to the ground, twitching and shaking and completely disoriented from reality. At that point, their dissociative trance is so profound that they become hypersuggestible in a way rarely exhibited in less consuming induction techniques, such as hypnosis or most half-hearted Western religious services.

The astonishing forms of dissociative behavior seen during Malaysia's famous religious festival of Thaipusam is also the result of dissociation generated with sensory bombardment. It is during this festival that certain participants impale themselves with large skewers and needles. Sometimes the entire weight of their bodies is hung from metal hooks that pierce deeply into the flesh. All this is done without any apparent pain. One of the best descriptions of this practice is given by Colleen Ward and Simon Kemp.[22] Their analysis includes a detailed account of the specific mode of sensory bombardment induction, one that can be seen to include physiological elements (i.e., dissociation) as well as social and cultural elements that give direction to the dramatic state of dissociation. Ward and Kemp write:

> A major precipitant of trance is an increase of exteroceptive stimulation and the presence of somatopsychological factors which affect biochemistry and neurophysiology. Sensory bombardment of repetitive stimuli—olfactory, auditory, and kinesthetic—plays an important role in evoking dissociation. Stimulation includes the chanting of Sanskrit prayers by temple priests with refrains from the attendants, inhalation of pungent incense, and in some cases repetitive stroking of the skin. Trance is further aided by fasting, contributing to hypoglycemia, and occasionally by hyperventilation practices.[23]

It is tempting to say that the above method contains all the essential elements of a *good* dissociative trance-induction technique. By "good" I mean one that draws on all the available internal and external agencies to help the person reach not only a deep state of dissociation but one that is utilized effectively with relevant suggestions. In analyzing the various components of this approach, we see that the unrestrained sensory bombardment creates the general atmosphere conducive to cognitive dissociation. The devotee becomes profoundly *absorbed* into repetitive religious stimuli that affect all five senses. Attention might shift and become a very narrow band of consciousness consisting only of prayers or religious images that repeat themselves continuously. Eventually, the individual surrenders to a dissociative trance state involving "selective attention, unusual bodily sensations and dissolution of body boundaries, sensations of lightness and 'blank feelings,' alterations in body image, analgesia to pain, internal orientation, concentration, alteration in the quality of thought, diminished logic, intense emotions including euphoria, temporal and spatial disorientation, selective amnesia, detachment from the external environment, and gross, uncontrolled muscular movements such as tremors and rigidity."[24]

Many aspects of this trance state will be seen to characterize various psychopathological states, which carry the label of abnormality since they make no sense in any recognized cultural context. Such forms of disturbance will be seen to be inefficient *personalized* strategies of trance induction and usage that entail autosuggestion. Although Thaipusam trance states overlap somewhat with pathological syndromes, they differ in very important ways. Most notably, they are relatively short in duration and very meaningful when judged

within the framework of that culture. They even enjoy the wholehearted support of its members, which includes their physical presence
and participation at all phases of the process, including the induction
phase. As Ward and Kemp observe, family members typically follow
the devotee around chanting and playing drums in order to sustain
the trance. They also make periodic ritualistic offerings (e.g., cutting
limes and breaking coconuts) in order to fend off evil spirits, a symbolic
gesture to reassure the person that he is safe. People from the
community at large also assist the devotee in these ways. So the
devotee enjoys not only a feeling of safety, but also one of "sanity"
in the sense of not being viewed as deviant or an outsider. This
occurs despite the fact that the person is engaging in behavior that
would be regarded as completely insane (i.e., removed from reality)
when judged by criteria from other cultures.

The value of the collective "other" in promoting trance is often
underestimated. Sometimes people think of hypnotic trance and the
intricate relationship between subject and hypnotist and make the
mistake of assuming that trance generally is best effected on a one-
to-one basis. It might seem logical that other people would create
distractions or make the subject self-conscious or anxious. Yet, as most
cultures have learned about trance, including religious trance, the
"other" is a very potent aid in the induction process. It can even be
said that dissociative trance is made more difficult when others are
not in attendance. All over the world, shamanistic practices that rely
on dissociative trance almost always draw on the power of the subject's
friends and relatives, and even unrelated members of the tribe.

Parenthetically, stage hypnotism is often dismissed as mere acting
since it seems inconceivable that anyone could enter into a real trance
under such conditions of public scrutiny. Yet our cross-cultural observations tell us that trance is best promoted when an audience
is actively involved and supportive. In fact, stage hypnotists often
insist that hypnotic trance is actually easier on stage than in one-
to-one settings. Given that the traditional format for induction is
a collective one, there is reason to believe that stage techniques can
be as effective, if not potentially more so, than some of the audience-
free approaches. Of course, this in no way suggests that stage
hypnotists have any of the magic abilities that they sometimes try
to convey with their spectacular promotional techniques. We are
still talking about an entirely natural ability that is shared by all
human beings.

Another misconception about trance induction concerns the
matter of relaxation. Some theorists, aware of the apparent part
played by relaxation in hypnotic techniques, have postulated that

relaxation is the cornerstone of hypnotic trance. However, this has been rightly criticized in terms of our historical and cross-cultural knowledge of trance.[25] Quantitative research is also available to indicate that relaxation is largely independent of the dissociative trance resulting from traditional hypnotic induction methods. Moreover, one could make the case that relaxation, as it is used by Western hypnotists, is an impediment to effective trance induction. We have already seen that heightened sensory *excitation* is the method of choice for trance inducers in the various cultures of the world. An emphasis on relaxation may create the impression in the subject that inhibition and sleeplike lethargy are expected, which may eventually inhibit suggestive responding. This can extend to the confusion that arises when eyes-closed induction shifts to the eyes-open phase. Starting with an eyes-closed approach while hoping to maximize relaxation may only act as an overall obstacle to the trance procedure. With this and the other points made above, we can now try to understand hypnosis in a new light and also to grade its quality as a trance-induction strategy. In turn, this will allow us to compare hypnotic approaches to those found in religion and psychopathology.

THE LIMITATIONS OF WESTERN HYPNOSIS

Current theories of hypnosis date from the Victorian era and before, when there were attempts to explain a number of "hysterical" disorders. The actual hypnotic induction techniques that followed ended up bearing considerable resemblance to the underlying dynamics of these and other dissociative syndromes. For instance, it will be seen later that the manner in which "multiple personalities" are constructed and maintained by the victims of that disorder are very similar to the methods used by hypnotists in altering the experienced reality of the hypnotic subjects. Hypnotic and psychopathological approaches to dissociative trance also share certain distinct limitations that make them less than ideal as systems wherein suggestions can be utilized for reality-altering purposes. Granted, hypnosis is sometimes used in an effort to return a person to actual reality when that person has already managed to distort reality in an independent (i.e., "self-hypnotic") manner. Yet this usually proves less than effective because of the shortcomings inherent in the traditional hypnotic techniques. This may even be one of the reasons that many pioneering psychologists turned away from hypnosis in preference for other therapeutic approaches. Likewise, despite considerable professional interest in hypnosis that persists to this day, it has failed in its present form to live up to its early promise as a treatment modality. As we consider the strengths and weaknesses of hypnotic inductions, the way will be paved for a discussion of more effective forms of trance promotion, in particular the religious.

Hypnotic induction, as we saw, frequently entails the use of *absorption points* that help the subject to narrow concentration, to dissociate, and thus to become more suggestible. But often these absorption points are vague and ill-defined, sometimes being restricted to the sound of the hypnotist's voice. If the points of absorption are specific, such as a thumbtack on a wall or ceiling, they are typically *meaningless* in terms of the overall objectives and goals of the hypnosis procedure. By comparison, the Thaipusam devotee uses as absorption points religious stimuli that are highly meaningful in terms of the trance behavior to follow.

Most of the moving and productive trance techniques found in the non-Western world are a consequence of either sensory bombardment or sensory deprivation. Often these become the actual points of absorption, as in the classical case of repetitive beating drums. But hypnosis does not avail itself of either deprivation or bombardment to much of an extent. This makes it less likely that its vague absorption points will be sufficient to engender a workable *degree* of dissociation. There are some people, sometimes labeled "hypnotic virtuosos," who will enter into trance despite the general inadequacy of the induction technique. In special cases, surgical operations can be performed on these individuals following hypnotic induction. But these represent only a small percentage of the population, probably less than 5 percent. When the more striking methods of other cultures are employed, however, a far higher proportion of the population can take maximal advantage of dissociative trance. That is, it is not just the "virtuosos" who become accessible with those more powerful trance techniques.

One might be tempted to say that hypnotic induction involves stimulus deprivation to the extent that the subject is narrowly focused (i.e., absorbed) and consequently removed from most sources of sensory deprivation. But even if there is some truth to this, the length of the deprivation state during induction would be so short that no real effects would be derived. It certainly would not compare to the previously described examples of sensory deprivation techniques involving complete isolation with extended fasting for days or weeks at a time. Therefore, hypnotic trance induction fails to take advantage of either of the two universal catalysts for trance induction. Instead, it is usually reliant primarily on simple absorption into irrelevant stimuli in order to encourage a state of dissociation.

When it comes to the deliverance of suggestions, hypnotic strategies again fall short because there is no accepted cultural foundation for trance achieved in this way. Granted, some people have read or heard something about hypnosis which would create certain expectations in their minds. Since prior expectations can propel and can shape one's behavior during the suggestion phase, these individuals might be assisted somewhat by their supposed understanding of hypnosis. In the example of the Ojibwa trance technique, we saw that culturally transmitted "knowledge" about the guardian spirit made it possible for the boys to make contact with the guardian spirit once a dissociative state was achieved. Unquestionably, they were highly prepared to give structure to the state of dissociation by way of self-suggestions that were born from their knowledge of visits from the guardian spirit.

Formal hypnosis is different in that the suggestions are delivered by an external agent. Until the suggestions arrive, the subject basically waits. If the subject has only limited knowledge, or no knowledge, of hypnotic responding, he or she waits in uncertainty and apprehension. The subject is naturally vigilant at these times and the conscious monitoring authority is inclined to remain engaged. The final result is that it becomes more difficult for the subject to relinquish control and to enter into a dissociative state. Even for those who have been previously versed in hypnosis, it is still difficult to be confident about one's "knowledge." The fact is that people are exposed to conflicting theories about hypnosis, with little chance of resolving that conflict.

Additionally, individual hypnotists vary considerably in their preferred modes of induction and their delivery of suggestions. Thus there is no common knowledge about hypnotic responding that is a permanent feature of our culture. Those entering trance by way of hypnotic induction techniques are unable to draw on culturally prescribed means by which to translate dissociation into meaningful misconstructions of reality. As such, hypnosis remains a curiosity in the minds of most people. In the absence of a cultural context for it, hypnosis will remain nothing more than a poorly understood clinical tool. Therefore, in its present form, it will continue to yield mediocre and generally disappointing results.

The true identity of hypnosis must be sought not in and of itself, but rather in wider contexts, especially that of religion. In fact, what we call hypnosis is actually a variant of the type of cognitive behavior that plays an integral part in collective methods of reality transformation. This is not surprising in light of the observations already mentioned concerning hypnosis, and hypnotic suggestion, as a distortive mechanism. Hypnosis quickly fades into the domain of religion once we realize that its workings are those that enable entire cultures of people to participate in the adaptive process of reality distortion and transcendence.

4 Religion: The Cultural Mask of Sanity

The central theme of this chapter is that, despite superficial differences, religious and "hypnotic" phenomena are the result of identical mental operations. Both involve techniques that, while again variable in appearance, are intended to produce a state of dissociative trance that will make people amenable to worthwhile reality-altering suggestions. Also, both employ methods whereby suggestions are implanted once dissociation is achieved. Religion, like formal hypnosis, entails a *deconstruction* process that is dependent on dissociation as well as a *reconstruction* process that is carried out via suggestion. That is, reality or a portion of reality is first somehow dismantled by way of the dissociation process, following which a reconstruction can proceed using suggestions.

Some worthwhile examples come to mind that would reveal the bridge between "hypnotic" and religious behavior. Consider the recently publicized miracle that took place when a figure of Christ on the cross began to shed tears. The cross was situated high against the front wall of the church, too high in fact for anyone actually to see the drops of water firsthand. Yet a great percentage of people who visited the church were convinced wholeheartedly that tears were being shed by the figure. At a later point, zoom cameras were able to show that there were no changes to the figure's eyes, even while people reported seeing the tears. Without doubt, people went into the church already armed with the suggestion that they would see tears. They stared at the eyes for long periods of time, which had a trance-inducing effect due to the visual monotony. At the same time, this staring caused eye fatigue and some inevitable perceptual variations, possibly even the result of increased watering of their own eyes. These effects were then interpreted in relation to believers' original suggestion, namely, that Christ's eyes would water. Hypnotists can do much the same thing by having subjects

81

visually focus for several minutes on a small object, and then suggest that the object is transforming itself in some way.

The miracle cures performed by religious faith healers also duplicate formal hypnotic procedures in most respects. They are the result of mass dissociation and suggestion, followed by selected indirect suggestion that works temporarily as a cure with highly susceptible members of the audience. In fact, as a point of departure, we might consider quantitative research showing a connection between religiosity and the capacity for dissociation and suggestive responding.

THE HYPNOSIS OF RELIGION: EXPERIMENTAL EVIDENCE

Very few investigators have made a theoretical interface of religion with hypnosis, or of religion with the dissociation/suggestion mechanism. As such, there are few empirical studies of the relationship between these phenomena. However, a small body of somewhat outdated work has been done in this area, a summary of which is given by Michael Argyle and Benjamin Beit-Hallahmi in their book *The Social Psychology of Religion*.[1]

One study measured hypnotic susceptibility in a large group of subjects using the Harvard Susceptibility Group Scale of Hypnotic Susceptibility. The same people were also surveyed as to the frequency with which they had religious experiences. The findings showed that individuals who were more responsive to hypnotic suggestions tended to be the same people who had the greatest number of religious experiences. The researchers explained these findings in terms of the assumption that religious experiences are the consequence of a response to suggestion. They also assumed that hypnotic behavior is a response to suggestion. Combining their results, they concluded that the ability to respond to suggestions within the context of hypnosis also better enabled a person to respond to suggestions in religious contexts.

If we change the vocabulary slightly, we can see that the above research also makes sense in terms of dissociation theory. Religious and hypnotic behavior are inextricably related because they are both the end result of a person's *ability to dissociate*. Thus it may be inferred that people who show an ability to be religious will show a similar ability to be hypnotized. In both instances, of course, subjects are drawing on their *relatively* superior dissociative abilities. From a statistical standpoint, this means that quantitative measures of religiosity should show significant correlations with measures of hypnotic susceptibility, as was the case in the previously mentioned study. Conversely, people with less developed dissociative capabilities should find it more difficult to respond to both hypnotic and religious induction techniques, since both again rely on a *prerequisite* state of dissociation.

Argyle and Beit-Hallahmi refer to two other studies that warrant mention here. One of these assessed hypnotic susceptibility on the basis of people's responsiveness to five psychomotor suggestions, such as those sometimes given to test depth of hypnosis. Fifty conservative religious subjects were compared in this way to an equal number who held opposing points of view about religion. It was found that the conservative group were more responsive to hypnotic suggestions than their less religious counterparts. Argyle and Beit-Hallahmi review a similar study carried out on a student population, which yielded the same results.

In another study described by Argyle and Beit-Hallahmi, the subjects were those who had experienced "sudden conversion" while part of a revivalistic or evangelical audience. Many of these people had also experienced the classic jerking and twitching movements that precede the religious collapse. These types of bodily reactions are similar to the automatisms displayed by certain individuals who are especially susceptible to hypnotic induction. When the "sudden conversion" subjects were examined under hypnosis, they were more likely than their "unconverted" counterparts to display hypnotic automatisms. This outcome suggests that the most religiously responsive people are also the most hypnotically responsive.

Let us describe the outcome more precisely in terms of dissociation theory. That is, those who are good hypnotic subjects are inclined to be good religious subjects since they are endowed with superior dissociative capacities. Thus, they can be expected to be *talented* at the entire range of skills demanding dissociative potential, and even (if necessary) the types of psychopathology that rely on dissociation. Interestingly, Argyle and Beit-Hallahmi mention a study demonstrating that extremely religious people scored in the high range on a measure of "hysteria," a class of psychopathology that has traditionally been viewed as dissociative in nature. Recent researchers have actually approached an understanding of these same types of psychological disorders from the point of view of hypnosis, even referring to these as "hypnotic" and dissociative in their origin. It is here that we can begin to comprehend that religion, hypnosis, and psychopathology come together as a common cognitive strategy that feeds off our brain's remarkable ability to process information on dissociated pathways.

Thomas Long also examined the interaction between religiosity and hypnotizability.[2] After administering tests of hypnotic responsiveness, he created two groups of subjects on the basis of their hypnotizability scores. Long then compared the religious behavior of these two groups and found that the highly hypnotizable subjects were significantly more religious than their less hypnotizable counterparts.

It is a widely held view that dissociation is the key to an understanding of traditional Western hypnosis. To this, many would add that dissociation can also explain the many cross-cultural practices that closely resemble Western hypnosis, but which carry different labels and are acted out in differing social contexts. Now we have some initial evidence that religion, in all its varied forms, must also be understood as an expression of our dissociative capacity. However, a firm conclusion cannot be based on the regrettably small number of studies described above. Much more sophisticated research is required, some of which will undoubtedly make use of the dissociation scales that have emerged recently. Even then, however, we may find ourselves faced with the inevitable problems of interpretation that plague quantitative studies of this sort. As a result, we may still want to opt for a broad spectrum approach to this general topic, one that puts the relevant issues in historical as well as cross-cultural frames of reference.

I would like to proceed in this manner while attempting to further my case that hypnosis and religion are largely synonymous in their essentially dissociative natures. This will be done while keeping in mind the caution expressed earlier, namely, that "hypnotic" behavior is only one of many possible expressions of the dissociation-suggestion mechanism. Furthermore, when I speak of hypnotic forms of religion, I am referring to patterns of religious induction and indoctrination that resemble the technique used by Western hypnotists. There are many other types of religious techniques that generate a workable degree of dissociation but that do not resemble the hypnotic methods used by hypnotists in Western society.

CROSS-CULTURAL PERSPECTIVES

As a point of departure, it might be worthwhile to give an example that shows religion as it is fostered and maintained by techniques resembling those of modern-day hypnotists. From such a starting point, we can then consider religion that promotes dissociation techniques that fall outside of those employed by Western hypnotists.

Ja'Far Hallaji details the religious practices of the semimonastic group of Afghanistan known as the Naqshbandi Sufis.[3] At the center of this community is the Hakim who spends sixteen years practicing Sufi methods and preparing himself to become a religious practitioner and healer. As an adjunct to formal devotional services, the Hakim holds weekly clinics in which a wide range of psychological and physical problems are attended to. Several assistants also participate in the procedure.

Patients at these religious clinics are brought to a large room containing numerous beds. After being assigned to the beds, they are made to lie on their backs and then instructed to fix their eyes on a nine-pointed symbolic diagram located on the ceiling. The patients are then told to chant, over and over again, the syllables "Ya Hoo, Ya Hukk." As they do this and continue to concentrate on the diagram, the practitioner goes from one patient to another, acting out certain rituals. He holds his hands together, palms down, and passes them over the body of each patient. His hands are moved rhythmically and repeatedly from head to toe, in a fashion resembling the early Mesmerists. According to Hallaji, the hypnogenic effect of this strategy is further enhanced by the periodic interruption of light due to the passing of the Hakim's hands in front of the person's eyes. As still another feature of the practitioner's technique, he rhythmically blows on each patient at the considerable rate of approximately two blows per second. Based on his direct observations of this "Chuff" induction method, Hallaji claims that it takes an average of only six minutes for patients to enter into a deep dissociative trance. This is a much faster result than that obtained by traditional hypnotists in Western society.

Once dissociative trance has been established, the practitioner proceeds to enter into the next stage of the process, namely, the giving of suggestions. He begins by beating a small gong next to the ear of each patient. Then he verbally identifies the symptoms that have brought the person in for help. At this point, the practitioner suggests five times to each patient that the curative powers of the spirit Baraka (Impalpable Force) are entering the patient's body and that these powers will cause the symptoms to disappear when the treatment session has finished. In addition, the practitioner makes two occult references, one of which specifies that the healing power was being transmitted through Sheikh Bahauddin Nakshbund, the founder of the Order of Sufis. It should be noted that, with this technique, no reference is ever made to sleep. Although it is not an element of the induction process, the patients nonetheless lapse into a deep state of dissociation that superficially resembles sleep.

The patients are eventually roused from this state when the practitioner shakes them by the shoulders. Once returned in this way to a general reality orientation, the patients gratefully kiss the hand of the chief practitioner.

Of the eighteen patients observed by Hallaji in the religious clinic, sixteen of those were obviously "hypnotized" by the Hakim. Quite remarkably, by contrast with the rate of effectiveness of Western hypnotherapy, fifteen of the patients reported that their symptoms had disappeared after a single session. The sixteenth patient, who had been suffering from impotence, was unable to report immediately on the status of his problem. Other symptoms reported by the patients included headaches, loss of appetite, anxiety states, intestinal upsets, and backache.

The parallels between this Sufi religious healing practice and that of Western hypnotism are so close that Hallaji is led to describe this religious procedure as a form of hypnosis or, more specifically, hypnotherapy. This is again misleading, since the term "hypnosis" derives from the specific Western induction techniques that constitute what we have also come to call hypnosis. In fact, it is largely a matter of coincidence that the Sufi religious technique for promoting a workable dissociative state resembles so closely that of Western hypnotic methods. This is despite the fact that both are aimed at generating the same final product, namely, a state of dissociation wherein suggestions can be planted in order to alter the person's understanding and/or experience of reality. Quite predictably, however, the Sufi method, like most other non-Western methods of dissociative trance induction, proves to be superior to that used by Western hypnotists.

In the above description, the Hakim, unlike the hypnotist in Western society, takes advantage of the *group* as a facilitator of dissociative trance. This involves treating people in a group setting, as well as on an individual basis. The Hakim has several assistants who also serve to extend the entire procedure into the more fruitful domain of society. Moreover, meaningful patterns of ritual are acted out in the context of recognizable aspects of the cultural heritage, including transcendent beliefs that are an accepted part of the community.

We can therefore say that this Sufi healing practice resembles Western hypnosis, except that its overall method makes it technically superior in most respects, as well as more effective. But this is also an example of a *religious* practice that has a long history among the Naqshbandi Sufis. This leads us to the next logical question: Does religion, in general, depend on induction techniques that promote dissociative trance, thereby making possible the dissemination of religious suggestions for the purpose of transforming reality? The answer is an affirmative one that requires us to consider the problematic nature of reality in relation to the primary goal of religion.

RELIGION AND DISSOCIATIVE TRANCE

In the conclusion of his book *The Transcendental Temptation,* Paul Kurtz analyzes the universal "temptation" of human beings to align themselves with constructions of reality that transcend logical and naturalistic principles.[4] While culturally sanctioned religion is the historical resting point for this powerful drive, it can also express itself in any number of paranormal beliefs and related rituals that operate on the social fringe. Kurtz does not rule out the possibility that some people seem able to resist the natural inclination to entertain constructions of reality that are, by all objective measures, erroneous. But, as I have been arguing, nothing is more uniquely human than deliberate and functional error, especially the variety that serves to modify earthly reality with positive bias.

Kurtz recognizes that reality distortion and transcendence (usually in the form of group religion) is common to all cultures, albeit not necessarily all individuals within every culture. This fact alone, as Kurtz concedes, forces one to consider the possibility that the transcendental temptation, as he calls it, might be tied to our unique biological makeup. On this subject, Kurtz even leaves open the possibility that the human brain is organized in such a way that predisposes it to accept propositions, such as religious beliefs, that are in active defiance of available information.

For the most part, human beings rely on various types of learning, and in particular social learning, in the course of acquiring a behavioral repertoire. As a result, we can see great diversity in behavior from one culture to another. Furthermore, it is only when a behavior is universal by strict definition that one is inclined to postulate biological predispositions. Religion, very broadly defined in order to encompass all unjustified reality biases, is one of these. But, even though Kurtz is sympathetic to biological interpretations of transcendental yearnings, he leaves us with a difficult question to answer: Why is it that some people seem able to live without religion or any other form of transcendental misperceptions of the world?

As simple as that question seems, it requires us to go beyond our usual notions of behaviors as biologically driven. In this case, I believe that we must search for the ways in which human biology interacts with social forces. This means that it may not be religion per se that is biologically determined, despite the fact that it is one of a very small number of human universals. Rather, we might be dealing with a biological *precursor* to religion that is utilized and regulated by cultural forces.

A dual level biocultural model would imply that, even though the biological requisites of religion are in place, religion only develops when the culture *exploits* these requisites in strategic ways. Since individual environments differ considerably, it follows that people would vary in terms of the *degree of exposure* to the cultural forces that act to synthesize religion from the biological raw materials. The end result would be that, in any given society, some people would be expected to be more religious than others.

It is also likely that, as with all biologically based human characteristics, some people are more endowed than others with the biological prerequisites for religion. Again, this would mean that some people should be more religious than others, even in situations where everyone has equal exposure to the cultural mechanics that manufacture religion. Additionally, a biocultural model would allow us to explain differences in religiosity in terms of the *intactness* or viability of any particular culture. History shows us that cultures evolve in much the same way that living organisms do. A cross-cultural analysis will reveal that, in optimally intact and fully functioning cultures, the vast majority of members are religious. On the other hand, cultures in decline, or in early stages of evolution, will be unable to avail themselves totally of the biology that makes possible religion. Thus we would expect to see that some entire cultures are more or less religious than others, which is clearly the case when we make cross-cultural comparisons of religiosity.

I believe that the main biological ingredient for religion is the brain-level capacity to dissociate itself into separate and largely independent streams of consciousness. In fact, the ability to achieve dissociative trance has always been a direct extension of human beings' fundamentally *theological* nature. When trance and suggestion are embedded solidly into a culture, the combination yields religion, however varied our expressions of religion might be. The historical roots of dissociation (as well as "hypnosis") lie outside psychology altogether, in the realm of religion where it *works* best. It is only a culture that has lost its way religiously that could "discover" something like hypnosis and fail to see it as a weak, skeletal version of the more powerful trances that have permitted human beings to religiously *transcend* their general condition. This transcendence has further enabled humankind to escape innumerable conflicts and crises that have arisen within that condition. Such a process has lain at the heart of our instinctive drive to contrive *order* at individual and social levels.

Dissociative trance makes possible all types of religion and quasi-religion, as well as the powerful experiences they often entail. Without our brain's capacity to dissociate and thereby process information along parallel channels, history would not have seen any of the estimated 100,000 or so gods that have come and gone.[5] Nor would we have witnessed the vast array of other religious beliefs that have functioned for ages as mental health prophylactics and overall positive distorters of reality. Religion and dissociation are so closely linked that one must understand them as *coevolutionary* phenomena that unite biological and cultural evolution. Dissociation, which is the result of our unique physiology, is the cornerstone of all religion. Grafted together with biology in the defining context of culture, dissociation is our historical vehicle to alternative constructions of reality that are *better* for us than the reality that would reach us by way of strictly rational cognitive processes.

It is possible, as will become clear in the next chapter, to enter into dissociative trance on one's own and to self-direct that trance toward some useful distortive outcome. In such cases, we usually call the final product psychopathology since the reality distortions are not recognized as normal (in the sense of "normative"). In this regard, we should contemplate the disaster that would ensue if everyone went about the business of biasing and distorting reality on an *individual* basis. Extreme problems of credibility would arise. One person's distortions would clash logically with those of other people, throwing into doubt the entire lot of distortions. Endless small-scale conflicts would appear as people naturally sought to suppress dissimilar misinterpretations of reality in order to maintain credibility. History has even seen some of this on a large scale as collective systems of reality distortion have come into contact with one another. When several corruptions of reality are allowed to exist together, they will inevitably contradict one another and threaten the integrity of them all.

When it comes to our passionate need to transcend and transform reality, *we need each other*. We must defy reality *together* or risk having our illusions exposed as ludicrous fabrications. Anthony Wallace touches on the need for religion to be *social* when he writes:

> Religious behavior is always social; that is to say, the adherents of a religion . . . come together as a group. There they perform (or watch) ceremonies, talk to the gods or to one another, dance

and play music, sing, eat and drink, and in other ways engage in acts rationalized by their relevance to the supernatural. Some religious behaviors may be performed by individuals in solitude, but no religion is purely an individual matter; there is always a congregation which meets on some occasions for the joint performance of ritual acts.[6]

In order for us to be fully convinced of the truth of false beliefs, such beliefs must be the result of a *group* effort whereby the group *normalizes* that particular "insanity" (i.e., *out-of-touchness* with reality). Beyond that, the *degree* of dissociative trance required to sufficiently override critical and analytical faculties is much more easily accomplished when in a group. All cultures know and take advantage of this fact.

What we call religion, therefore, is in effect a cultural-level system involving *group dissociative trance induction techniques* for purposes of instilling reality-distorting suggestions that can be *agreed upon* and therefore not questioned. On the topic of the adaptive value of dissociation, Arnold Ludwig writes that dissociation enables us to "escape from the constraints of reality."[7] Again, however, the actual *content* of our new formulations of reality depend entirely on the suggestions we receive while in a dissociative state, or trance. Once dissociated and released from the constraints of reality, we are free to improve on reality, something religion can do on a collective level. Consequently, religion should be viewed as the main benefactor within any given culture in that it acts in the service of the delusions that have evolved there. This remains valid even though we know that some products of religion (e.g., eternal damnation) may prove distressing to individuals. The *net* contribution of collective religion in its role as reality reformer is usually positive. I say this even though there are known costs that come with religion in the area of personality development and cognitive functioning.[8] From time to time, there are also dysfunctional religions that are selected out and replaced with more functional ones. Religion, like elements operating in the natural world, is subject to evolutionary forces that strive to maintain fitness.

So it makes perfect sense that religions in all cultures contain measures to assist people into dissociative trance. People thus become maximally receptive to the type of suggestions that modify our conceptions of the world and ourselves. Only through dissociation is the person *indoctrinable* or suggestible enough to incorporate the massive distortions of reality that we find in religion. On this subject, E. O. Wilson writes in *On Human Nature* that religious belief became possible in our species only when it had evolved the cerebral capacity of *indoctrinability*.[9] This is the ability of the brain to interrupt its own logical and reasoning faculties in favor of passive modes of information processing that permit indoctrination, or "brainwashing," from external sources. In that description, we see that we are actually talking about dissociation as the technique by which cultural institutions neutralize our higher-order cognitive skills as they seek to promote constructions of reality preferable to those that would be made by our higher functions alone.

On the related topic of human "docility" and "bounded rationality," Herbert Simon extends our knowledge of the coevolution of biology and culture. He does this in the greater context of the biocultural dynamics of altruism. Yet I feel that his insights are equally relevant to an understanding of religious behavior. By docility, Simon means "the tendency to accept social influence."[10] The term "bounded rationality" refers to the end product of evolutionary forces that seek to set upper limits on human rationality, and to make possible patterns of irrationality that contribute to the overall fitness of our species. While proposing that human beings are genetically *selected* on the partial basis of the ability to think *uncritically*, Simon writes:

> Much of the value of docility to the individual is lost if great effort is expended evaluating each bit of social influence before accepting it. Acceptance without full evaluation is an integral part of the docility mechanism, and of the mechanisms of guilt and shame.[11]

Therefore, it may be that successive generations of natural selection have resulted in a species genetically designed to accept, without independent criticism or analysis, constructions of reality that are skewed in any number of ways. Still, culture remains a vital part of the total process, both in the way it magnifies this predisposition toward the irrational and also in the way it provides beneficial alternatives to the real.

A theoretical connection exists between "docility" and conformity. That is, by creating "docile" people, one should also be creating people who are more inclined to conform without imposing critical thought on the directives offered to them. Clearly, group religion is tantamount to conformity since it requires large numbers of individuals to conform to highly specific sets of beliefs and related behaviors. If religion is "hypnotic" or dissociative by its essential nature, we would also expect to find a relationship between conformity and indices of dissociation, such as hypnotic responsiveness. Morris Shames conducted a test of this relationship while measuring both conformity and hypnotizability in a group of sub-jects.[12] As could be predicted on the basis of the above reasoning, Shames found a significant positive correlation between conformity and hypnotic susceptibility, thus providing still greater support for the theoretical model under discussion here.

This takes us to some of the culture-based methods by which dissociative trance is achieved in the framework of religion.

RELIGIOUS INDUCTION TECHNIQUES

When religion is viable and functioning optimally, it is capable of producing one of the most sublime states of *ecstasy*, in addition to the other personal and social benefits described previously. Associated with this ecstasy are feelings of oceanic bliss, and a sense that one is of supreme importance in the unseen eyes of a supreme force. Words usually do not suffice as people try to describe the joy and rapture that ensue when religions are *working* according to their intended biocultural blueprint. Of course, this sounds grossly exaggerated to the average modern Westerner who has rarely, if ever, felt the full power of religion. Most have no notion of the manner and degree to which religion can take hold of a person and throw open the welcomed doors of new imagined worlds, no less inviting than the glorious chemically constructed worlds of addictive drugs.

On this note, Karl Marx was not, in fact, the first to describe religion as an opiate. More likely, he was one of the last, since the Western world was by then losing high-grade religion. Historical developments had left religion in the West largely incapable of orchestrating human thought and emotion in dramatic fashion. Specifically, a social climate emerged in the West that was no longer conducive to the type of religious techniques that could propel people into the religious trance that gave birth to full expressions of religion, including the experience of ecstasy. This climate persists to this day, although numerous small- and medium-scale movements are attempting to revitalize religion and so restore it to its former glory, maybe even its former infamy.

In his work titled *Ecstasy or Religious Trance*, Ernst Arbman draws a close parallel between ecstasy and religious trance, while depicting both as *states of suggestive absorption*. Says Arbman:

> The ecstasy can from the psychological point of view only be under-stood as a specific form of suggestive absorption in the complex

of beliefs which in the state preceding it has constituted the sole, exclusive, and totally dominating object of the consciousness.[13]

To this, Arbman adds that, in the throes of religion, it is even possible for a dissociative split, or what he terms a *doubling of the personality*, to occur. Such terminology takes us back to our previous discussion of dissociation and "hypnotic" phenomena, especially as witnessed in many non-Western societies. It also begins to sound like clinical descriptions of psychopathological conditions, such as the distinctive "splitting" that occurs in certain disorders entailing large amounts of cognitive dissociation. As we proceed, the overlap of these different phenomena should become even more apparent. While on the topic of religion, however, we should explore further the processes of religious trance techniques as they employ strategies of absorption and suggestion. In doing this, I will make further comparisons between Western and non-Western religions in terms of their techniques and how well these techniques work.

Stated concisely, religions rely upon the usual two-stage process of trance induction, with dissociation followed by the imposition of suggestions in order to give structure to the dissociated state. Before speaking of the religious suggestion process, let us consider the ways in which religious "services," as they are often called, go about inducing a dissociative trance in people. There are as many such techniques as there are religions. But certain important commonalities regarding *technique* exist that reinforce the argument that religion is, first and foremost, a dissociative phenomenon.

Music, Monotony, and Religious Trance

On a somewhat whimsical note, we might ask why it is that music is an integral part of all collective religious practices in virtually every culture of the world. It is difficult to think of a single exception. Why, when the Tibetan diviner is seeking spiritual guidance from another world, do priests approach him from both sides and repeatedly blow thighbone trumpets into his ears? Why do the Kotoko of Chad play harps and water drums as they go about their religious possession ceremonies? Among the Vezo of Madagascar it is the zither and, more recently, the accordion. Then there are the gongs used by the Hakim in the earlier example given of Sufi religious healing. In Bali, religious practices involve *gamelan*, or gong music, while small flutes and drums are common in several Vietnamese religions. Small mouth organs and symbols are used in some of the religions seen in Laos, whereas a type of fiddle is part of the religious ceremonies of the Songhay people of Niger. The list goes on and on. I might even ask why, during my own religious services, I was exposed relentlessly to the organ and to choral singing.

Anthony Wallace provides an answer summarizing a vast body of anthropological research. He makes the broad statement that "there are few, if any, religious systems in which dancing, singing, chanting, poesy, and the playing of musical instruments does not play an important role."[14] Then, with specific reference to the *musical* nature of virtually all religions, he writes that "we may suspect . . . that musical media are preferred because of their effect on the human performer and his audience and that sometimes, as in voodoo dancing and drumming, . . . musical performance facilitates entry into a desired state of heightened suggestibility or trance in which . . . religious experiences can be expected to occur.[15] In other words, music is an ideal medium by which to engender a state of dissociative trance and the concomitant hypersuggestibility that is the cognitive foundation for the construction of religious belief systems.

A similar answer is ventured by Gilbert Rouget, author of the illuminating book *Music and Trance*. There he writes unequivocally that "it is music that throws people into a trance."[16] Rouget is so emphatic about music as the universal trance inducer that he feels one need not look much further than music in order to understand the effectiveness of the myriad of trance-induction techniques that are part of the religious and quasireligious activities of human beings. Even so, Rouget is the first to admit that the music-trance relationship is a varied and complex one, even within the confines of his special area of interest, namely, spiritual possession trance. While I hope to show that more is involved in dissociative trance creation than music, it should not be surprising that music is the universal facilitator of trance. Certain forms and patterns of music enable a person to disengage from the conscious monitoring authority and the generalized reality orientation. The music itself can be the focal point for total absorption, with dissociation and greatly enhanced suggestibility following automatically.

Rouget speaks of the neurophysiological repercussions of the systematic and repetitive use of *accelerando* and *crescendo*, and the way in which these pave entry into trance. Some people have even suggested that certain musical time signatures are better than others at bringing about dissociative trance in religious contexts. The ethnomusicologist Alain Danielou observed the inevitable presence of music in religion, while writing more specifically that "in all religions of the world the rhythms employed to produce trance states are always odd, in 5, 7, and 11 time."[17] Danielou even claimed that square rhythms in four or eight time had no "hypnotic" value whatsoever; that is, no value as a generator of dissociative trance.

Rouget disputes the assertion that rhythms in four and eight time have no trance value, giving many examples of religions that achieve excellent dissociative trance results with such rhythms. On that, I would agree with Rouget, since I know that I went into dissociative trance with musical time signatures in four that were used on me during past religious services. But it was probably not as deep a trance as those achieved with more irregular time signatures. Maybe it was also not as forceful and all-consuming as some of the music played as part of powerful *sensory bombardment* trance-induction approaches. Yet I was unquestionably *under the influence* as a result of the musical time signatures in four that I knew in my former days as a practicing Catholic.

As a sidelight, let me add that the word *practicing* is most appropriate when used in the context of religion. Many observers of hypnosis have pointed out that hypnotic (i.e., dissociative) ability can be improved with practice, even for those people with relatively low levels of ability in this area. With continual practice over extended periods of time, it becomes quite simple to use certain cues to enter dissociative trance almost instantly. Therefore, if the ability to be religious is dependent upon the ability to foster a dissociative trance, it follows directly that one can *practice* religion. Beyond that, hypno-therapy with many types of problems is optimally effective when the person receives regular "booster" sessions, ideally every week or so. Otherwise the effect of the suggestions tends to fade, with a consequent return of the unwanted malady. In the same way, it is no coincidence that religious "services" are typically spaced out in time at the same approximate distance as one would space out hypnosis sessions if one wanted maximal results. This allows for the necessary amount of practice in order to keep the process activated.

Studies of the neurophysiological effects of music as they pro-mote trance have often focused on the drum since so many cultures make use of that particular instrument for trance-induction purposes. Analyses of various drum recordings from non-Western religious ceremonial procedures tend to show that "hypnotic" drumming of this sort has a frequency range somewhere between one and five cycles per second, with a mean of approximately three cycles per second. A number of investigators have pointed out that, during dissociative trances of all kinds, the brain generates theta waves in roughly the same frequency range as that of the drums.[18]

Therefore, they have taken the simple logical step of concluding that certain patterns of drumming facilitate entry into states of dissociative trance. Such a conclusion has the support of endless naturalistic studies in which the "acoustic driving" (Etzel Cardeña's term) of drumming can engender deep trance states in very short periods of time. In summing up work in this area, Raymond Prince suggests the possibility that auditory driving of the type generated by drumming is the "commonly used portal of entry into the dissociative state."[19]

Regarding the relationship between music and trance, it is not the music itself that forges a trance in those who experience the music. Instead, the key component is a high quality of *obsessive monotony*. The term "obsessive," as it is used here, refers to a type of musical presentation and influence that is difficult, if not impossible, to resist. Hultkrantz wrote about the dynamics of religious possession in Siberia, pointing out the dissociative methods employed by the trainee shaman as he enters into a state of possession via "hypnotic" trance.[20] It is observed how the procedure revolves around highly monotonous activities that produce an "obsession" which, according to Hultkrantz, easily develops into a state of religious possession. In turn, the possession itself unfolds according to cultural plan. The young shaman, like all those before him, is harassed and finally "killed" by certain invisible spirits, only to be resuscitated by these same spirits, leaving him with new power and magical abilities. The following description by John Pfeiffer of an ancient ceremony illustrates how overwhelming obsessive monotony can be produced in a religious context:

> Everything they knew and believed, the full force of ancestral authority and tradition, came to a growing white-heat in ceremony. What began with a shaman performing in a trance among people around camp fires culminated in spectacles conducted by high priests and their cohorts from platforms elevated above the multitude. There was singing and chanting, words said over and over again, recited in singsong metrical patterns with punctuating rhymes at the ends of lines. Music, setting the pace in the background and echoing and rising to crescendos and climaxes, reinforced the beat. Dancers with masks kept time to the words and the music as they acted out the roles of gods and heroes. Spectators moved with the rhythms and chanted ritual responses.[21]

Griffith Wynne Williams points out that "whenever anthropological records are adequate, monotony is always mentioned as an aid in inducing trance."[22] It happens that music is an ideal sensual modality by which to subject a person to persistent monotonous stimulation. If, as some have argued, certain forms of music facilitate trance better than others, this is probably owing to the differing quality and intensity of monotony contained in the music. Too much melody, for example, can have the effect of diminishing the trance-generating effect of music by creating too much distance between similar beats, thus diluting the amount of useful monotony available to the listener. In fact, increasing amounts of melody have infiltrated many Western religions over the past few centuries, something that may account for the decline in those religions over the same time span. Without an effective mode for delivering dissociative trance, religion cannot proceed and people cannot believe the otherwise unbelievable. Therefore, as a starting point for a revival, religious leaders in the West should assess the overly melodious music that is failing to engender an optimal degree of trance in their constituents.

The trance-yielding monotony of music can also be depleted when it has too much of an intellectual component. Too many words or words that make rational and literal sense, can cause a left hemisphere shift in cortical activity, or prevent the previously mentioned right brain shift that is an aspect of both dissociation and its products, including religion. As a result, the music, which also has as its processing center the right hemisphere, is less able to translate itself into dissociative trance. In this way, I feel that the Roman Catholic church dealt a blow to people's ability to enter trance when it switched languages from Latin to English. Once that type of event transpires, religion does not survive long under rational scrutiny. Had the church continued to make no sense to me, maybe I would have remained susceptible to religious trance and thus not inclined to impose sense on it. Non-Western religions, taken as a whole, seem to possess more wisdom in this regard. As such, cross-cultural observers usually note that their religious inductions do not contaminate trance-generating strategies with left brain material, such as meaningful and attention-demanding words.

Rouget cites numerous examples of the *intended* music-trance relationship in his discussion of spirit possession, which is an important part of some non-Western religions. It has also been noted that, in many cultures, "possession by the God is the supreme religious experience."[23] Included here would be the religions of such groups as the Shango in Trinidad, the Candomblé of Bahia, and the Kung of Botswana. With few exceptions, drums are the musical instruments employed as an integral element of the trance induction underlying the entire process. Specifically, the repetitive driving beat of the drums has the effect of producing a state of dissociation that paves the way for the experience of being taken over by the various spiritual identities. Collectively, the phrase "falling with the drums" has been used to describe the way in which prolonged drumming can send people into the trance that, in turn, enables them to become "possessed" (via autosuggestion) by transcendent spirits and deities.

There is typically a high degree of culturally relevant action with spirit possession ceremonies. This sometimes comes in the form of chanting, rhythmic dancing, and excited crowd activity around ceremonial fires. When performed at night, there is frequently a stroboscopic effect wherein darkness is punctuated by light when bodies move in front of the fire. This alone goes a long way toward trance induction. The same is true of ceremonies that use only candlelight to break the darkness. The effect is to create intense and unmistakable absorption points that also make easier the person's entry into trance. Additionally, it has long been known that stroboscopic photostimulation, such as that caused by the natural movement of fire, produces "photic driving." This refers to the promotion of the type of brain electrical activity that makes people more conducive to dissociative trance.[24]

Without question, this use of fire to create absorption points and photic driving is far more effective than the now familiar and very humble church candle. Over recent years, fewer and fewer candles have been lit in Western religious services, and the candles themselves have become smaller and more difficult to use as points for absorption and subsequent dissociation. This is especially true for followers seated well away from the candles, since they even lose the all-important flickering movement that goes so far in a trance/suggestion setting. Church leaders would be wise to rethink their priorities and not to scrimp on candles. They represent an ancient and time-proven aid to trance induction and to the process of religious suggestion that is thus made possible. Many other improvements could be made as we study the religious methods that survive in some non-Western cultures.

As a trance inducer, the modern church organ deserves some serious criticism. It pales by comparison with the historical methods of drumming, gonging, or clapping people into dissociative trance. The same is true of the present-day choral music that fails to muster the same dissociative effect as widespread emotional chanting, usually accompanied by acoustic driving, as seen in traditional societies. But this generalization should be qualified somewhat by stressing the fact that Western religious music lost most of its "hypnotic" punch only in recent centuries. The past few decades can even be singled out as those that have seen the most rapid loss of Western religion's ability to "monotonize" and absorb followers into a state of dissociation.

As late as the sixteenth and early seventeenth centuries, religious music was still largely alive from the point of view of trance induction. Music, the time-honored harbinger of dissociative trance, remained highly sophisticated in this regard, one of several factors that serves to explain the comparative ease with which religious suggestions could be implanted. It also explains why atheism and other expressions of irreligion were virtually nonexistent until approximately three hundred years ago.[25] Until that time, the process of religious suggestion operated smoothly and efficiently in conjunction with religious induction techniques in order to establish and maintain distortive (i.e., religious) belief.

In terms of music, as just one example of the trance generators that have made possible religious suggestion and thus belief, we might consider the master works of the great English composer Thomas Tallis (1505–1585). His church music was crafted in an exquisitely dissociative fashion, so much so that the ensuing religious trance came as quickly and effortlessly as the trance deriving from the traditional drums and gongs found in non-Western cultural groups. Musicologists attribute this to the endless looping and repetitive cycling of sounds that are part of Tallis's spellbinding religious works. In addition, the notes themselves are sustained for exceptionally long periods of time, and the actual pieces last much longer than their modern counterparts.

By stark contrast to premodern religious music in the West, or that of many non-Western societies, the music found in contemporary Western religious services is insipid and half-hearted. It provides the basis for only the slightest degree of obsessive monotony and absorption. It makes dissociative trance largely impossible, which also means that the service lacks the physiological basis for the successful delivery of trance. Consequently, we should expect that this infirm type of music would not contribute significantly to the establishment of religious beliefs.

The tentative quality of modern church music, and modern religious trance techniques generally, may reflect what Émile Durkheim saw as the increasingly "inward" nature of contemporary Christianity.[26] Additionally, the current Christian trance methods have probably suffered from the self-consciousness and emotional inhibition that have pervaded this particular religious tradition, especially in recent decades.

Although the current trance techniques, and in particular the music, have some effect on the exposed group, they certainly lack the irresistible acoustic driving that will generate the intense obsessive monotony that quickly sends the religious subjects into deep trance in very short periods of time. Rouget elaborates on this point while outlining the interrelationships between emotion, music, and trance. He observes that music is closer to the emotions than any other mode of human expression. Consequently, since "trance is clearly an emotional form of behavior," it is only natural that emotion-arousing music becomes institutionalized as the trance-inducing component of cultural religions.[27] Rouget reiterates that this sort of *emotional trance*, while shaped and patterned to some extent by culture, is nonetheless a universal property of the music itself.

PHYSICAL MOVEMENT AND RELIGIOUS DISSOCIATION

Religion has always been a highly *physical* enterprise. In a myriad of ways, it seeks to promote physiological and biochemical changes that are instrumental in the induction, indoctrination, and maintenance phases of the religious process. In order to better appreciate this fact, we must look beyond some of the relatively "motionless" religious practices of some Western religions. The body phobia underlying their intensely bashful relationship to religion is the result of peculiar historical developments that constitute a flaw in their methods. These modern religions should be understood as a rare exception to the larger picture of religion as a physical, as well as mental, operation. To this effect, Anthony Wallace writes that "physiological manipulation of the human body, by any means available, to produce euphoria, dissociation, or hallucination is one of the nearly universal characteristics of religion."[28]

The physical dimension of religion is also stressed by Gilbert Rouget.[29] After establishing music as the historical harbinger of trance, he goes on to note that energy expenditure in the form of physical movement is also a ubiquitous element of almost all religions. Rouget gives detailed accounts of religious dissociation procedures in which vigorous dance and music function in close harmony. In fact, dancing can magnify the trance effect of the music, and vice versa. Rouget cites examples of the religious practices seen among the Russian Shlustes, the Bushmen of southern Africa, and the Shakers of the United States. He notes that, in combination, music and dance can generate great emotional effervescence and a *state of monoideism* whose psychophysiological conditions are highly favorable to the emergence of dissociative trance.

The value of dance undoubtedly lies in the fact that, like music, it can be the source of trance-fostering obsessive monotony. This is especially true when the dance is emotionally engrossing and culturally choreographed in order to yield a high degree of *repetition* in its specified movements. The communal trance resulting from this type of religious induction exercise is due largely to *ritualized* music; that is, music that contains additional dissociative potential in the form of monotonous movement.

Dance, within a religious context, has another important asset, namely, the ability to bring about a state of total *physical exhaustion*. In turn, this promotes neurophysiological changes and depletions, whose resultant effect is to lessen the participant's ability to resist the core instruments of the trance-induction operation. If one could begin to speak of *ideal* methods for the induction of collective religious trance, one would certainly want to include dance or some other mode of repetitive physical involvement that leads to a significant degree of exhaustion. This component is lacking almost entirely in conservative Western religions. Granted, some mainstream religions in the West still employ ritualistic alterations of positions from standing to sitting, sitting to kneeling, kneeling to standing, and so forth. It could be argued that some physical fatigue is generated by this tactic, but it would not approach the quantity of exhaustion needed to facilitate trance entry.

Other people might point to the anthropological literature demonstrating that prolonged physical discomfort is another ancient religious technique for assisting followers into dissociative trance. They might even single out painful kneeling as a trance aid that persists in some contemporary Western religions, such as Catholicism. Yet we only have to look at the thick padding that now covers present-day kneelers to cast doubt on that theory, not to mention the fact that the duration of the kneeling is insufficient to make much difference in terms of easing entry into dissociative trance. Incidentally, it is worth mentioning that Western hypnosis methods also fail to take much advantage of physical movement. This becomes increasingly important when we discuss the limited value of Western hypnosis in light of the largely ineffective techniques of Western religious services, both of which are beginning to rely on very similar mechanisms.

In many of the new charismatic and revivalistic religions, there remains a creative use of exhaustive physical movement that operates conjointly with music in the promotion of trance. These same religions, it should be added, make use of ebullient and driving musical forms that are much more suited to the promotion of dissociative trance. It is therefore no coincidence that membership in revivalistic and charismatic religions is growing rapidly in relation to other religions. I believe that this trend is a response to the deficit of workable dissociative trance in the orthodox religions. For without effective techniques for dissociative trance, there is no belief, and thus no religion.

Throughout human history, selected physical movements have been used by religious leaders to assist followers into a viable state of dissociation. This category of movement, while not necessarily intended to exhaust the participants, nonetheless functions to engage or *absorb* people's attention, with dissociative trance as the goal. We see this today, even in religions that are floundering seriously in the area of religious induction and indoctrination. In many services, for example, the priest or minister makes slow repetitive movements to the left and right, while performing some aspect of whatever religious ritual is involved. Such movements are intended to facilitate trance entry in much the same manner as letting one's eyes follow the proverbial swinging pocket watch on a chain. If done correctly, exposing people in an appropriate setting to this type of left-right movement will in itself produce cortical changes (sometimes referred to as "cortical irradiation") that help greatly in the trance process. This remains the case to some extent even when the followers are only passively involved. It should be added here that priests and ministers are not consciously aware of their role as "hypnotists" as they use ritualistic movement and other techniques toward the goal of trance induction. Instead, these rituals are the end result of cultural evolution in relation to religious practices.

In a more highly refined and more effective way, this particular use of movement for purposes of trance can be seen among Iban spiritual healers of Borneo who are known in their language as Menang. The Iban shamans of Borneo's Sarawak region are re-nowned for their ability to generate trance states in their "patients" in a very short span of time (usually five minutes or less) and to effect cures in almost all cases. We will return to these religious healers in a later discussion of the etiology and treatment of psy-chopathology, Here, let us simply make note of one part of the trance-induction technique in the Belian ceremony, which is used for treating more serious conditions.

In this, we see the Menang seated in a dimly lit room, empty except for an open fire. He puts a ruglike cloth over his head and then lets his body sway from side to side. This slow and repetitive swaying motion is only occasionally punctuated by brief periods of abrupt convulsions on the part of the Menang. According to German hypnotherapists Bärbel Bongartz and Walter Bongartz, who made a study of Menang trance-induction methods, these periodic convulsions are designed to retain the attention and concentration of the patient, while simultaneously serving to enhance suggestibility.[30] Of course, the patient's ability to respond to subsequent suggestions, aimed at relieving painful symptoms, is dependent upon the hypersuggestibility made possible by dissociative trance. It so happens that the Menang operates within a cultural context wherein historical pathways to trance remain relatively intact.

The physical layout of most Western church services is not such that movement can be utilized extensively in the course of the trance-induction phase of the service. Much better are naturalistic settings where people can gather around the spiritual leader in two broken semicircles, thus allowing for the entire group to become visually and cortically responsive to repetitive movements if that is part of the trance process. As with other potentially valuable trance techniques that have become eroded in Western religion, the effective use of movement as a trance catalyst has fallen out of the repertoire of most Western religious service conductors. Not only is movement limited and restricted, but it lacks the vital feature of repetition which is crucial in providing the obsessive monotony upon which absorption, trance, and suggestion rely.

Stage evangelists, especially those of the unabashed charismatic variety, often do a much better job of utilizing repetitive movement as they prepare their audience for trance and the ensuing suggestions. In their wisdom as religious hypnotists, they frequently make use of the entire stage, pacing from one end of it to the other. The most gifted evangelists know instinctively to pace at varying distances from the midpoint of the stage (also the midpoint of the visual field). This enables those near to as well as far from the religious leader to be influenced by this repetitive left-right movement as one of several monotony-generating trance techniques.

Television evangelists appear to vary in their knowledge of the potential for repetitive movement to promote trance. Some of them make very good use of their hands, which are moved in the characteristic up-down motion. This creates a certain degree of monotony if the visual sequence is held sufficiently long and if the camera distance is such that the eyes of television viewers will follow the evangelist's hands in the angle range that best promotes absorption and trance. Obviously, this must be done in close conjunction with a properly trained camera operator.

Televangelists frequently use left-right pacing, just like their counterparts who operate on live audiences. When this is done, however, it is essential that the camera not follow the religious pacer.

Instead, the operator should maintain the camera in a fixed central position so that the eyes of the television viewer can move left to right across the screen. In doing this, the camera distance should again be adjusted so that the viewer's eyes move rather quickly from side to side. If the distance is too great, the eyes will move too slowly as they follow the leader, and the monotony effect will be sacrificed.

It should be quite apparent by now that most conventional Western religious services are not physically organized and ritualistically choreographed in order to make extensive use of movement as an aid to dissociative trance. Furthermore, the recent trend toward deritualizing in Western religious services has resulted in the loss of some of the few good movement-based trance devices that were once a regular feature of these services. One that comes to mind is the shiny incense burner that swings hypnotically from a gold chain. It has almost disappeared from some services. In his simple body-sway technique, interrupted by tactical convulsions, the Iban Menang does more toward the goal of trance and suggestion than can be accomplished using all the fragmented and unproductive movement techniques remaining at the disposal of Western religious leaders.

With regard to movement and trance, we see here still another example of the way in which contemporary religions are failing technically as they go about the business of indoctrinating their followers with much-needed misconstructions of reality. One cannot expect masses of people to believe the unbelievable unless they are provided with group-sanctioned strategies by which they can actively *dissociate* from relevant constellations of memory and those modes of mental activity that disallow nonsense, illogic, and distortion. In our well-meaning effort over recent decades to bring religion down to earth, we have unknowingly stripped religion of many of its historical vehicles for trance, thereby also forfeiting the central mechanism by which religious suggestions are made palatable, or believable, to people. It is, therefore, not surprising to find a large world-wide migration toward charismatic and so-called primitive religions wherein dynamic and high-powered dissociative trance techniques play a vital role.

RELIGIOUS TRANCE, LANGUAGE, AND EMOTION

In some modern Western religious induction strategies, words substitute partially, or even entirely, for music. When this is done,

one notices that additional amounts of emotion are employed in an effort to induce dissociative trance. Consider again the television evangelists or the administrators of group faith-healing sessions. We are so accustomed to high levels of emotion being associated with their words that we rarely question the reason for all that emotion. The explanation for this predictable phenomenon is that emotion facilitates and accelerates entry into trance. Just as emotional music is advantageous in this way, so, too, are emotional words.

The most talented religious trance inducers sometimes work themselves up into a spellbinding emotional pitch of such intensity that it spills automatically onto the exposed group. This promotes a state of dissociation and increases the likelihood of acceptance of the suggestions that are incorporated into the trance procedure. When agitated pacing is added, emotion can be amplified. This is especially true if vigorous gestures (ideally of a repetitive nature) can be made with the hand, arms, and upper body. If these are done well, the emotion thus derived will combine with whatever monotony is mustered in helping followers to achieve dissociation and to suspend critical faculties, thereby opening the door further to distortive suggestions.

Word-based religious induction techniques are interesting for another reason. The words themselves are not delivered as they would be in normal speech. Instead, they are frequently expressed in complex arrhythmic patterns, giving the effect of primitive beats in odd musical time signatures. In charismatic and revivalistic Western religions, this is often done with considerable emotion. The final result is the creation of gripping "verbal music" (not so unlike modern "rap" music) that enlists the emotions and creates an excellent atmosphere for easy entry into dissociative trance. When words substitute for music in this format for religious induction, the words can be compared to the drums used in so many non-Western religions.

The above description of words as alternatives to music applies to religions that rely on "acoustic driving" in order to facilitate dissociation. But words can also replace or supplement music, although less efficiently, in religions that depend on sensory deprivation methods of trance induction. This would include the majority of mainstream conservative Western church services in which words are used to create a droning sound that generates monotony by avoiding pitch variation. When actual music is an aspect of these religious inductions, it also tends to lack intonation, yielding monotony in the form of a sustained tone that becomes the focus for total absorption and eventual dissociation. When words accompany music in sensory deprivation services, they are also devoid of expression, adding to the slow "hum" that is ultimately featured in trance techniques of this nature.

Although words are sometimes used to accompany sensory bombardment religious techniques, they usually play a lesser role than sensory deprivation approaches. When they are found in bombardment religious inductions, they again resemble a musical modality, except that they are highly expressive, percussive, and consistent with the overall driving beat of the religious practice. If one can keep partially alive one's critical faculties during a sensory deprivation service, it becomes apparent that the outcome is to entrance the congregation even further. Once the congregation is suitably prepared, the suggestions embedded into the sermon can be imparted, hopefully with some success.

A curious situation develops when trance induction is reliant primarily on word-based inductions, such as those of television evangelists who do not use musical backups. It means that the words must serve as *both* the basis for trance induction via "musical" monotony and the vehicle by which suggestions are delivered to the religious subjects once dissociative trance is achieved. This is not an ideal tactic for two reasons: Most obviously, and like all other word-based methods, it does not take sufficient advantage of music. Second, it demands an exceptional skill on the part of the speaker. He or she must possess a mastery of words, not only as they can be used to drum people into a trance, but also as they must be able to deliver suggestions that steer followers into modified versions of reality. Despite the high degree of talent needed here, there are some religious figures who have developed this into a fine art, not to mention a thriving business venture.

If we stand back for a moment and survey the larger picture, we can make some additional observations about the relationship between religious services and classical hypnosis. For one, the stereotypical hypnotic situation mirrors only certain types of religious induction techniques. In particular, it roughly parallels conservative noncharismatic Western religious services that lack a strong musical foundation for trance induction, thus opting usually for sensory deprivation methods for the instilling of dissociative trance. Also, services associated with this type of religion mirror classical hypnotic sessions in that both involve an external agent whose role it is to orchestrate the trance techniques. This agent is also largely dependent upon words, but can gain some additional assistance from mild sensory deprivation that derives from the actual environment in which the procedure is conducted.

Certain potential shortcomings are also shared by these

superficially different manifestations of dissociation. As word-based strategies, the value of both techniques is hampered by whatever limitations the external agent has in terms of verbal ability and the performance skills needed to facilitate the trance process. To reiterate, only the most talented of people can have high impact results using words alone for dual purposes of trance and suggestion. This is true whether they be hypnotists or conductors of religious services.

In this context, reports of the purported effectiveness of hypnosis are very misleading. We saw, for example, that only about 5 percent or so of people are "hypnotic virtuosos." This term refers to individuals with exceptional ability to enter dissociative trance via so-called hypnotic induction techniques, and to be highly responsive to suggestions that are offered while in a state of trance. Immediately, one is compelled to ask why it is that such a small percentage of people have this particular ability. On the matter of the effectiveness of orthodox Western religious methods, many observers have noted that the bulk of religious followers have only a half-hearted degree of religious commitment. My personal experience would lead me to judge that, as with classical hypnotic techniques, only about 5 percent of devotees are "religious virtuosos," or what has elsewhere been called true believers, or true holders of the faith. These estimates could be accurate, given the relative feebleness of the dissociative trance techniques currently found in most mainstream Western religious services.

Still again, there cannot be wholehearted belief in the otherwise unbelievable unless people can first dissociate themselves in order to disengage critical thinking faculties. Likewise, classical hypnosis will continue to yield lackluster and mediocre results until its techniques are enhanced in light of new insights into the dissociation process. Therefore, in a curious way, a common basis exists for the failings of both modern religion as well as contemporary applications of "hypnosis" in therapeutic ways. Conversely, if both are to survive, similar sorts of technical modifications would need to be introduced in an effort to amplify the trance effect, thus making it possible to disseminate suggestions with far more success than is now obtained.

RELIGION, DRUGS, AND DISSOCIATION

From the vantage point of contemporary Western religion, it might seem outrageous to argue that drugs and religion usually go hand in hand. But this is precisely the case. Throughout human history, drugs have enabled people to gain access to moving religious experiences that were highly important at the level of the individual and society. Spiritual healers in a multitude of cultures made regular use of hypnotic drugs in order to make contact with the divine spirits and forces that would empower the healer to bring about cures. In many instances, young people were formally introduced to the transcendent beliefs of the society while under the influence of such drugs. Related rituals, which were then performed while in this socially prescribed altered state of consciousness, took on special meaning and left indelible impressions on the initiates. The controlled use of drugs as a method of religious indoctrination can still be seen in some non-Western cultural settings, typically those in which the religious systems are largely intact and functional.

Religions have varied enormously in their methods of employing drugs, whether the drugs are used by the followers, the leaders, or both. Yet certain consistent patterns emerge that help us to further understand religion as a product of dissociation and suggestion. A specific example might serve to illustrate this pattern while simultaneously drawing attention to the problems of Western religions as they seek to promote their spiritual wares without the benefits of chemical hypnotics. Some excellent descriptions are provided by Charles Grob and Marlene Dobkin de Rios.[31] One of these deals with the Chumash Indians of California, whose religion was intimately tied to *Datura*, a potent hypnotic and hallucinogenic drug. This drug, more commonly called Jimsonweed, was once used by the Aztecs and probably reached northern destinations via early Aztec trading routes.

Among the Chumash, Datura was highly regulated, and so, too, was the reality of the people. Members of that culture first encountered Datura in a custom in which youths made formal passage into adulthood. Before this transition could be accomplished, it was necessary for the youth to make contact with a guardian spirit and to enlist the spirit's lifelong help and guidance. Among other things, this would allow the person access to the supernatural world and enable that person to achieve knowledge of future events. Datura was important in this process since the invisible spirits somehow had to become visible to the youth. The Chumash believed that the drug itself had paranormal properties that could transport the young person into the unseen world inhabited by the guardian spirits.

Upon closer inspection, however, it becomes apparent that the Chumash rite of passage ceremony is still another variation of the use of dissociation and suggestion in order to instill misconstructions of reality. The key difference is that, unlike traditional hypnosis or

Western religious services, dissociation is greatly facilitated through ingestion of a chemical hypnotic. Beyond that, the degree of dissociation made possible by this drug is increased far beyond the level that could be achieved by most people exposed only to non-chemical pathways to dissociative trance. It follows logically that the implantation of suggestion would be much aided by this hyper-dissociated state, and also that the affected person would be responsive to suggestions with a higher than usual degree of distortion. This is evidenced by the fact that, almost without exception, these Chumash youths "see" and "communicate" with the invisible spirits, and carry these beliefs with conviction into their adult lives.

The class of drugs known generally as hypnotics acts on the brain in order to promote deep dissociation. To call them "hypnotic" drugs, however, is misleading to the extent that the word "hypnosis" implies not only dissociation, but responses to suggestion that derive from external, or sometimes internal, sources. Strictly speaking, it would be more accurate to describe these drugs as "dissociatives" since the drugs, by themselves, only bring about a state of dissociation. In such a state, the person loses touch with the conscious monitoring authority and related abilities needed to scrutinize critically incoming information. Nonetheless, the drug-induced dissociative state is a largely vacuous one that needs direction in the form of suggestions. These give structure and meaning to the chemically produced state of dissociation, done in much the same way by the hypnotist who follows up trance induction with hypnotic suggestions or the priest who follows up religious trance induction with religious suggestions. Otherwise, a problematic situation would arise, not unlike a person who was given sodium amytal prior to an interview, but then not interviewed.

The Chumash are very skilled when it comes to managing and directing the dissociative trance made possible by Datura. Such skill is indispensable to the long-term perpetuation of Chumash religious belief systems. In this regard, it is necessary for certain designated tribal members to make sure that the youngster sees and experiences what is culturally appropriate. Individual "sponsors," prior to the actual ceremony, instruct the initiate in all facets of religious lore, including descriptions of the guardian spirits with whom contact will soon be made. This represents a set of suggestions that will be acted upon at the specified time and under the specified condition, in this case, the trance state engendered by Datura. As a safeguard, the "sponsors" guide the ceremony itself, thus ensuring that the initiate is exposed to the correct suggestions. We see here that *auto*suggestion is at the heart of this procedure, but also that these suggestions stemmed originally from an external source (i.e., the sponsor). Additionally, the initiate's autosuggestions are supplemented and guided by the sponsor as needed when the initiate is under the influence of the hypnotic, or dissociative, drug. When all goes according to plan, the invisible guardian spirits become "visible" and the young person is successful in forging a permanent relationship with a guardian spirit. While this spirit is fictitious in terms of actual or primary reality, it is certainly real to the young initiate and real in that it exerts a positive influence over the life of the new adult.

One traditional role of the guardian spirit was to make the young man a successful hunter. I have no doubt in this regard that the young person's hunting ability was enhanced. The guardian spirit, which existed in his *personal* reality, could easily increase courage and confidence, and consequently the likelihood of success as a hunter. We saw this to be the case with religion generally. With some exceptions, both mental and physical health benefit from religious involvement. In turn, we could expect these advantages to extend to people's everyday life, in their ability to perform tasks more effectively, and to be more successful within their defined social roles and duties. While this originates in "docility" and the ability to suspend higher-order cerebral functions, it translates into final sets of behaviors that prove advantageous to the individual and society. Drugs, such as Datura, have been central to this total process since the dawn of amplified consciousness in our species. This occurred when we evolved the capacity for dissociation and religion, and when drugs could serve us well toward these ends.

Grob and Dobkin de Rios observe that the use of Datura within religious contexts varies considerably from one cultural setting to another. In part, this reflects the different beliefs and rituals that evolved across the Indian cultures that have employed this drug as an aid to dissociative trance and the conveyance of religious suggestion. In some cultural groups, for example, Datura is strictly controlled and its use limited to a very small number of ceremonial events. Sometimes it is used only a single time, that being during the ceremony marking passage from youth to adulthood.

Both men and women can be seen in some cultural settings to ingest Datura in order to have religious visions. But in others only men are allowed to use the drug. In the Cahuilla Indian society, located in the mountains of southern California, women take Datura for a variety of purposes in addition to religious ones. They frequently take this drug during childbirth, in order to reduce pain. This analgesic effect is not the direct result of the drug. Instead, as a "hypnotic" drug, Datura brings about a state of dissociation and hypersuggestibility. In turn, the woman can readily respond to suggestion, in this case the suggestion that pain will vanish. In Cahuilla society, such a suggestion does not need to come from an external source, since members "know" (i.e., have already received the suggestion) that Datura diminishes pain during pregnancy. Even so, others are typically present during childbirth to reinforce that existing knowledge by implanting pain-countering suggestions while the woman is under the influence of the drug. This resembles a situation in Western society wherein a hypnotist might train a woman in self-hypnosis so that she can put herself into a dissociative trance at the time of birth, and then be able to suggest to herself that she feels no pain. The main difference would be that, in the Western scenario, a drug is not used to facilitate dissociative trance. Also, the suggestion that the woman will feel no pain originates from an independent external agent rather than existing at the cultural level, as in the case of the Cahuilla. This factor takes on much greater significance when it concerns religion, as will be seen when we take up the issue of pathological religions that do not enjoy social sanctioning.

The age-old interaction of drugs and religion can be further illustrated by considering the Shangana-Tsonga culture of Mozambique and the northern Transvaal region of South Africa. This group of people is also noteworthy for the way in which they reveal how religion can constitute an ongoing *adaptive* response to group-level problems that could threaten the survival of the entire group. To understand this latter point, we must recognize that, in an impoverished rural society, rates of infertility and infant mortality are exceptionally high. It is estimated that 30 percent of Shangana-Tsonga women are infertile, and that 35 percent of infants die in the first year of life.

The religious practices of these people include the employment of a hypnotic drug extracted from the *Datura fatuosa* plant, one closely related to the plant used by the Chumash Indians. Not surprisingly, many religious rituals in Shangana-Tsonga culture revolve around the issue of female fertility. This can be seen clearly in the coming-of-age ceremony in which the wife of the chief inserts porcupine-like quills into the young girl's vaginal area, a symbol of pubic hair growth and, indirectly, a symbol of fertility. For her part, the initiate wraps her legs around a tree that contains a white sap ("semen") and mimics the act of intercourse with the tree.

As part of this particular religious ceremony, *Datura fatuosa* is given to the girl in order for her to make contact with the fertility god who has the power to remove any witchcraft that was causing sterility in the girl. Her job is to translate the drug-based dissociative trance into visions of the fertility god. The young girl must also hear the voice of this god. This is accomplished by suggestions that were given to her during the course of preparation for the formal initiation, ones that can be self-delivered in a manner similar to that of the person who autosuggests during a state of self-hypnosis. But an external agent is also present at the Shangana-Tsonga ceremony in order to administer preselected suggestions that will help the female initiate see and hear the fertility god. Grob and Dobkin de Rios do a fine job of highlighting the essentially "hypnotic" nature of this overall religious process and the final outcome, including the role of the drug. They write:

> The main goal of the rituals is for the girls to hear the voice of the fertility god, stimulated largely by the suggestions of the officiant who is knowledgeable about Tsonga ritualistic lore. . . . The officiant psychologically manipulates the group of novices to ensure group conformity during the rituals. The plant [i.e., drug] enforces a diminution of the girls' critical faculties, and there is a decreased reality testing and hypersuggestibility . . . the dissolution of self-boundaries under the plant's influence evokes primary process thinking where external suggestions assume a concrete reality and a supramotivational state ensues.[32]

In this description, we can see all the elements of religion as a dissociation-based procedure that can be assisted by the managed use of a "hypnotic" drug. This sequence of events directly follows what we have said thus far about the joint operation of dissociation and suggestion. We see that the Shangana-Tsonga avail themselves of a chemical substance that generates the desired state of dissociation, with the usual fading of critical and analytical thought processes. In relating this to a discussion of memory, we could likewise conclude that the subjects also become dissociated from memories or knowledge of the natural world that would interfere with the implantation of distortive suggestions. Following the establishment of a dissociated state, cultural suggestions that are both self-delivered and other-delivered come into play in order to give religious structure and meaning to the largely vacuous state of dissociation created by the drug. Once this has been done, the girls readily hear the voice of the fertility god who communicates to them about the importance of having many children, looking after the home, growing food for the family, and so forth. At this point, one recognizes the *adaptive* value of this particular expression of religion among these people. It serves to instill religious beliefs that translate into actions that will sustain population growth and combat the problems of infertility and infant mortality. At the individual level, the girls have an increased sense of their own importance as they enter officially into the adult world. This and many other personal mental health benefits derive from this type of religious practice, which owes its effectiveness in part to *Datura fatuosa*.

We would be completely mistaken in viewing the Shangana-Tsonga religious system as "primitive" or somehow less rarified than the religion with which we are familiar in the West. In fact, if we judge this mode of religion in terms of its effectiveness, we realize that it is far superior to the Western variety in many respects. It is technologically more advanced in the sense that it is more in tune with the workings of dissociation. The specific strategies for trance induction and the ensuing transfer of religious suggestions are closely aligned with the intended and natural mechanisms by which religion is manufactured at the cultural level. The Shangana-Tsonga have not lost sight of the benefits of controlled drug administration as an effective point of entry into a state of dissociation. They do this in a highly managed way, limiting drug usage to its rightful place, namely, religion.

Aside from their adroit application of drugs, the high degree of religious sophistication among the Shangana-Tsonga is evidenced by their simultaneous deployment of repetitive music of the forceful "acoustic-driving" variety. Of this, Grob and Dobkin de Rios write that "music plays an important role in evoking stereotypical visionary patterns linked to the presence of the fertility god."[33] Furthermore, the entire ritual is enacted in a *group* setting which we know to be an asset both in terms of trance achievement and the individual's ability to absorb suggestions during trance. The presence of an actively participating group serves to *normalize* both the bizarre induction procedures and the reality-distorting suggestions to follow. Experiencing these as normal reduces anxiety and suspicion, and prevents the person's higher-order critical thinking capabilities from creating interference.

Drugs are a very sensitive issue in Western society today, and most people would recoil at the thought of introducing them in order to improve our flagging religions. They would not readily understand that drugs are extremely valuable religious tools that, for thousands of years, have offered viable pathways to dissociation and suggestive responding. Terrifying images would come to mind of masses of folk irrevocably addicted to mind-altering chemical substances. Yet, in those societies where drugs are utilized in this appropriate manner, one rarely finds drug abuse, dependency, or addiction. Instead, a much different situation arises when a society is unable to offer sufficient dissociation within the framework of religion. Then we see that people are forced to take *personal* responsibility for the achievement of dissociation (and a positive biasing of reality). This is all too often done with drug taking that is uncontrolled, contextless, and thus addictive in a truly destructive way. As creatures who historically have given in to the "transcendental temptation" (Paul Kurtz's term), we were meant to be addicted to religion, without being directly addicted to the drugs that have been a part of religion for so long.

RELIGIOUS SUGGESTION AND ITS PREPARATION

Until now, we have been concentrating on the first phase of the religious process, namely, the imposition of cognitive dissociation. From the perspective of religion, this is the vital process allowing followers to become susceptible to beliefs and related behaviors that would be difficult or impossible while a person was planted firmly in the general reality orientation. Dissociation, as it is achieved in religious contexts, permits the implantation of religious suggestions. As a mode of conveyance for distortive suggestions, religious dissociation techniques are to be partially understood as a form of preparation.

We saw how adept the Shangana-Tsonga were at *preparing* initiates to participate fully in the religious practices of that culture. This entailed well-conceived trance inductions that were sufficiently powerful to promote a state of dissociative trance in virtually any person subjected to these methods. The Shangana-Tsonga are worth further mention here since they also exemplify the effective delivery of suggestions within a religious context, once the dissociative state has been achieved.

I emphasize the word *preparation* here since it is essential that certain expectations be well established in advance of the more formal induction service. For some time prior to the Shangana-Tsonga initiation ceremony for young girls, for example, the initiate is coached by adult women who have already been through the procedure and made contact with the fertility god. This sort of dialogue might have little meaning or significance to the young person at that stage and her attention to this information might be less than total. But when it comes time for the actual ceremony, these earlier interactions become all-important because they serve as the basis by which the young woman will *structure* the dissociated state that is brought about by the drug and the other trance techniques of the religious leader. Specifically, the messages given to her in the weeks leading up to the ceremony translate readily into self-deliverable verbalizations, or *autosuggestions*.

In the absence of such social preparation, it would be quite difficult for the young woman to "see" and "hear" the fertility god. Such would be the case even though the conductor of the ceremony is also giving suggestions aimed at steering the girl's dissociated state toward the fertility god. We know that the autosuggestions used by the girl in this instance stem from external agents in her social environment. Even so, they become her own to the extent that, ultimately, she is primarily responsible for guiding herself toward the god of fertility. Other people are an integral component in the process, but it comes down in the end to the individual delivering to herself/himself the suggestions that provide distortive shape to the dissociative state. This is precisely why Ernest Hilgard wrote, on the topic of traditional hypnosis, that all forms of hypnosis are ultimately displays of *self*-hypnosis. The same is true of religion. Religious suggestions, even when delivered directly from outside sources, are self-suggestions. Yet we see how necessary it is for others to play a role in *readying* the person in such a way that the correct suggestions are self-delivered in order to achieve the intended final outcome.

The Chumash Indians, as we also saw, used very similar trance-induction strategies as part of their religious services, again involving a "hypnotic" drug that greatly facilitated a state of dissociation. In their case, however, the young person encounters the guardian spirit who communicates a different message. These religious experiences, despite some variation among individuals, are highly specific and closely aligned to the belief systems of the culture. To describe the drugs as "hallucinogenic" in nature is potentially confusing due to the connotation carried by such a label. That is, such a name leads one to think that the drugs themselves produce certain specific mental images, or that the "hallucinations" appear to the person in a haphazard or random way. The fact that very similar drugs produce very different specialized images tells us that one should view these chemicals as "dissociatives" rather than hallucinogenics. True, they subsequently allow the person to "hallucinate" in the sense of seeing and communicating with someone who does not exist in actual reality. But this is the result of the *suggestions* that are used as the mental building blocks of a biased construction of reality *once the dissociative trance has been achieved* (in this instance, with the help of a drug).

As with the Shangana-Tsonga, the Chumash engaged in educational practices in preparation for the religious ceremony that would eventually give life to mental constructions in the form of the guardian spirits. Unquestionably, the messages contained in the Chumash dialogue entailed content different from that of the Shangana-Tsonga. Thus, despite a dissociative trance of very similar design and origin to that of the Shangana-Tsonga, the Chumash youth delivered autosuggestions that gave an entirely different structure to the state of dissociation. The same observation can be made when considering religious practices in almost any culture. In nearly all instances, people are exposed to image-generating verbalizations that can be used as autosuggestions, or *autoverbalizations*, once they are needed in a religious context in order to structure a dissociative state.

Frequently, the preparation of society's members for religious autosuggestion is a subtle extension of the broader process of *cultural suggestion*. By this is meant the messages or themes that are communicated to people simply as a consequence of their existence and participation in that culture. Until recent times, cultural suggestions had a high degree of overlap with those that were part of the religious indoctrination process. This would be expected since general understanding of the world did not deviate greatly from religious "knowledge," and very often the society itself was governed by religious figures of various sorts. Only in the past few centuries have dominant secular suggestions emerged, which fall outside of the culture's religious beliefs. Even today, in certain non-Western societies where religion has not waned significantly, one can still see how religious messages, or suggestions, permeate everyday communications. There, as with nearly all functional cultures of the past, people's thoughts were never far away from the gods, the spirits both good and bad, and the endless magical forces that also featured in their religious comprehensions of their world. The mutual exchange of such information was, in effect, cultural suggestions that kept people armed, or prepared, to self-deliver relevant culturally based religious suggestions.

A culture's religion is greatly aided if there exists this close relationship between religious suggestion and ongoing cultural suggestion. The advantage is derived from the fact that members are continually preparing themselves for successful formal religious involvement as they and others keep alive in their minds the verbalizations and images that can become autosuggestions. After these suggestions are cemented as beliefs during religious ceremonies entailing dissociative trance, the process of cultural suggestion reinforces these beliefs on an ongoing basis. This cycle, which is crucial for the maintenance of a viable and wholehearted religion, involves each member of society acting in the minor role of a "hypnotist" to the extent that religiously pertinent suggestions are regularly shared by people within the society.

A much different picture presents itself in contemporary Western society where, for the most part, religion has become *compartmentalized.* That is, the practice of religion is tightly time-limited, and usually involves no more than the one hour per week when people show themselves at the service. And, as is well known, attendance at religious services today is sporadic with many individuals, a factor that erodes the continuity of available religious autosuggestion even further. Stated simply, the religious practices of Western people today do not contain sufficient *practice,* or preparation, in terms of the suggestion process. With the exception of a small percentage of true believers, the remainder of the modern man's or woman's life revolves around activities totally divorced from religion. If anything, most people today become self-conscious and embarrassed by talk of religion that surfaces in the course of their social interactions. At best, the secular world of today has a very hesitant and uncertain relationship to religious allusions (and potential self-suggestions) that occur outside of religion's narrowly defined place and time.

This is but one aspect of the overall erosion of Western religion that has been witnessed since about the seventeenth century. The offshoot of this in terms of religious suggestion is quite serious from the point of view of the ingredients for a dynamic and *functional* religion. An almost insurmountable obstacle is faced by the religious leader when he or she must somehow indoctrinate a group of people who are *unprepared* for the procedure at hand. The congregation lacks the communicative rehearsals, or the religious *practice,* that will assist the leader toward the goal of indoctrinating the group with valuable distortive beliefs, perceptions, and experiences. It is true that church members generally have some vague ideas about the set of religious doctrines from which these distortions will be drawn. Yet, if Christianity can serve as an example, we must recognize that many modern Christians rarely read the Bible, which could be helpful to the leader once the service is in motion. Also, they tend not to talk about the content of the Bible, just as they avoid discussing most elements of their religion. Once again, then, conductors of the religious service encounter a daunting task as they seek to orchestrate what are essentially group hypnosis sessions. (Certain fundamentalist Christian sects might be excepted since they strongly emphasize the Bible and its messages.)

Being a teacher, I am reminded of a situation in which students come to class not having read any of the required readings, and not having discussed or even thought about any of the material that is to be learned. They come in *cold*, not unlike the bulk of today's so-called faithful who show up cold at a religious service. By contrast, we saw the close interaction between religion and everyday life that characterized traditional societies, a factor that increased the power and persuasiveness of the religious leader. There the power of the suggestions was magnified since the religion had been *practiced* on an ongoing basis. This was done despite the fact that such practice did not entail the dissociative trance techniques that are a part of the official religious ceremony. When religion is an *ongoing* aspect of people's lives, members of that society have a readily available pool of "prehypnotic" suggestions that ready them for formal induction and indoctrination. Moreover, this same *living* religion provides the "posthypnotic" suggestions that reinforce and continuously normalize the distortive suggestions lying at the heart of the religion.

THE NATURE AND FUNCTION OF RELIGIOUS SUGGESTION

In most non-Western cultures where religions remain intact, one sees that religious suggestions are often *indirect*, or indicated simply through the enactment of a ritual or the introduction of a religious symbol. This does not diminish the power of the religious leader's *implied* suggestions, again because the participants are so well versed in the religious content and meanings. Stated more technically, cultural members enter into socially sanctioned indoctrination procedures with clearly defined *cognitive* sets that minimize the need for overt and direct suggestion following trance induction. On their own, these well-rehearsed cognitions, which might be described by contemporary cognitive psychologists as "self-talk" or "internal dialogue," transform readily into autosuggestion. But this is only possible when religion is central to the daily life of a society.

It is also true that many non-Western religious services have assistants of various sorts whose role it is to deliver more *direct* suggestions to individuals who are targeted for some specific religious purpose, such as healing or initiation. We saw this in the Chumash ceremony where the officiant acted as a sort of hypnotist's assistant while directing suggestions to the entranced subject. In that case, the dissociative trance was made possible by a combination of a drug and the induction techniques of the religious leader. Turning to what remains of religious services in the West, we can draw some useful comparisons with those of non-Western suggestion methods. We could even take a specific example to illustrate how suggestions are delivered in a familiar Western religious context. A useful example would be that of a small northern Baptist congregation, with which I have had recent personal experience. It is especially interesting since it demonstrates how religions can be brought to the point of crisis if the practices of those religions are not satisfactory in terms of trance induction, and consequently in the delivery and implantation of distortive suggestions.

The actual religious service was representative of thousands of other such current Western services, except possibly that its techniques had weakened even further than most. An extremely small amount of ritual and drama was featured in the service. The minister merely draped a black robe over an ordinary business suit. Absorption points were virtually nonexistent. Also absent were candles, the standard focal points for trance entry. Each service was punctuated with hymns, but they were sung unemotionally in unentrancing ordinary (i.e., even) musical time signatures. This produced only the slightest amount of stimulus deprivation, hardly a sufficient beginning point for the trance-suggestion process. "Communion," was carried out only once a month; therefore, the congregation was deprived of the benefit of a regular group-binding ritual. The minister gave a sermon toward the end of each service which did contain a certain number of religious (i.e., distortive) suggestions. Yet these sermons tended to lack emotion and were presented without the aid of "hypnotic" movements or verbalization patterns.

Curiously, just prior to the start of the sermon, children under the age of ten or so were allowed to go to the church basement to play. Research shows that suggestibility peaks in human beings at around the age of nine or ten. This meant that children were absent from the sermons during the years when we would expect them to absorb most readily the suggestions that were embedded into the sermon. If one wants to ensure the perpetuation of religious beliefs from one generation to the next, special efforts should be made to expose nine- and ten-year-old children to all sermon material. In fact, they should be present from a very young age even if it seems on the surface that they are not picking up on the suggestions. This is simply another aspect of the larger process of keeping people *prepared* to become indoctrinated. However, the reverse was the case in the Baptist congregation under discussion here.

Predictably, as regards what we know about the inner workings of religion, membership in this particular church began to fall and continued to decline for many years. As a result, a financial crisis developed that further threatened the church's future. Special efforts were made to retain current members and to encourage potential new members. From time to time, concerned church deacons consulted with one another as they sought possible explanations for the declining membership as well as potential solutions. But membership continued to dwindle, especially in the younger age groups, throwing further doubt on the longterm viability of the church.

While this is a common scenario in many Western religions today, many religious leaders still do not realize what lies at the heart of the problem. But our example makes it clear that religious services are almost entirely devoid of the necessary ingredients that have, throughout our history, made us into creatures of religion. In their present state, religions like the one above lie at the other end of the spectrum from those misnomered "primitive" religions that still manage to retain their emotional, psychological, and social grip on the people fortunate enough to be members of those societies.

Religions, like all other living organisms, can evolve in order to improve their capacity for survival. This happens continuously as a response to environmental changes of all kinds, including the inadvertent collapse of the religious techniques required to manufacture and maintain religion with a culture or subculture. As one symptom of its evolutionary experimentation, the congregation in the above example went through a period in which new ministers came and went, almost as if the church were sampling different ministerial approaches. Then, with the recruitment of one particular minister, the unconscious group mind of the church seemed to recognize in him the basis for positive evolutionary change.

This new minister touched a nerve in the congregation when he openly announced his intention to make the religious services into "charismatic" ones. As he spelled it out, these would resemble, but in a tempered way, the high-energy charismatic services of Southern Baptist congregations. Without, of course, labeling the new strategies as dissociative or hypnotic, the minister demonstrated them to the congregation and even conducted some preliminary services wherein he coached people through the new set of rituals and activities. For their part, the congregation was expected to raise their hands in the air and move them repetitiously left to right. This was to be combined with singing and chanting that was far more acoustically driving than what they had been accustomed to. Clapping in unison, which yielded a weak drumming effect, was also demonstrated, as were physical movement rituals aimed at producing mild exhaustion.

In an effort to orient the group to this radically different operation, the minister demonstrated to the congregation what he would be doing differently from previous ministers. For instance, he would move about much more in front of people, pacing frequently and showing higher degrees of emotion in his actions as well as in his voice. The minister pounded at the air with his fists in an up-down fashion, and his head and upper body followed suit. His words were delivered with the arrhythmic beat that sometimes works so well when used by the highly skilled Pentecostal and evangelistic leaders discussed earlier.

We see here that this enlightened minister was teaching people about recognized religious techniques for entering into a state of dissociative trance. These were to replace the hopelessly diminished methods that had been failing in all regards in that congregation as evidenced by continually falling church membership. Beyond that, the minister tried to show people how to structure the dissociative trance once it was in place with these new methods. The core feature of this was "speaking in tongues," which required people to come before the group and utter emotionally charged messages, however incoherent and nonsensical, from the Holy Ghost. He demonstrated this and even fell to the floor as followers often do when overcome by the Holy Spirit. This is where the minister's religious revitalization work probably broke down. That is, he did not go far enough in terms of giving people direction and guidance for structuring the trance. Many of the congregation were completely unaccustomed to the high degree of improvisation required when one speaks in tongues. In fact, it is a type of improvisation with a predictable form and structure that comes with a gradual acclimatization to the practice, such as happens when people are exposed to the techniques from an early age.

Approximately half of the congregation were shocked and overwhelmed at the prospect of change of a seemingly spectacular sort endorsed by the new minister. But this did not stop the other half, mostly the younger members, from responding with enthusiasm to the move toward a charismatic service. A fascinating situation arose that reflected evolution's singular motto: "Change or die." We know that the religious practices of that church had deteriorated in effectiveness to such an extent that an evolutionary crossroads had been reached. One route was the very well-trodden route to extinction, which in this case meant the imminent closure of the church. The other was the way of survival linked to religious innovation and adaptability. The matter reached a climax when a committee was established in order to arrive at an either-or decision. It was biased in favor of those who were reluctant to introduce change. Consequently, a decision was made against the proposed move toward charismatic services and the minister was dismissed.

Feelings ran so high about this issue that the procharismatic half of the congregation followed the discharged minister to his next placement which was in another part of the city. This cut in half the already small number of people who belonged to the church, leaving its future in grave doubt. By contrast, membership has risen sharply in the church now headed by the charismatic minister. New members were drawn from a number of churches in the area, in addition to the dying one under discussion here. It is likely that those other churches were also not offering their people the necessary technical ingredients by which they could achieve a dissociated state and then bias reality in a positive direction.

The above example illustrates a situation being witnessed all too frequently in the Western world. Today, self-consciousness about emotion and loss of control, combined with religious ambivalence, is creating religious induction techniques that are unable to promote a workable degree of dissociation. As a result, congregations are unprepared for the distortive suggestions that should, under correct conditions, become the religious beliefs that benefit us in so many ways, both individually and collectively. Ultimately, they are deprived of the reality-biasing cognitions that, when subsequently self-suggested, constitute the *normal* delusions that combat psychologically toxic elements of primary reality.

Non-Western cultures with intact religious systems generally have the trance induction methods that enable indoctrination with distortive suggestions, however symbolized or indirect these might be during the official indoctrination procedure. The religious beliefs, or functionally errant cognitions, that crystallize from these suggestions are useful because they are *unworldly* and *nonsensical*, just as religion was always meant to be by definition. As healthy religion removes people from this-world interpretations, they benefit from a sense of *ultimate* meaning and the illusion of ultimate knowledge.

The suggestions delivered during a typical conservative Western service can hardly be called suggestions in the strictest sense of the word. The word "suggestion" implies a message that, if assimilated, will lead to a construction of reality that would otherwise *not* be made if the person were processing information while in full contact with her/his conscious monitoring authority. Others have described suggestions in terms of falsifications that become possible when, first, there takes place a neutralizing of the general reality orientation. Such descriptions return us to our earlier discussion of suggestion and the essential point that suggestion must be understood as the *central distortive mechanism* underlying misperceptions and misconstructions of primary reality. But the trend we see in Western religion is for these suggestions to become more and more *nondistortive* in nature. This is clear when one analyzes sermon suggestions over the past few centuries, and especially the past several decades.

Prior to the rise of modern industrialism, religious suggestion was still largely a viable enterprise. Religious leaders, in their roles as suggesters, were able to sell, so to speak, suggestions that were gross and flagrant distortions of primary reality. Malicious devils and guardian angels were alive and well, as were literal understandings of even the wildest biblical stories. People went to hell for doubting the word (i.e., religious suggestions). A sin was still a sin, and God waited with open arms for those who lived according to His clearly specified religious plan, however ludicrous that plan might seem to religious liberals now. Because religion was at least adequately operational, it was able to achieve a type of "insanity," founded on religious suggestion and delusion, that biased sufficiently people's perceptions of the world, their place in it, and their future in this life and the next. That is, religion was still able to manufacture *religious madness for the sake of mental health.*

The same is not true today. Gradually, but relentlessly over the past few centuries, religious suggestions have been drained of their other-world properties. According to James Turner, church leaders are partially to blame for the current decrepit state of Western religion since they "too often forgot the *transcendence* essential to any worthwhile God."[34] Religious suggestion today has lost much of its former transcendent content, traceable to the religious trance induction techniques that can no longer support suggestions that depart radically from primary reality. This trend has nothing to do with a waning desire for reality transcendence on the part of modern Western people. They always have, and always will, seek pathways that let them achieve *an ideal level of illusion,* thus explaining the present world-wide migration toward more *dissociative* religions and cults. Rather, the current failure of religious suggestion is the result of the incompetence of our now familiar religious trance-induction techniques. Where once we saw the requisite gap between ourselves and the gods, we now see suggestions that cannot offer us any useful distance from ourselves and this-world understandings. This has gone so far that, in some cases, we are left virtually to our own devices to make sense of both this world and the other world, including God himself (or herself). Even in my own lifetime I have witnessed this trend toward a "do your own thing" brand of religion.

RELIGIOUS SYMPTOMS OF PSYCHOPATHOLOGY

David Berman argues the point that "religious beliefs and behaviors can themselves be pathological."[35] He compares the strict patterns of avoidance of pork by Jews and Muslims to the behavior of phobic people who avoid nonreligious objects or animals, such as spiders. For purposes of illustration, Berman singles out the famous case of Judge Daniel Schreber, who was convinced that God wanted him to turn into a woman in order that God could copulate with him. While most clinicians now agree that Judge Schreber was a paranoid schizophrenic with delusions containing religious content, Berman asks why we should not also label as psychopathological the person who believes that he or she is loved literally by God. Additionally, he sees no basis for exempting from a diagnosis of mass delusion such devotions as the medieval belief in the devil, or the seventeenth-century belief in witches. In Berman's well-reasoned view, psychopathology does not cease to be psychopathology simply because large groups of people happen to participate in it. The more subtle aspects of this stance have important implications for our understanding of both religion and mental disorders.

To speak of the "symptoms of religion" is to violate the usual methods of diagnosis used by mental health professionals, while also offending the religious sensitivities of religious followers. However, I have argued elsewhere at considerable length that religion must be regarded as a class of mental disorder since it involves the same types of cognitive, affective, and perceptual distortions seen in "clinical" types of mental disorders.[36] As others have done in the past, I made the equally contentious case that, because of *problematic* levels of awareness, the human being was eventually destined to become a *creature of psychopathological symptoms*, whether those be religious or nonreligious in nature. The distinct advantage of having religious symptoms is that they are given a normal status by way of their wide acceptance. This will become more obvious in the next chapter when we analyze pathological symptoms that operate like religion, but fall outside of that particular definitional framework.

At this stage, I would like to mention some of the specific symptoms and syndromes that religion affords people. This will be done in the spirit of Freud's insight that religious symptoms are beneficial to the extent that they often make it unnecessary for people to construct symptoms at the individual level. However, I do not mean to imply that, by accepting religious pathology, people automatically forego the need for symptoms that extend beyond the usual offerings of religion. Even within the confines of religion, some will need to make more use than others of the symptoms that function as mental health prophylactics. Also, in extreme cases, even when the pathology is of a religious nature, certain individuals can be identified as *clinically* disturbed, even by members of that religion.

The religions of many non-Western cultures are able to absorb even blatantly psychotic individuals. Sometimes their wild hallucinations and bizarre actions indicate that these people have made contact with the unseen forces that operate behind the scenes of ordinary consciousness. As a result, it is quite common to observe societies in which the shamans or religious leaders are flagrantly disturbed by Western criteria, often fitting the clinical picture of schizophrenia. This is above and beyond the ability of these cultures to offer ordinary religious pathology, for its usual therapeutic and preventative purposes, to the bulk of the community. The anthropological literature is full of examples of this phenomenon.

The history of Western religion shows us examples of decidedly pathological individuals who, because their behavior made *religious* sense, functioned as very high-profile religious leaders. For reasons still unknown, certain brain disorders cause many of the afflicted individuals to develop high degrees of religiosity. This can be seen with paranoid schizophrenics who, upon the onset of their illness, are engulfed by thoughts and delusions of a religious nature. When these have sufficient organization, and when the social system is sufficiently oriented in terms of religion, such individuals can sometimes be slotted into positions of religious authority. It is also well documented that temporal lobe epilepsy, in and of itself, causes some of its victims to experience a dramatic and sudden religious conversion, sometimes accompanied by striking visions and hallucinations of a religious nature.[37] This is probably the result of stimulation of brain centers that play a central role in the chain of neurological events culminating in religion and related cognitive behavior. Even so, history is replete with cases of epilepsy-provoked religious conversions that gave birth to great religious figures. Notable examples are St. Paul, St. Teresa of Avila, St. Catherine Dei Ricci, and St. Thérèse of Lisieux.

While referring specifically to St. Paul, the impartial William James wrote that Paul's conversion could have been the result of excessive physiological discharge such as that seen in several forms of epilepsy.[38] Jerome Frank, in his book *Persuasion and Healing*, writes about the personal qualities that enable a religious leader to engage in successful "thought reform" as it culminates in religious conversion.[39] He discloses that many of history's very best evangelists were schizophrenic or otherwise psychotic, except that they had exceptional organizational ability, the capacity for vivid imagination of an emotional and religious nature, a sensitivity to audience response, and a talent for translating their bizarre delusions (and often hallucinations) into convincing religious form. The end result, according to Jerome Frank, was the ability of these gifted psychotics to alter powerfully the *assumptive worlds* of their followers, thus greatly raising the status of the religious healer.

Let me add parenthetically that Jerome Frank refers to some of the more gifted evangelists of modern times. However, he also cites statistics demonstrating that, on average, only 2 to 5 percent of those attending present-day revivals are sufficiently "thought-reformed" in order to experience religious conversion. Furthermore, only half of the converts studied were active after one year, and only 15 percent of those remained permanently converted. Jerome Frank extrapolates from the limited amount of historical evidence concerning the success rate of the great evangelists from previous eras (e.g., John Wesley and Jonathan Edwards). He concludes in this regard that their rate of conversion was far higher than that of contemporary evangelists. This is explained partly in terms of Wesley's gripping high-emotion technique, whereby he fully entranced people with explicit images of God's wrath and the terrors of damnation. Equally important is the fact that religion, including God's wrath, had a much more central position in the cultural consciousness of the eighteenth century. It seems that people no longer respond so completely to religious beliefs that are packaged and presented as they were in former ages.

Returning to the matter of religion and psychopathological religious leaders, the point has been made that religions are able to disguise mental disorders such as schizophrenia or organic brain syndromes. But that is not my primary interest. Rather, I am intrigued by the potential for religion to *create* and maintain psychopathology that is actually beneficial at the level of the individual and the group. While religion simultaneously disguises these symptoms, more is involved than simply hiding the symptoms under the umbrella of institutionalized (i.e., normal) psychopathology. We might begin by considering delusion as a class of symptom that is present in all religions of the world.

Religious Delusion

Delusion is an indispensable *cognitive* aspect of religion since it is the springboard for the even more valuable symptoms that are *ritualistic* in design. It can be seen in all working religions. Furthermore, as Joseph Westermeyer observes and supports with quantitative research, delusions in previous ages were confined largely to religion. It is only recently that delusions with secular content have emerged, a phenomenon that is the consequence of a diminution of religion and its themes.[40] This fact takes on increasing importance when one approaches the topic of "clinical" psychopathology in light of the decline of Western religion.

A discussion of the cognitive delusions that exist within religion must be founded on an understanding of dissociation and the manner in which cognitive dissociation makes possible reality distortion in the form of collective delusions. Of this, Gilbert Rouget writes that dissociative trance techniques exist only because they are *in the service of belief* and because trance constitutes a cultural model whereby these beliefs are integrated into a revised representation of the natural world.[41]

It is no coincidence that dissociative trance induction, whether subtle or explosive in its mode of delivery, is a key element of intact religions in all parts of the world. This would not need to be the case if the desired outcome were not reality *distortion*. People could retain all their critical and analytical thinking abilities if religion were merely for the purposes of imparting information that was accurate and in line with the workings of the natural order. If, for instance, the goal of particular religious services were to inform people of the workings of the human heart as an organ involved in pumping blood through the body, then the priests could extinguish the flickering candles and set aside the incense burners that swing mesmerizingly from their chains. The choirs of monotonous singers could put away their hymn books, the evangelical preachers could rid their collective voice of its entrancing arrhythmic drum beat, and the congregation could stop clapping. Such techniques, and their related rituals and accompanying paraphernalia, are only necessary if the aim is to promote *delusional* beliefs and *distortive* experiences based on those beliefs. In terms of the interaction of dissociation and memory, we can also say that such techniques are also required if people need to temporarily neutralize memory traces that contain accurate information about primary reality. Once more, this is done by shifting those traces, during belief, to an information-processing pathway that does not have access to conscious awareness.

The word "delusion" might strike some people as a rather strong word to use with reference to religion. We are accustomed to safeguarding religion from the reach of definitions that would depict it as psychopathological in nature. But let us see if there is any sound reason to give religion an exemption when it comes to this issue. Since a great deal of what we call religion entails religious *belief*, we should first strip away biases that protect religious beliefs from the label of abnormality.

The fields of psychiatry and clinical psychology have done their part in depicting religious beliefs as normal, even though identical beliefs would be deemed as abnormal if they occurred outside the context of religion. The *Diagnostic and Statistical Manual of Mental Disorders* (*DSM*) is the hallowed guide used by mental health professionals for purposes of diagnosis. In the latest, fourth edition (*DSM-IV*, 1994) beliefs are considered to be delusional if they are false in the sense of being *based on incorrect references about external reality*. It adds that delusions are bizarre if they are "implausible, not understandable, and not derived from ordinary life experiences."[42] To illustrate what is meant by a bizarre delusion, *DSM-IV* offers an example of a person who believes that a stranger has removed his or her internal organs and replaced these with someone else's organs. The *DSM-IV* makes no mention of religious beliefs even though many such beliefs could fit easily into the category of bizarre delusions. It only makes the general observation that "bizarreness" might be difficult to judge, especially when one tries to do this across cultures. The earlier, 1980 edition of *DSM* (*DSM-III*) went further in defense of religious beliefs in specifying that a belief is no longer delusional if it is "ordinarily accepted by other members of the person's culture or subculture (i.e., it is not an article of religious faith)."[43] In a similar vein, E. Tory Higgins and Marlene Moretti conceptualize delusions in terms of the *social-evaluative process*. They write:

> We propose that aberrant beliefs and delusions reflect atypical or nonnormative *judgments* and *interpretations* of information. Further, we suggest that judgments and interpretations will be deviant to the extent that normative considerations have to be violated in the *selection* and the *application* of standards during information processing.[44]

Following the logic of such definitions, we are led to the dubious conclusion that a belief cannot be delusional in nature if it has the endorsement of the majority of people. But clearly this is not the case if we take even a fleeting glance at history, where we can cite endless examples of blatantly delusional beliefs that had widespread acceptance by entire societies. We could even find numerous instances of group-sanctioned delusions that existed within a culture's dominant system of religious beliefs.

As an example, let us say we hold the religious belief that we must kill some of our neighbors, tear out their hearts, and hold those hearts above our heads as a sacrifice to the gods. We also believe that the universe would cease to exist unless this were done on a daily basis. More exactly, we believe that the sun would fail to rise in the morning if human hearts were not offered up in this way. While modern people are still largely ignorant of the workings of the cosmos, most would agree that the rising sun is not dependent upon the daily delivery of hearts to an unseen god. They would be so sure of this that they would call such a belief delusional on the grounds that it was based on an erroneous reference about external reality. Yet for centuries the Aztecs held such a religious belief and, consequently, sacrificed up to 20,000 people each year.[45]

Before we ask ourselves if all religious beliefs are delusions that can be explained in terms of dissociation and suggestion, we should first try to find satisfactory alternative explanations that could protect religion from the label of madness. What about the Aztec belief about sacrificed hearts and the rising sun? In an essay titled "Delusions and the Construction of Reality," David Heise argues that "delusions fall out of the psychiatric realm if we give the believer social commitment and modify the belief so it has social significance."[46] This statement rests on his assertion that psychologists and psychiatrists have the responsibility of maintaining the general population at a satisfactory *balance between social commitment and individuality*. Therefore, in specifying what is or is not a delusion, mental health professionals must exercise their "authority to define the limits of individuality, the breakdown of social commitment, and the development of excessive egocentricity."[47] Heise's thesis culminates in his conclusion that delusional beliefs are highly *individualistic* mental constructions that lack "social currency" and hence constitute a reality that others do not want to share.

There is no reason to doubt that Aztec religion *worked* at the individual level. As with most functional manifestations of religion, it offered a total and absolute explanatory system that was far more conducive to personal mental health than earthbound modes of understanding. Mental health benefits flowed even to those who knew they were to be eventual objects of sacrifice, since they were automatically rewarded with a blissful afterlife.

Given the longevity of Aztec religion, it also probably worked well at the social level, providing a cohesive way of organizing and controlling people and directing their energies for purposes of survival. The thousands of people who were lost for this end were apparently *affordable*, and not too high a social cost in relation to the benefits obtained. But this in no way means that the Aztecs' religious beliefs were anything but delusional.

The core of Heise's definition of a delusion bears close resemblance to the basic approach used by psychologists and psychiatrists to diagnose abnormal behavior. That is, someone is abnormal if he or she *deviates* significantly from the norm, especially if the direction of the deviance runs counter to the prevailing notions about prosocial behavior. If we take Heise's model of delusional belief and transpose it to our example of Aztec religion, we end up with a potentially perverse situation. It means that an Aztec would have been delusional if he or she held the contrary *individualistic* belief that each new morning came of its own accord and had nothing to do with the ripping out of people's hearts. Such a person would have been great cause for concern, no less than someone today who would suggest that we begin tearing out human hearts in order to keep new days coming.

In the time of the Aztecs, measures would have been taken to deal with the individual who held the "delusional" belief that the rising sun was not dependent upon human sacrifice. We obviously know now that the "delusion" would be delusional only in the sense that the belief did not correspond to mainstream group-endorsed religious beliefs within Aztec culture. Moreover, it would be not at all delusional in terms of *actual*, or primary, reality. New days *do* arrive regardless of hearts that may or may not be extracted from people's bodies and sacrificed to the god in question. Yet, in the context of *cultural* reality (and the personal realities of the people whose beliefs were shaped by culture), our Aztec who perceived primary reality correctly must be deemed delusional according to the "statistical" model proposed by Heise and others. This is especially the case in the Aztec example, since our wayward individual held a belief lacking any social currency; that is, any opposition to the human sacrifice belief threatened the lives of all Aztec people, and all living things. Naturally, no one would want to know about that and, as such, it would remain unshared and deviant within the context of cultural reality.

The myth of progress that is part of modern consciousness would lead some religious defenders to claim that modern religious beliefs are somehow more aligned with reality. They might compare it to technological progress that has seen us increase our knowledge of the physical world. But functional religion has always dealt with the *unnatural*. Religion is unnecessary in terms of what can be comprehended in naturalistic ways. When new discoveries are made that contradict religious explanations and beliefs, they are expelled from religion, thereby confining religion to the domain of the unexplainable, where it belongs. In some religions of the past, thunder and lightning were explained according to the actions of the gods in whom the people believed. Once convincing naturalistic explanations came along, however, these religions responded by ejecting thunder and lightning beliefs. In so doing, these religions showed themselves to be flexible and capable of evolving in order to remain unfalsifiable and safe from critical scrutiny.

Pushing this line of thought to its logical conclusion, we are faced with the prospect that religion is only needed in order to support beliefs that would otherwise be rejected by our available cognitive methods for testing the veracity of information. Stated more succinctly, religion is involved in manufacturing, supporting, and sustaining *delusional* beliefs, and in particular collective delusional beliefs. Such a view has the welcome advantage of taking religion beyond the reach of cultural relativism, a model that deems beliefs to be "true" within any particular culture, regardless of the disharmony between those beliefs and primary reality. A strict cultural relativist would even have to regard as true the belief that sacrificed human hearts ushered in each new day. It would also be true that Catholics actually incorporate the body and blood of the son of God when they ingest an unleavened piece of bread during the Communion ceremony. Therefore, religions are best envisioned as a socially constructed haven for delusions that are not diagnosed as insanity due to majority acceptance. Those same beliefs would, however, receive the diagnosis of insanity if they were to appear *outside of* a religious framework.

Even within the confines of clinical psychology and psychiatry, religious beliefs fulfill most criteria for the formal diagnosis of delusion. Take, for instance, the set of criteria set out by John Strauss.[48] According to Strauss, a belief is to be regarded as delusional in the psychiatric sense if it: (a) is held with conviction, (b) constitutes the basis for preoccupation, (c) is implausible, and (d) is not the result of cultural determinants. While religious beliefs are unquestionably the consequence of cultural determinants, it is clear that most religious beliefs fit the other three criteria for the diagnosis of delusion. Beyond that, we must reject definitions of delusional beliefs that view such beliefs as normal on the grounds that they have "social currency" or general social sanction, as we see in religion. Not only that, we can single out religion as a home for beliefs that *must* be considered delusional because they are religious in nature. Once more, this is because religion is reserved for the construction of beliefs that are, by their very nature, *abnormal* in the truest sense of the word. They are even to be regarded as delusional by DSM-IV criteria since they are based on inferences about what is real that do not correspond to external reality.

The third edition, revised, of DSM (DSM-III-R, 1987) describes a delusional belief as a "false" one that is so extreme that it "defies credibility."[49] To illustrate what a delusion is *not*, it offers an example of a person who claims that he or she is terrible because that person did something to disappoint family members. In the eyes of DSM-III-R, it seems that this type of mental construction is not the stuff of which delusions of clinical severity are made. But then it gives a second example that does illustrate a delusion, namely, that of being a person who "claims he or she is the worst sinner in the world."[50] DSM-III-R equates this with the delusion of the very underweight individual who believes unwaveringly that he or she is fat, as is found in those who suffer from the eating disorder anorexia nervosa.

The sin example leads one logically to ask if one is also clinically delusional for believing that one is not the *worst* sinner, but instead a *very bad* sinner. And what about people who believe themselves to be average sinners? Where along the continuum of sin are people allowed to bail themselves out of a diagnosis of delusion? Surely it is not as simple as stating that a normal sinner becomes abnormal after an arbitrary point of sinning badness.

Instead of addressing directly the issue of religion, as was done in the 1980 DSM-III, the DSM-III-R tries to skirt the issue while mixing extreme examples of religious behavior among a number of diagnoses, including that of delusion. For instance, it describes people with obsessive-compulsive personality disorder as being "excessively conscientious, moralistic, scrupulous, and judgmental of self and others—for example, considering it sinful for a neighbor to leave her child's bicycle out in the rain."[51] All right, let us take a leap and accept that it is not a sin to leave out in the rain our children's bicycles. We will say that such a belief is, in fact, a delusion. But then I must also ask about a former Catholic nun who taught that one was sinning at the go-to-purgatory level for stealing goods valued at less than twenty dollars, and sinning at the go-to-hell level for stealing twenty dollars and up. Should her beliefs, despite their religious content, be diagnosed as delusions? In my mind, she was not too far away from the bicycle-in-the-rain delusional belief, and one is tempted to refuse her the label of normality on the grounds that hers was a religious belief.

Magical thinking is defined in the DSM-III-R in ways similar to that of a definition of a delusion. Specifically, it says that, in magical thinking, "the person believes that his or her thoughts, words, or actions might, or will in some manner, cause or prevent a specific outcome in some way that defies the normal laws of cause and effect."[52] Immediately following this statement we read: "Example: A man believed that if he said a specific prayer three times each night, his mother's death might be prevented indefinitely." This official diagnostic manual even states that magical thinking of this sort can be labeled as delusional if "the person maintains a firm conviction about the belief despite evidence to the contrary."[53] The only possible thing that could save our praying man from the diagnosis of delusion is for someone to argue effectively that his convictions were not *despite evidence to the contrary*. In actuality, such a person has absolutely no evidence to the *affirmatory*. No evidence exists at any level that his prayers should be expected to make a difference as they intercede via an invisible being for whom there is also no affirmatory evidence. One would have a solid case for insisting that a total absence of affirmatory evidence should, in fact, constitute evidence to the contrary.

Such a position is supported by many cognitive psychologists. In describing the cognitive deviances in delusions, for example, Loren Chapman and Jean Chapman write that delusions are born when a person "constricts the information that they consider in reaching a conclusion . . . and ignores or gives inadequate weight to data from his or her other experiences, some of which may contradict the delusional belief."[54] They cite the case of a person who relies on incomplete information in reaching the delusional conclusion that "Life is more meaningful than it seems."[55] We obviously know this particular delusion to be one that rests at the heart of all religions, as well as many secular religions and some types of psychopathology. The work of Aaron Beck centers on the isolation of cognitive distortions that exist within people's thought patterns. One type of distortion to which he refers is that of *arbitrary inference*, i.e., faulty thinking wherein conclusions are drawn either when confirmatory evidence is lacking or when support exists for a contrary conclusion.[56]

At the very least, the *DSM-III-R* seems to allow for the diagnosis of magical thinking for someone who prays to God in the *unrealistic* expectation of results. It stops just one step short of permitting outright the diagnosis of delusion for such behavior. Yet it is very easy to see why many objective observers, including myself, see no acceptable reason for exempting religion from diagnostic categories that imply distortions in the thought process. This is precisely the goal of religion, namely, to establish at the group level the cognitive distortions, or delusions, that skew reality in desired directions. Without "symptoms" of a delusional nature (i.e., in the strict sense of *deluding* the person), religion would be of no avail to followers.

Although the *DSM-III-R* is unable to deal diagnostically with religion, its system for subcategorizing delusions and other mental disorders does throw some light on the specific psychopathologies that reveal themselves in religion. Let us enumerate some of these. One of them, which is magical thinking, was already alluded to briefly. Certainly it is an unmistakable feature of religions around the world. Furthermore, the fact that magical thinking is even mentioned in the official diagnostic manual of mental disorders tells us that it is not unreasonable to describe as pathological this type of aberrant cognition as it appears in religious settings.

One sees in many societies a pattern of religious delusion that, in *DSM-III-R* terminology, would be classified as *Delusional (Paranoid) Disorder: Persecutory Type*. According to the *DSM-III-R*, this pattern of delusion can be either simple or elaborate in nature, and can be composed of single themes or multiple connected themes. These themes can include the delusion that one is being followed or spied upon, harassed or conspired against, or deliberately obstructed in the pursuit of long-term goals. It is very easy to see how certain common religious beliefs would fit into the category of persecutory delusions: for example, "God is always watching" or "The devil is always lurking nearby, plotting your downfall" or "You won't get to heaven if you use a condom."

Many parallels exist between the implantation of religious suggestion and what is sometimes called "directed fantasy" in psychotherapy circles. French psychologists Roger Frétigny and André Virel wrote a book about directed fantasy and mental imagery, relating it to the strategies used by various world religions as they *compete with the factual world* through the mass inculcation of religious fantasies.[57] Their reasoning is founded on the premise that the human mind would quickly become crippled if it dwelled only in the world of facts, or what we have here been referring to as primary reality. Frétigny and Virel speak of a balance between fact and fantasy that can be seen in all cultures of the world, with the fantasy usually being delivered by way of formal religious mechanisms. Consistently with some of my previous comments about the decline of Western religion, they write about the past three centuries which have witnessed a shift in balance between fact and fantasy.

This development has resulted, for both religious and non-religious people today, in a degree of exposure to the factual world far in excess of that seen in previous ages. At the same time, Frétigny and Virel speak of the ebb and flow of fact and fantasy as civilizations evolve in one direction or another. They also comment on the stirrings of a global tension reflective of a cultural desire to divert its collective attention away from the factual world and to restore greater amounts of transcendent fantasy. This last statement is especially relevant as we look around us and notice the proliferation of ways in which people today grope desperately for alternative methods by which to combat the factual world.

The term "guided imagery" is often used by Western cognitive psychologists and, interestingly, it is frequently deployed as a therapeutic technique while the subject is in the state of dissociation following hypnotic induction techniques. It resembles as well the procedure used by religious leaders around the world, except that the suggested images are disseminated at the group level in most religious settings. With this comparison in mind, it should be apparent that conductors of religious services can direct, or structure, the content of religious delusions in an endless number of ways. Depending on the cultural source of the religious suggestion, for instance, it is quite possible to establish the collective delusion that one is being loved and cared for by an invisible spirit or god. This, in formal *DSM-III-R* language, would probably fall into the category of a *Delusional Disorder: Ertomanic Type.*[58] Symptom patterns of this nature have as their preeminent theme the delusion that one is loved by another person, usually one of higher status or in a position superior to the subject. The ertomanic type of delusion is not sexual, according to the *DSM-III-R*. Instead, it involves the faulty conclusion that one is the subject of idealized romantic love or a spiritual unionship. The latter would be the typical delusional format with most religious delusions wherein gods are invested with loving attributes, except in rare cases like Judge Schreber who believed that God wanted him/her physically as well as spiritually.

Perusing further through the *DSM-III-R*, one comes upon another type of delusion that appears in many religions, namely, *Delusional Disorder: Grandiose Type.* Here, the symptoms take the form of an unwarranted conviction that one possesses some extraordinary insight, or ability. One could imagine any number of religious scenarios in which the people are convinced that they have the remarkable ability to communicate with an infinitely powerful force, or deity, and that they can actually influence earthly events as a consequence. The *DSM-III-R* concedes that "grandiose delusions may have religious content, and people with these delusions can become leaders of religious cults."[59] Ernest Becker, in his book *Escape from*

Evil, was aware that, when human beings are at the peak of *transcendent creativity,* they are likely to "strain toward the grandest illusion."[60] We could easily rephrase this by saying that, in the throes of fully functional religion, people generally end up with delusional symptoms of an unabashedly grandiose nature. This, however, may be less true in the temperate religious climate in which we find ourselves today in Western culture. The *DSM-IV* rephrases slightly the definition of *Delusional Disorder: Grandiose Type.* It also makes the point that this disorder can have a religious content, but then gives a new example, that of a person who believes that he or she has a special message from a deity. Since it is common knowledge that many religious people believe they are the recipients of special messages from God, one could easily argue that they qualify for this particular psychiatric diagnosis.

Earlier I alluded to David Berman's reference to the *phobias* that are featured in many of the world's religions. These are fueled by the delusional belief that a great threat exists in an object or situation which, in reality, is harmless or much less harmful than is believed by the phobic individual. The *DSM-IV* devotes considerable space to this particular diagnosis, and it would be a simple matter to make the case that this is still another type of desired psychopathology produced by means of dissociation and suggestion in religious contexts. Superficially, it might seem counterproductive from a psychological and social standpoint for religions to instill unrealistic fear in their members. Yet every religion has a set of taboos that can generate considerable emotional distress if they are violated. Malevolent devils or evil spirits are always invented along with the benevolent gods and spirits, and religions predictably spell out behaviors that expose one to the merciless whims of treacherous forces. Sometimes, as in Christianity, a single god is endowed with positive as well as negative attributes, and the violation of taboos can bring wrath from the dark side of the god.

The Catholicism I followed in years past had a taboo against biting down on the host (i.e., the body and blood of Christ) when it was in one's mouth during Communion, or touching the host itself. Many other religions share taboos that forbid the touching of sacred symbolic objects. One taboo that occupied much of my time and energy was that against taking Communion while in a state of mortal sin. A considerable portion of my mental activity as a youth focused on the status of my soul, since we went to church and took Communion every day. And in the Catholicism of my youth, sexuality was riddled with enough taboos to keep one phobic or paranoid for several lifetimes. Indeed, mild phobias and mild paranoia are an inevitable part of the religious picture *when those religions are working well.*

In *The Elementary Forms of Religious Life,* Émile Durkheim makes an observation that has important implications for our understanding of both religion as well as psychopathology. He writes:

> All known religious beliefs present one common characteristic: they presuppose a classification of all things, real and ideal . . . into two classes or opposed groups, generally designated by two distinct terms which are translated well enough by the words profane and sacred.[61]

This means that all religious beliefs create the basis for a conflict between opposing forces, whatever those forces might be. A god rarely exists alone without some sort of devil to represent the antithesis of the god. No religion in the world has only benevolent spirits. If there are codes for desired behavior, you will also find taboos that spell out undesirable behavior, and so forth. But, for Durkheim, the value of religious beliefs as they organize themselves into inevitably opposing camps needs to take account of the great benefit that human beings derive from the enactment of ritual.

Taboos play an integral role in the manufacture and consumption of ritual since they indicate what is "profane." This profanity then *magnifies* the size and intensity of the sacred. Personifications of profanity in the form of devils or evil spirits go further in this regard. In a sense, we know the gods better because of their opposites. The creation of profanity serves to involve the person at an *emotional* level through the engagement of emotions (e.g., fear or anxiety) that might not otherwise be tapped by sacred ideology alone. Taboos can also concentrate, or *absorb*, attention very successfully, again due to their close relationship with strong emotions.

Several classes of *clinical* psychopathology, as we will see in the next chapter, utilize a "devil" of one type or another in order to establish the foundation for highly focused attention, or absorption. This then becomes the basis for an autodissociative syndrome, structured with self-suggestion, that allows the person to become removed from certain aspects of reality. Yet group-sanctioned religion is much more efficient, and less problematic, than psychopathology as it goes about the job of translating reality.

Take as an example the orthodox Jew who complies with the food-related taboos that require the faithful to follow complex rules regarding food selection and preparation. An entire lifestyle crystallizes around food taboos, one that would be deemed clinically pathological were the behaviors removed from the religious context. Such a lifestyle would have a distinct flavor of phobic, paranoid, and compulsive thought and action.

The food taboo in Judaism rests partially on the delusional belief that dire consequences befall people if the kid (i.e., baby goat) is boiled with its mother's milk. This translates into behaviors ensuring that milk and meat are kept separated. Fears of contamination enter into this, as food preparers go to great lengths to keep milk from meat dishes. If milk accidentally gets mixed in with a pot of meat, the pot is ruined and rendered inedible. However, if the contamination is less than one part in sixty, it is not officially (i.e., religiously) contaminated. This might happen if only a drop or two of milk were allowed to enter a meat dish. But if this reached eight or ten drops in the average-size meat dish, then it might exceed the one-sixtieth contamination mark, and would then be off limits. If Jewish food regulations are followed strictly, preparers should use separate drying linen for cookery using milk and that using meat, respectively.

The psychopathology of such religious belief and behavior should not cause us to lose sight of the value of religious insanity. The source of phobic and paranoid behavior is also the rich source of religious delusion. Furthermore, these delusions establish the groundwork for modified and positively biased versions of reality. Even though one might not look forward to the prospect of a lifelong need to avoid making contact between milk and meat, each ritualistic repetition of the taboo avoidance behavior reinforces the delusional belief. Taboos, therefore, can energize and give additional impetus to the cognitive supports of a religion. At the same time, they constitute a justification for active participation in religious ritual that is connected to the taboo-related delusional system.

The Delusion-Ritual Complex

I would like now to move on to religious symptoms that, while also reliant on the dissociation/suggestion process, have a large *ritualistic* component. As with clinical expressions of psychopathology, symptoms are rarely only cognitive in nature. Those studying religion often speak of the *myth-ritual complex* in which myths translate into physical action. Durkheim, for instance, felt that one could not understand religion outside of the context of ritual. He saw religion as the *unity* of myth and ritual, and gave special emphasis to the social and psychological fruits of the ritual process. For the sake of conceptual consistency, I feel it is more worthwhile to refer to the *delusion-ritual complex*. This allows for an easy transition from a discussion of religion to that of psychopathology. Additionally, the word "myth" can lead us astray since it does not imply belief to a sufficient extent. I enjoy reading Greek mythology, and myths surround us in various forms. But as we have come to know the word "myth," it is possible to be involved with myth without believing in it. The word "delusion," by contrast, conveys not only the idea of belief, but the idea of *distortion* which is central to accurate conceptions of religion and the types of psychopathology to be considered later.

In terms of psychopathology, mental health professionals do not often encounter cases of delusions or obsessions lacking pathological *behavioral* patterns (i.e., rituals) that are energized and shaped by whatever cognitive symptoms are present. Therefore, it is appropriate to speak of both religious and nonreligious manifestations of psychopathology in terms of the interplay between distortive beliefs and physically enacted behavior. The parallels between religious and clinical expressions of pathology are not always exact, owing to the fact that religious symptoms are constructed at the level of the group. Clinical symptoms are created with much more input from the individual (but with *some* influence from the surrounding culture). Let us begin with ritualistic symptoms as they emerge within dominant cultural religions.

RITUALISTIC SYMPTOMS OF RELIGION

Durkheim writes about the intimate relationship between religious ritual and belief when he observes: "At the heart of all systems of beliefs and of all cults, there must necessarily be a certain number of fundamental *représentations* and ritual attitudes which, despite the diversity of forms they have each been able to assume, have everywhere the same object meaning and universally fulfill the same functions."[62] Ritual is such an integral part of religion that some thinkers have been inclined to equate religion with ritual. Yet, many Western people are still of the mistaken view that religion is largely ideology. This may be owing to the diminished quantity and quality of conventional Western religions, as well as their exaggerated intellectual component. Instead, religion deals almost entirely with the *rituals* that are made possible because of myth or ideology. In this respect, then, religious myths (i.e., mass delusions) should be regarded at least partially as *excuses* for ritual. Ritual can be intensely *absorbing*, with a "hypnotic" or dissociative life of its own, which keeps the delusional belief viable. In turn, the delusion allows further participation in the ritual.

Nearly fifty years ago, in *The Origins of Religion*, Lord Raglan took up the matter of the relationship between ritual and religious beliefs.[63] There, he comes close to equating religion with ritual. He says quite unequivocally that "religion . . . consists in the due performance of ritual," and that *religious beliefs give reasons why these rituals should be performed*.[64] This again locates ritual at the center of religion. In light of the psychotherapeutic value of religion generally, it also leads us to suspect that ritual (including religious ritual) is advantageous from a mental health point of view.

Joseph Campbell, in *Myths to Live By*, writes that "it is the rite, the ritual and its imagery, that counts in religion, and where that is missing the words are mere carriers of concepts that may or may not make contemporary sense."[65] He exclaims the importance of ritual and underscores its therapeutic value as it structures human reality at a deep meaningful level. According to Campbell, this structuring process has been traditionally of a *religious* nature. He, too, sees myths as the "mental supports" of rituals, or what he also calls the "physical enactments of myth."[66] By way of a prelude to ritual as it appears in clinical psychopathology, however, Campbell also points to the modern dearth of ritual, particularly its disappearance from traditional religious sources. The "slack" that this has caused in the Western cultural system is taken up by secular varieties of ritual, which will be another departure point for our transition into pathological ritual.

Janet Jacobs, in her essay "Religious Ritual and Mental Health," shows us that ritual is psychologically beneficial for a number of reasons,[67] one of which is the *cathartic* effect of group-enacted ritual. She provides cross-cultural evidence that the performance of religious ritual can be an outlet for a wide range of emotions. Jacobs draws on the work of Thomas Scheff, whose theory of ritual catharsis states that ritual has the potential to create *emotional distancing*.[68] That is, ritual enables people to establish distance from the intensity of emotional experience. Jacobs emphasizes both the therapeutic and preventive benefits of ritual as a mechanism for emotional distancing. And, like Scheff, she stresses that rituals of a religious nature are necessarily dependent upon religious myths that constitute the rationale for such rituals.

Barbara Myerhoff goes further in outlining the close relationship between ritual and fictional understandings of the world. She writes that "rituals not only fuse disparate elements but they also make assertions, claims that are at the same time denials of unacceptable realities."[69] Thus, when ritual is performed successfully, the participants become convinced of the truth of fictional constructions of reality. According to Myerhoff, this applies to secular as well as religious ritual, a point made increasingly meaningful as we contemplate ritual as it is acted out by "abnormal" people in an effort to prop up a set of relatively private fictions.

Let us now look at additional definitions of ritual and scrutinize more closely the nature of ritual as we seek to isolate ritualistic religious symptoms.

The Nature of Ritual

A ritual is seen by Barbara Myerhoff as "an act or actions intentionally conducted by a group of people employing one or more symbols in a repetitive, formal, precise, highly stylized fashion."[70] The following definition of ritual is offered by S. J. Wolin and L. A. Bennett: "A symbolic form of communication that, owing to the satisfaction that . . . members experience through its repetition, is acted out in a systematic fashion over time."[71] Another definition, put forward by R. L. Grimes, depicts ritual as "those conscious . . . repetitious and stylized symbolic actions (including verbal behavior such as chant, song and prayer) that are centered on cosmic structures and/or sacred presences."[72]

Ritual is defined by K. Helmut Reich as "an aspect of *social engineering* by means of the emotional experience of a charismatic leader, of intense fellowship, and/or through the psychological reinforcement effect due to repetition."[73] Reich adds that collective rituals *engineer* society by breaking down the barriers between reality and unreality, and between fact and fiction, thus transforming or *reconstructing* reality in useful directions. This is akin to Ernest Becker's description of ritual as a social "technique of manufacture that renovates nature," except that Becker portrayed ritual as a "preindustrial" technique.[74]

According to Eugene d'Aquili, a ritual is "a sequence of behavior which is structured or patterned; which is rhythmic and repetitive (to some degree at least), that is, it tends to recur in the same or nearly the same form with some regularity."[75] Erik H. Erikson defines ritual as a group-bound process that provides "a catharsis of affects . . . while becoming familiar through repetition."[76] Erikson postulates that ritual satisfies the human need for structure and order. He also sees ritual as developmentally important in that it helps to promote "basic trust," while also *countering a fear of loss of control* at the personal as well as existential level. This bears some resemblance to Victor Turner's assessment of ritual as a social drama that assists "actors" in the pursuit of resolving conflicts and restoring psychic and social equilibrium. Of this, Turner writes that rituals actualize myths in order that the myth (via the ritual) may symbolically alter human experience, perception, and understanding.[77]

All the above definitions mention *repetition* in relation to ritual. For some action to be a ritual, and to function as a ritual, it must be something that is repeated in a stereotyped fashion. This is true of ritual as it appears in all religions of the world, and also of secular ritual, whether "normal" or "abnormal" in nature. Therefore, we are led to wonder what it is about repetition that is so vital to ritual. We could also ask if repetition generally is of value to human beings and if one of religion's main offerings is that of repetition and its effects. The answer would be an affirmative one if we accepted that repetition represents an important ritual base that yields dissociation and enables reality-altering suggestions to be implanted. While this is traditionally done in a religious context, the use of repetitive rituals is not restricted to religion. For example, Jerome Frank's book *Persuasion and Healing* outlines the thought-reform and brainwashing techniques that have been used on people for political reasons. Many of these can be compared to the more benign indoctrination methods used by religious leaders. Significantly, Jerome Frank shows us that, as in religion, the effectiveness of brainwashing is highly dependent upon repetition. He writes: "The same material was gone over again and again, and the interrogators never tired of repeating their demands. . . . Many prisoners of war stated that most of the techniques used gained their effectiveness by being used in the repetitive way until the prisoner could no longer sustain his resistance."[78]

The topic of repetition is taken up by Eugene d'Aquili, who observes that human beings tend to cope with their environment through motor activity that is of a repetitive nature and structured into society in the form of group ritual. Repetition, he says, produces brain-level changes that culminate in lower anxiety levels and an increased sense of order and harmony, as well as enhanced cohesion among participants. As an example, d'Aquili mentions the repetition entailed in many forms of prayer and the cadence and chanting of words that contribute to the repetition seen in various religious rituals. He also notes that "the slow rhythmicity of a religious procession or the fast beat of drums or rattles all serve to drive the ergotropic [sympathetic, energy-expanding] system independent of the meaning of words."[79] A passage from Konrad Lorenz's book *On Aggression* also reveals the ubiquitous *repetitions* that fill our lives, both in and out of the religious context:

The deans of the university walk into the hall with a "measured step"; rhythm and loudness of the Catholic priests chanting during mass are all strictly regulated by liturgic prescription. The unambiguity of the communication is also increased by its frequent repetition. Rhythmical repetition of the same movement is so characteristic of very many rituals, both instinctive and cultural, that it is hardly necessary to describe examples.[80]

Repetition, as it falls under the label of religious ritual, begins to make sense as we understand it in terms of the processes of dissociation and suggestion. After all, we saw that dissociative trance is largely dependent on the *obsessive monotony* that is typically achieved when people are exposed to *repetitions* of various sorts. As a result of this monotony-driven dissociation, people's conscious monitoring authority eases and they slip away from a general reality orientation. In relation to ritual, Barbara Myerhoff writes that, during the performance of ritual, higher-order thought processes wane as fictional cognitions are entertained. On this, she states that "critical, analytic thought, the attitude which would pierce the illusion of reality, is anathema to ritual," while adding that "the enemy of ritual is one who is incapable of or unwilling to voluntarily suspend belief—the spoilsport."[81]

In his book *The Interpretation of Culture,* Clifford Geertz echoes a similar sentiment while observing that rituals transport participants into another mode of existence that relies on *the suppression of the commonsense perspective of the everyday world.*[82] Likewise, Etzel Cardeña writes about specific types of ritual as they operate via repetition toward the elimination of critical thought. As a leading authority on dissociation, Cardeña ties together ritual and dissociation in describing the *narrow deployment of attention* that exists during ritual. In the midst of ritual enactment, the subject experiences "absorption," which is one of the key ingredients for all trance. He notes that changes in *memory* are thus promoted, which can include not remembering, or distracting oneself from remembering, one's own identity. This type of *amnesia,* Cardeña correctly observes, is simply part of "the common thread of amnesia that underlies the dissociative process."[83]

As the topic of ritual returns us to our earlier topics of dissociation and memory, we must keep in mind the crucial role of *memory interference* in the religion process (and, as we will see, in the psychopathology process). When adequate techniques are applied that include those categorized as ritual, the person should be able to dissociate from memory traces containing knowledge that would compete with delusional constructions of reality. Furthermore, as we also discussed, this can be "knowledge" that is the result of *nonhappenings* and information that is acquired when we experience what is not an aspect of primary reality. In arriving at my former religious belief that by saying "Jesus, Mary, Joseph" I would erase seven years from my purgatory time, for instance, I had to somehow momentarily relinquish my memory (i.e., knowledge) that no single shred of evidence was ever encountered to support such a conclusion.

We also know that dissociated memories are not forgotten, but rather temporarily displaced onto an information-processing channel that has an amnesic barrier between it and conscious awareness. In terms of dissociation theory, this means that there is really no such thing as an *ongoing* believer in the delusions that make up religion or any other vehicle for transcendence. Such errant constructions of reality are entered into only when techniques are successfully employed, whether externally or internally based, in allowing a person to dissociate from certain constellations of memory. It is at these same times that critical and analytic thought capabilities are also suspended, thereby preventing new scrutiny that would jeopardize the alternative reality.

Obsessive-Compulsive Behavior: Religious Type

If, indeed, human beings are *symptomatic* creatures by design, it follows that some symptoms might be more effective than others at detaching/distracting people from unsavory realities. We might even speak of *symptoms of choice* in much the same way that health professionals speak of treatments of choice. When one looks across cultures, one finds a religious symptom that might be called the universal symptom of choice for religion. This is a united combination of *obsessions* and *compulsions*, all of which become normalized by the religious context in which they emerge.

Essentially, an obsession is a recurrent thought or cognition, whereas a compulsion is a repetitive physical action. The obsession provides the reason or rationalization for the compulsive act. Or, conversely, the compulsion is justified in terms of the content of the obsession. One nurtures the other in order to keep the entire syndrome of delusional thoughts and bizarre actions alive. It is quite easy to recognize the ritualistic nature of religious compulsions since one sees directly the repetition of physical actions. But obsessions must also be regarded as ritualistic since the patterns of cognitions are similarly inflexible and stereotyped, as well as the subject of monotonous repetition.

Prayer is one very common religious package for the beneficial types of obsessions and compulsions that we are discussing here. Under the protective label of religion, people can repeat to themselves a prescribed set of verbalizations that make sense in relation to (and *only* in relation to) certain group-sanctioned beliefs. At the same time, they can engage in repeated stereotyped actions that correspond to the verbal (i.e., obsessive) symptoms. With regard to prayer, Anthony Wallace observes that virtually all religions of the world offer its members a clearly specified set of instructions for partaking in prayer:

> In almost every culture in the world there are customary ways of addressing supernatural beings. Such address is generally conducted by speaking aloud while the body is held in a conventional posture and while standardized gestures intended to express fear, love, respect, threat, or other motives are made; the style of speech is also apt to be stereotyped. The purpose and content of the address, of course, vary with culture and, within the culture, with the occasion. Often such address is made in public, at a sacred location and with special apparatus, such as incense or smoke from a fire, to expedite the message.[84]

Wallace's description captures both the obsessive and compulsive dimensions of prayer. He refers to the verbal elements of prayer as *stereotyped*, and the physical component as involving *standardized* gestures. In this respect, we must again acknowledge that both these aspects of prayer are ritualistic in their construction, and thus can provide the important benefits that were previously mentioned in relation to religious ritual. Prayer is also an example of an ideal type of symptom since it engages the person in ritual physically as well as mentally. Another advantage of prayer is that it can be employed at the group level, such as during a ceremony or church service of one type or another. Alternatively, individuals can transport this mode of ritual to their personal lives and participate in a private manner. This allows them to exploit this technique to whatever extent is judged necessary in meeting their ritual requirements. Unquestionably, some people will experience more of a need than others in this regard.

Given the depleted state of religious prayer ritual as we find it in the West, we may be forgiven for resisting the notion that prayer is the historical paradigm for therapeutic obsession and compulsion. Yet this is unmistakably obvious when we look beyond our religiously insipid surroundings and concentrate on cultures where prayer ritual is still propagated by more intact religious systems. Consider, for instance, the type of traditional Jewish prayer witnessed at the Wailing Wall in Jerusalem. Initially try to do so while divorcing what one sees there from its religious context. Men face the wall and repeat familiar prayers, either aloud or to themselves, while also rocking their upper body back and forth in such a way that their heads alternately move toward and away from the wall. One could hardly imagine a better designed strategy for the self-promotion of a dissociated state and the subsequent or simultaneous filling of that dissociative void with relevant, socially prepared religious material. The obsessive monotony that the prayer method offers comes via repetition at the cognitive as well as motor level.

Many cultures of the world still have high-profile prayer techniques containing similar ritualistic elements that reflect the prayer's ability to serve as an *autodissociative device* as well as a cognitive instrument for reinforcing one's alternative constructions of reality by means of the actual religious content of the prayer.

Jacques Janssen and his colleagues insist that praying should be understood in light of the fact that "people constantly have to shape and reshape the world they live in."[85] Prayer, in their estimation, is ritual in the manner of "a concentrated preparation to change or rearrange elements of everyday life, . . . a mechanism to construct and interpret one's experience."[86] This, they maintain, is part of the general *construction process* for restructuring reality and increasing one's feelings of control and order.

Research reveals that prayer is still very common as a pattern of individualized ritual, with one large study showing that 54 percent of Americans pray on a daily basis.[87] However, the same study found that only 37 percent of young people (those between the ages of twenty and thirty) prayed every day. A similar study in Germany found that 37 percent of youths prayed regularly, as compared to 43 percent for their parents. In The Netherlands from the years 1967 to 1979, there was a drop from 69 percent to 53 percent in terms of those who considered it useful to pray; for Dutch youths in the 1979 study, it was only 42 percent. In a 1989 Dutch study, the percentage of youths who prayed regularly had decreased to 29 percent.

Janssen remarks that many of those who continue to pray do so despite the fact that they are not church goers or even overtly religious. Some do not even profess to believe in any definite conception of a god. Even so, it appears that the act of prayer contributes to the sense of happiness and well-being of people. In explaining this, Janssen introduces the concept of *noncommunicative prayer*, as well as the categories of nontheistic and meditational prayer. He reveals that, for many people, prayer is structured as an internal *monologue* where the main value is derived from the self-directed talk, rather than from a communication with an external agent. This is consistent with Janssen's research which found that only 33 percent of prayer involved any form of asking or wishing. It also suggests the need to conceptualize prayer as not only a ritual, but a type of *cognitive* ritual that has a desired effect even when it is removed from its religious roots.

The findings of Janssen's research team helps to explain how it is possible for nontheistic prayer to operate even though it does not have a clear religious blueprint for promoting the goal of dissociative trance. In other words, how can someone employ prayer on a strictly private basis in order to acquire the dissociative benefits normally achieved by clearly defined religious modes for the execution of prayer? Janssen et al. argue that, when prayer is "turned inwards" like this, people frequently achieve a dissociated state by entering into prayer in a naturally recurring twilight state, just prior to sleep. They describe this in more detail in relation to the type of prayer that is becoming more common as traditionally theistic prayer begins to wane:

> Our hypothesis is that, when the institution of prayer is fading away in secularizing society and when praying—as we maintained— indeed has important psychological functions, people will reconstruct a mode of praying on their own. It seems understandable that this noninstitutionalized reconstruction will take place at the moment most suitable from a physiological point of view. At night in bed, people are finally on their own and have an opportunity.[88]

Janssen et al. go on to describe presleep prayer as a time when brain activity is automatically reduced and when people spontaneously enter into "a mode of passive receptivity," as they term it. This sounds very much like dissociation, even though the presleep approach prayer lacks a cultural context to some extent as well as a standardized set of prayer-specific actions that allow the person to indulge in prayer at any time. Janssen et al. found that this presleep form of prayer was the most common type of prayer among the youths they studied. The ritual involved, they state, is highly individualized and minimal in nature, while still providing a mechanism for the therapeutic consumption of ritual. They even suggest that, in our secular age, this could represent "the prototype of a new way of praying."[89]

The *improvisation* that has occurred with regard to prayer is part of a much larger process of improvisation wherein people strive to compensate for the failings of religion that are apparent in the West. With prayer, we see an example of improvisation that takes place within the confines of religion. But we also see that some New Age religious prayers have a high degree of *privacy* and even secularism about them. Improvisation extends far beyond religion into many realms of the secular world, even though this compensatory exercise can be traced to the erosion of religious systems of belief and related ritual. The case has been made that the principal value of religion lies in its ability to equip followers with "symptoms" that go undiagnosed as dissociation-based psychopathology. When religion is fully functional, these symptoms serve the individual and the larger social body. The entire existence of a person can become engulfed with the "normal abnormality" that is the historical cornerstone of human behavior. But we also know that the vestiges of religion, especially in contemporary Western culture, have driven people's symptoms into the domain of psychopathology where they are deemed not to be normal.

In relating this to our discussion of religious suggestion, however, we find that the fruits of religious insanity (i.e., delusional beliefs and related rituals) are critically reliant on the quality of the religious suggestion process, as well as the dissociation-generating techniques that pave the way for suggestive responding. If they are technically weak, or poorly rooted to the culture within which they occur, the suggestions that are instilled publicly will not convert readily into autosuggestions that operate to keep the reality distortions alive at the individual level as people go about trying to cope with day-to-day existence.

A similar situation would arise in traditional hypnosis if the hypnotic induction techniques were inappropriate and faulty in design. The hypnotist, or hypnotherapist, like the religious leader, might want to give the subject suggestions that will be effective on an ongoing basis as the subject *autosuggests* in the days or weeks following the formal hypnotic procedure. If these hypnotic methods are inadequate in design and execution, however, they will not provide the subject with the means by which to take over responsibility for the delivery of these suggestions. Just as all hypnosis comes down to self-hypnosis, it is also true that, ultimately, all religious suggestion is autosuggestion. Yet religion can normalize symptoms, something not possible when symptoms are constructed in the absence of a normalizing institution.

The religion that I grew up with in my early years had retained at least *some* of its ability to engender religious insanity, while also *confining* that madness to the realm of religion, its rightful home. But, unfortunately, I found myself growing gradually more self-conscious and less self-confident about the religious things I was thinking and doing. Eventually, I gave up my religious obsessive-compulsive disorder. The autosuggestions that I was employing had somehow lost their ability to activate and sustain the dissociation required to engage in, *without self-consciousness*, my normal religious pathology.

This occurred, not unexpectedly, around the time that the Roman Catholic Church underwent the already mentioned radical changes to its induction and indoctrination services. When the dust had settled, I found myself in a much more streamlined and deritualized religious ambience, one that carried with it messages (i.e., suggestions) different from the ones that had been delivered to me over the years of my church attendance. These were also very different from the messages that had become the autosuggestions upon which my obsessions and compulsions were founded. I recall quite clearly when, at one Sunday service following the changes in liturgy instituted by Vatican II, a polka band was substituted for the usual somnambulistic organ. While it is true that church organs are not the most superior source of absorption and dissociation-fostering monotony, the polka band music left me feeling completely cold from a "spiritual" standpoint. In terms of Rouget's claim that music is the traditional pathway to dissociative trance within religious contexts, it could be said that the polka music was devoid of almost all dissociative value. If anything, it served to irritate and to impede the necessary relaxation of the general reality orientation and the conscious monitoring authority.

Not only that, when the new messages arrived via sermons and the religious symbols that had survived although in highly diminished and unmagical form, the actual content of the suggestions had been changed. Even sins were no longer sins as I had come to know them. Instead, after a final blast of "Ave Maria" polka-style, it was suggested that such infractions were a matter of personal conscience, and that God did not want anyone to go to hell. Common sense was thrust upon the congregation along with other amorphous suggestions that cast doubt on the very existence of a hell or a purgatory. These, it was suggested in a hesitant way, were possibly only figurative places that served to highlight the importance of living in a loving way, in harmony and peace with one's neighbor.

Many other such suggestions were to follow, all intended to plant religion's feet more firmly on the ground. Behind the scenes, religious leaders worried about declining membership. The theory propelling the changes was that people would be ·more inclined to involve themselves in a religion whose format and design were recognizable to them in demystified ways. But, in relation to the whole argument before us, we know that church reformers had it all backwards. Followers were falling away because their religion had become increasingly *demystified* over the course of three hundred years. In direct opposition to all the ill-advised liberals spearheading the earthward movement of their church and its practices, Catholicism was actually crying out for an *amplification* of mystification and otherworldliness. Religious leaders failed to realize that, for their religion to *work*, it must remain *out of this world* and beyond the reach of reason and potential falsification.

As Rodney Stark observed, religions eventually disintegrate if they become "too worldly and too emptied of supernaturalism."[90] That was the crux of the problem facing the Roman Catholic Church, but it was misdiagnosed and treated in a counterproductive fashion. Thus an even more severe state of organizational precariousness faces that particular religious body today. Indeed, the future of all Western religions, in their present liberal forms, is in peril unless religious madness can be restored to the largely disoriented followers who now beg for more dissociation. The modern craving for dissociation is evidenced by the emigration of people into more "hypnotic" (i.e., dissociative) religions. Simultaneously, they seek religious suggestion techniques capable of producing delusional beliefs that translate reality to a greater degree than is now possible with so-called enlightened styles of religion. The last thing people want is for religion to come down to earth, and for them to be told that it is up to them to make sense of both this world and the other. Historically, people have sought religion for nonsense, and certainly not an additional dose of sense that only exacerbates the toxic effects of primary reality. Religion, by design, must provide *alternative* modes of understanding that positively bias primary reality in the process of promoting the illusion of order, control, and predictability.

Freud, despite his errant ideas about many subjects, was most astute when it came to recognizing religion as a pathological mental health prophylactic. On the surface, this seems like a contradiction in terms, and it is, given our current definitions of mental health and mental disorder. Freud maintained that well-functioning religions offer a socially acceptable and relatively painless type of psychopathology that makes it unnecessary for the individual to develop *personal* neurosis.[91] This useful insight was reached when he disallowed religious symptoms to be treated and diagnosed separately from the symptoms we typically associate with psychological disturbance. In agreement with Freud, we would achieve a better understanding of both religion and psychopathology by being truly objective with regard to psychological symptoms, whether or not they are religious in nature. There is a good case for doing just this, especially since religious and nonreligious symptoms quickly become blurred once we drop the protective barrier that safeguards religion from psychiatric diagnosis.

I would like to approach the next chapter, which deals with psychopathology, in a broad enough way that religion can be comprehended as one of several possible *syndromes* (i.e., sets of symptoms) that provide human beings with cognitive mechanisms for coping with noxious aspects of reality. These can be macroscopic in nature, such as the existential anxiety stemming naturally from an unnerving awareness of our insignificance and mortality. Or these can be syndromes enabling people to better cope with any number of distressing situational difficulties that might arise in the course of their everyday lives.

In fashioning a model of mental "disorder" that encompasses religion, I will attempt to show that it is comparable to the psychopathological syndromes which occupy the time and energy of mental health professionals, including addiction counselors of various sorts. Hopefully, this will add another dimension to the principal goal of this book, which is a broad and integrated theory of reality regulation.

5 Psychopathology: New Perspectives

As a clinical psychologist, I have been struck many times by the parallels between religious and psychopathological behavior. It is so common to see people simultaneously adopt pathological and religious symptoms. Some of the most impressive displays of religion that I have ever witnessed were by people in mental institutions. The reason for this seems quite obvious in terms of our knowledge of symptom formation as a coping device. Thus, when people turn to certain patterns of psychopathology, many would be expected to find additional coping value in the rituals and beliefs of religion. Quite literally, both are forms of *conversion*, and the symptoms of both are established and maintained in similar ways. Indeed, it is appropriate to introduce this chapter on psychopathology by restating some of the same principles that were covered while introducing the topic of religion. Let me recapitulate slightly while creating a foundation for an overlapping model of religious and psychopathological behavior.

Human beings possess a cerebral ability that enables them to escape an unremitting awareness of potentially unsettling situations and/or events. Otherwise, the hyperconsciousness of which we are capable could easily translate into chaos accompanied by debilitating emotional distress. Many of the realities that are within the grasp of our extensively developed brains have no apparent solutions, and the means for some sort of emotional retreat from reality allows us to escape nervous system overload. To do this, the human brain evolved a system for the *simultaneous* processing of both rational and irrational information. This process of dissociation is a parallel one that gives a high degree of independence to irrational and rational modes of information processing, thus preventing reality-based conclusions (and memories) from neutralizing irrational constructions of reality.

In the previous discussion about religion, we saw that nonrational understandings of the world and ourselves are usually engineered at the level of culture through the use of socially sanctioned methods for promoting dissociation and disseminating suggestions once a dissociative state has been achieved. When all goes according to plan, culturally endorsed suggestions are absorbed by masses of people, giving them delusions and patterns of ritual that prove beneficial to both the individual and the group. These cultural forms of "deviance" (i.e., deviations from primary reality), however insane by absolute standards, are always considered normal since they are patterned into group consciousness. However, this deviance does not retain the status of normality once it is no longer embraced by culture. Here is the exact point at which religion fades into psychopathology; that is, the point where pathological beliefs and actions lose their social sanction, and where one must speak of clinical rather than religious symptoms.

While it is true that we are "hypnotic" creatures who by nature seek pathways to dissociation, this was meant to operate at the collective level. The reasons for this are twofold. It comes back to the problem that the fruits of dissociation (e.g., religious ideologies, grossly inaccurate conclusions about the world, extremes of "ignorance," and associated practices and behaviors) are often absurd and ludicrous. If these were not played out on a collective stage, the healthy translations of reality afforded by dissociation and suggestion would be unobtainable. Quite simply, it is much easier to accept and maintain inaccurate constructions of reality if they are patterned into *group* consciousness. Social chaos would ensue if people used their dissociative abilities to transcend reality and themselves on an individual basis. There would be endless misperceptions of the world, most of which would compete with each other for credibility. Potentially healthy fictions would clash and negate each other. Confusion would reign and social bonding would be unlikely as individuals withdrew from one another in order to protect their personalized alterations of the world about them.

Culture and Coping

On the subject of religious ritual, Ernest Becker writes that "the fundamental imperative of all ritual is that one cannot do it alone . . . and cooperation is necessary in order to make that technique work.[1] The same can be said of religion generally. Becker's unflinching gaze allowed him to see that culture is the intended mediator between illusion and reality. The main body of "symptoms" that we have relied upon historically in order to cope with reality have come to us on the platter of culture. Anthony Marsella and Alice Dash-Scheuer address the important relationship between culture and coping. They begin by offering a definition of coping that views this process as "the active utilization of biological, psychological, and social resources which assist in controlling, mastering, and preventing the distress imposed by external and/or internal demands experienced by the organism."[2] They then show that all human cultures are direct reflections of the coping patterns for the individuals within those cultures, and add that cultures evolve and develop as a response to our natural inclination to adapt to all elements of our environment. By way of summation, Marsella and Dash-Scheuer make the simple but highly perceptive statement that *"culture is coping!"*

Numerous anthropologists and cross-cultural psychologists have pointed out that cultures are always religious to varying extents. This is because religion, which is the inevitable product of culture, should also be regarded as a style of coping, both for individuals and the society as a whole. In fact, we saw in the first chapter that religion tends to function as a coping mechanism in relation to its effects on personal adjustment. We also know from the work of Durkheim and others that religion and related ritual have important adaptive value in terms of social integrity and cohesion. But we also saw that religion must be understood as a type of psychopathology, both cognitive and ritualistic in nature, that evades a formal diagnosis due to social sanctioning. Speaking about culture as the generator of necessary delusion about primary reality, Ernest Becker states:

> True, there is a great deal of falseness and self-deception in the cultural *causa sui* project, but there is also the necessity of this project . . . cultural illusion is a necessary ideology . . . a dimension that is life itself to the symbolic animal . . . to lose the security of cultural illusion is to die—that is what "deculturation" of primitives means and what it does. . . . Life becomes possible only in a continual alcoholic stupor.[3]

As with religion, an analysis of the dynamics of psychopathology requires us to examine people's relationship to reality. Mental health professionals take the liberty of imposing a diagnosis of mental illness on individuals who are supposedly out of touch with their (i.e., the professionals') notion of reality. Sometimes they feel quite confident in doing this, as in the case of so-called psychotic thoughts and behaviors, such as those frequently witnessed in victims of schizophrenia.

Yet, even in extreme instances such as this, it is not always easy to separate pathology that is normal (i.e., socially sanctioned) from that which is abnormal (i.e., not agreed upon by the group).

As an example, I could mention a former client of mine whom we might call Thelma. She was referred to our mental health center because of her staunch belief that she had died four years earlier. The date of birth given in her file indicated that she was thirty-nine years old. Yet she insisted that she was only thirty-five, since she stopped having birthdays upon her death. There was logic within her illogic, for one would stop having birthdays if one had died. But was Thelma out of touch with reality and therefore worthy of the diagnosis of mentally disturbed or mentally ill? Complicating matters more was her equally strong conviction that God had taken away her soul four years ago, when she had let herself give in to the sexual advances of a stranger who approached her one day in a park. This came to the fore when, in the middle of the first session, Thelma dropped to her knees and shouted toward the ceiling, asking God to return her soul and reassuring God that she would refrain from sex forever. She demanded that, for my own good, I, too, should get down on my knees and beg forgiveness for my sexual offenses so that God would not also call in my soul. I refused.

Had I been a radical relativist, I would have been forced to agree with Thelma's pronouncement of herself as dead. In so doing, I would have conceded that there is no such thing as a real reality, but rather only the endless private realities of individuals. But contrary to this sort of nihilistic relativism, I made the bold conclusion that, on the basis of empirical information reaching my sensors and processors, Thelma was indeed alive. Moreover, prior to age thirty-five, she herself processed that same data in order to arrive at the conclusion that she was alive. It was only during Thelma's thirty-fifth year of life that something happened, causing her to construct a belief that did not correspond to primary reality.

Most people would not hesitate in agreeing with me about Thelma's being alive. But again, I could have been wrong. After all, it is possible that we are all dead and already part of some twisted afterlife. Or we could be mere ghostly actors in a memory trace that lingers in some unknown dimension of time and space. Admittedly, such possibilities are erroneous in terms of empirical reality, in the sense that no empirical data would lead us to such a conclusion. Yet it is possible, however inconceivable or improbable it might be. By sheer accident, some supposed falsehoods may turn out to be true when gauged according to data that are as yet completely beyond our reach.

As another example, consider the person whose personal reality includes the "knowledge" of the existence of flying saucers, even though that person has never seen a flying saucer or received any empirical data that would lead to such knowledge. While the certainty of this individual's knowledge is currently unjustified on the basis of empirical information, astronomers may one day detect such objects. If that happens, empirical reality will be altered in such a way that knowledge about the existence of flying saucers will be justified, and even expected. Therefore, empirical reality in no way implies absolute reality. Although absolute truths about the nature of the world and ourselves probably exist, the empirical information available to us is never complete. Even if it should become available, certain limits exist on our capacity to absorb and interpret that information.

That aside, let us cautiously assume that my client Thelma was actually alive. This then exemplifies, in a rather dramatic way, how personal reality can deviate from empirical reality. More precisely, her personal reality was *in error* in relation to data available from the empirical world. But what about Thelma's religious beliefs concerning her sexuality and her soul? The Aztecs, as we know, cut out thousands of human hearts in order to pacify their god and make the sun rise in the morning. Judged against the Aztecs, Thelma's beliefs seemed quite reasonable and moderate. But Thelma's religious beliefs, like her "I-am-dead" belief, had to be viewed as clinical (rather than religious) psychopathology since she did not belong to a group that shared that particular belief. If she had, then her religious beliefs would need to be viewed as normal. If that same religion perpetuated the belief that God punished sexuality by repossessing the soul, then Thelma's delusion about being dead would also be labeled as *norm*-al.

In Thelma's defense, we should note that some cultures have such religious beliefs. People who break certain religious taboos are robbed of their souls by the offended spirits, often causing the offender to suffer great physical and mental distress. That would be explained in normal religious ways. But again, Thelma's symptoms could not be normalized by religious beliefs that had the endorsement of a sizable portion of the cultural body. Quite obviously, the belief that one can be dead while also alive is not an element of the collective reality of Western society, nor is it featured in the religions of the West.

Thelma's case is illustrative in that it shows once more how deviance in the form of reality distortion is deemed to be pathological when and only when it falls outside the bounds of the reality constructions and misconstructions of the respective culture. It hardly matters how deviant from actual reality those constructions are as long as they can be normalized by the group. In previous ages, this was not much of an issue. Members of society could be highly pathological in the sense of being out of touch with reality while remaining normal and enjoying the feeling of being in harmony with reality as seen through the eyes of culture. On this note, Gehan Wijeyewardene makes the important observation that, in premodern times, *religion was a total way of life.*[4]

Until recently, human beings were surrounded by collective religious ideologies that made unnecessary the modern question about a person's degree of contact with reality. In short, culture as a religious enterprise immersed its people in abundant quantities of the irrational, or what could also be described as deviations from primary reality. This led the eminent culture theorist William T. Hall to describe culture quite succinctly as *an irrational force.*[5] Hall elaborates by saying that logic is largely a Western invention that can be traced to the time of Socrates, Plato, and Aristotle. Moreover, Hall speaks to the inherent strength of the historical cultures that arrived at "truths" via the irrational instead of the "linear, low-context, logical frames" that have infiltrated modern constructions of reality.[6]

In relation to our joint treatment of religion and psychopathology, it should be pointed out that "clinical" psychopathology as we know it does not exist in all cultures. There is no depression whatsoever among the Kaluli of New Guinea, to give one example. Such cultures have become the focus of scientific study, and they may help us to understand our current mental health problems. Of special relevance here are the findings of medical anthropologists and cross-cultural clinical psychologists who have sought to gauge the prevalence of mental disorders. Since schizophrenia is a brain disease, it is not surprising that the rate of schizophrenia does not vary much from one culture to another.[7] But remarkably, many "untouched" non-Western societies display virtually no "neurotic" symptoms as we know them in the West. The situation changes quickly for the worse, however, once they come under the influence of Western culture. By stark contrast to intact non-Western cultures, we in the West now make frequent reference to the *mental health crisis* that seems to have befallen us. This includes the full range of "neurotic" symptoms that are present in an unfortunately large percentage of Western society.

The absence of psychopathological symptoms among members of some non-Western cultural groups seems to contradict the fact that people, regardless of their culture of origin, experience the stresses, worries, and situational difficulties that we generally associate with the emergence of psychological symptoms. No matter what a person's cultural base, loved ones get sick and die, food sources come under threat, events beyond our control generate anxiety, and so forth. It seems that these groups would fall prey to "clinical" symptoms, just as those in Western cultural settings do. But this does not seem inevitable.

Three explanations for this present themselves, all of which I feel have some validity. The first is that some of these psychologically "symptom-free" societies were still *intact* as social systems that were structured in order to meet the needs of its members. Joseph Campbell expands on some of the ideas put forward by Oswald Spengler in *The Decline of the West*.[8] Campbell speaks of the relative *fitness* of cultures, in much the same way that Spengler uses the term "in form" to describe cultures that are operating in an optimal fashion. Spengler compares cultures to athletes, arguing it is possible for both to be in any degree of form, or lack of form. If a culture is "in form" it will, among other things, provide people with the necessary ingredients for a sense of mastery, belongingness, transcendence, and sense of purpose. These and other such cultural bestowals combine to produce a group of people who do not need to employ *personal* exercises that serve to compensate for a lack of cultural form.

Erich Fromm also recognized that the psychological and emotional well-being of people is largely the result of macroscopic forces operating at the level of culture. In *The Sane Society*, Fromm outlines what he calls our *human needs*, similar to those stated above (rootedness, belongingness, sense of identity, transcendence, and frame of orientation).[9] Fromm then distinguishes between sane and insane cultures, arguing that a sane society is one equipped to meet all of those needs. Fromm is often criticized for promoting the "happy savage" idea, since he points to "primitive" non-Western cultures as the only ones that have retained sufficient cultural form to meet our needs and produce healthy-minded members. Yet, in my experience, those criticisms are completely unjustified.

Fromm, like Joseph Campbell, has written convincingly about the miserable *lack* of form that exists in Western society, as well as the devastating social and psychological aftermath of this loss of form. By comparison, the cultures that have not suffered the same sort of erosion of form should be expected to contain members who are more "sane," as Fromm would put it. Therefore, it is no great surprise that cross-cultural investigators often find hardly any signs of clinical psychopathology among the so-called savages. It also comes as no surprise that the destruction of their cultures by Western peoples has left many acculturated groups in desperate shape in terms of psychological and social health. We imposed on them an even greater mental health crisis than our own since many were left with no culture at all, and thus no means of coping.

A second explanation for the apparent absence of mental disorders in the sane societies of which Fromm speaks is that their religions are in form to a degree that can conceal as normal even highly symptomatic usages of religion. That is, religion in such cultures is still the all-embracing *total way of life* that Wijeyewardene described. Consequently, there is virtually no end to people's ability to indulge in cognitive as well as ritualistic religious symptoms, without being identified as abnormal in any sense of the word.

I recall a time in Thailand when my wife and I were eating in a small open-air restaurant. A young man riding an elephant stopped the elephant near the front of the restaurant, at which time an elderly woman bent down and walked underneath the large beast. She did it over and over again, leaving no doubt in our minds that the woman was suffering from a mental disorder accompanied by suicidal tendencies. But several other people then approached the elephant and, after giving money to its rider, walked under the elephant in the same way done previously by the elderly woman. Suddenly it all became normal since it was clear that their behavior had some religious significance, something that was later confirmed by some locals.

A third possible explanation for the relative healthy mindedness of the "savage" has to do with the superiority of their psychotherapeutic techniques. These can be used in extreme cases in which religion is not able to contain a person's madness. Unlike our own, these techniques enjoy exceptionally high success rates since they have much more grounding in an agreed-upon cultural reality, usually one that gathers increased power from religion.

If we imagine a culture possessing a total-way-of-life religion that is beyond any doubt, we can also imagine that a person could be religiously symptomatic to any extent without risk of attracting a label of insanity. One could, for example, walk under elephants almost continuously and still not be exhibiting behavior identifiable as either abnormal or cause for concern. As Durkheim realized, religion and reality contradict one another and must therefore be kept apart. Once religion is successfully segregated from reality by an in-form culture, then members of that culture have unlimited access to the unreal, with total permission to draw on it to whatever extent is needed. In such a cultural climate, there is almost no need to speak of normality in the sense of being in touch with reality since people have full license to participate in the unreal, and do so readily without inhibition. We might be tempted to argue that some people from "sane" societies are overexercising their cultural right to be religiously out of touch with reality. But the fact remains that these individuals do not feel, and are not perceived to be, mentally disturbed.

In terms of certain in-form cultures, therefore, we have a situation wherein the social structure leads to lower rates of psychological disturbance, as well as a mechanism whereby symptoms can be masked and absorbed by in-form religion. Consequently, a discussion of psychopathology as we usually think of it can only be done in the larger context of out-of-form culture and out-of-form religion. And that is exactly what we see as we look around us. Joseph Campbell, for instance, referred to the *destruction of form* in Western culture, including the religions of the West.[10] He was especially struck by the loss of form in relation to religious ritual.

Similarly, Heije Faber writes about the failure of ritual in Western society, in particular its disappearance from traditional religious contexts.[11] Beyond that, Faber gives us insight into the formation of the systems of secular ritual that are emerging as substitutes for religious ritual. Yet we are reminded that, historically, rituals were enacted in *group* settings and that they lose much of their value under circumstances where people feel driven to engage in ritual without a normative foundation. Private ritual of this nature cannot support the transcendent belief systems that also gain their credibility as a result of their group endorsement.

Rituals, according to Barbara Myerhoff, are "dramas of persuasion" that draw their lifeblood from the group: "all must collude so as not to spoil the show, or damage the illusion that the dramatic reality coincides with the 'other, out-there reality.' "[12] Yet modern religions have become technically inadequate as cultural vehicles for reality transformation, including the manner in which the collapse of ritual has contributed to the evolution of psychopathology no longer identifiable as religion. On this topic, Victor Turner observes that

> under the conditions of social differentiation and in times of secularization, participation in rituals is more or less reduced to superficial experiences. . . . Instead of a deeper experience of social or individual transformation, there often remains nothing but a reduced liminality, called *limnoid form of transformation*.[13]

According to Turner, religion and its rituals constitute social dramas that reflect collective values. Under ideal cultural conditions, the *integrative function of ritual* has powerful transformative powers. Conflicts and tension, both at the level of the individual and society, can be resolved. Today, however, we continue to witness the disintegration of the collective pathways to reality transformation. Our myth-ritual complexes have become culturally unfit, thereby catapulting people into a new psychological and social terrain in which they find themselves operating as *islands* of transformation. Increasingly, we are forced to contest reality without the help of the cultural bodies whose role it is to structure as well as normalize our out-of-touchness with reality. This means that, in the wake of eroding mainstream religions, there has been a scattering process involving increasing numbers of small-scale and private religions, cults, quasi-religions, and poorly functioning paranormal attempts at reality rejection.

In terms of ritual, Harvey Cox writes in *The Feast of Fools* that the failure of modern Christianity has had the effect of *driving the dancers out into the streets*. He quotes the following verses, written by a Christian mystic in the tradition of St. Bernard, suggesting that Jesus himself made good use of ritualistic dance as he exerted his influence on potential followers:

> Jesus the dancers' master is
> A great skill at the dance is his
> He turns to right, he turns to left
> All must follow his teaching deft.[14]

The "dance" of people in Western cultures is clumsy, out of step, and lacking the form that can only come from culturally choreographed belief systems and the rituals that give movement and physical reality to those beliefs. If St. Bernard is correct, Jesus probably knew the power of dance as it can foster the state of consciousness that gives birth to religious beliefs. From our knowledge of dance as one of the traditional pathways to dissociative trance, we should not be shocked that Jesus' appeal could have sprung from his irresistible dance movements.

From the classic anthropological work of Erika Bourguignon, we know that virtually all viable religions employ systems of dissociative trance.[15] Furthermore, Bourguignon refers to the resultant states of altered consciousness associated with systems of belief. These beliefs, she writes, are *cultural inventions* in the same way that the trance-inducing techniques are cultural inventions. A global picture emerges in which we see a predictable tendency for people in all cultures to participate in patterned reality alterations that rely on culturally constructed methods for entry into dissociative states that can temporarily suspend the general reality orientation. A serious question arises, however, concerning the manner in which reality deconstruction and reconstruction are achieved in the face of cultural diffusion, part of which involves the waning of traditional religion as the usual mechanism for accomplishing this. Given the universality of the drive for cognitive bias as well as the dissociative exercises that make possible our bias, it seems implausible that these core aspects of human activity will simply disappear. Instead, in recent times, the dissociation/suggestion process has been spread out into marginal domains of religion as well as into the domain of psychopathology.

When culture as a coping device with historical ties to religion was relatively intact, there was much less need for the personal expressions of psychopathology that have become so familiar to us today. Also, history has never seen the degree of proliferation of so-called paranormal beliefs and their associated rituals as we see today. This is despite the fact that paranormal belief/ritual is always in the ascendant during secular ages when religion undergoes change. Unique historical factors appear to be at work today, causing an unparalleled degree of gravitation toward misconstructions of reality that are unable to attract the label of normality. As such, they must be understood as private, rather than universal, psychopathology. An analysis of the specific patterns of psychopathology might begin with the types of "paranormal" beliefs and activities that must be classified as pathological due to their minority endorsement.

PARANORMAL PSYCHOPATHOLOGY

Durkheim made a useful distinction between religion and magic, one that captures the essential difference between religion and the paranormal, and between religion and psychopathology generally. In the words of Durkheim, the belief in magic

> does not result in binding together those who adhere to it, nor in uniting them into a group leading a common life. . . . Between the magician and the individuals who consult him, as between these individuals themselves, there are no lasting bonds which make them members of the same moral community, comparable to that formed by the believers in the same god or the observers of the same cult.[16]

While traditional religion can certainly be regarded as paranormal in the sense of being located beyond the normal, I will use the term paranormal to describe beliefs/rituals that do not possess the "common life" (i.e., majority endorsement) to which Durkheim referred. In the previous chapter, a body of research was presented showing that religion correlates with dissociation as measured by scales of hypnotic responsiveness. This would be expected if the assumption is correct that religious alterations of reality are dependent upon the human capacity for dissociation. We should also suspect that paranormal adjustments to primary reality are related to people's ability to dissociate, even though those dissociations are not an extension of the dissociative strategies of mainstream cultural religion.

The small amount of quantitative research in this area supports the assumption that, like religion, the paranormal is also a manifestation of dissociated consciousness. For example, Douglas Richards administered the widely used Dissociative Experiences Scale to 184 attendees of a meeting of The Association for Research and Enlightenment.[17] This sample was selected since most of these individuals had high levels of paranormal experiences, including telepathy, clairvoyance, apparitions, psychic dreams, trance channeling, out-of-body experiences, precognition, and extraterrestrial encounters. Richards obtained significant correlations between dissociation scores and the frequency with which people had the following paranormal experiences: telepathy, clairvoyance, apparitions, psychic dreams, psychokinesis, trance channeling, out-of-body experiences, precognition, spirit guidance, past life encounters, and extraterrestrial meetings.

Also of interest was Richards's finding of a significant correlation between positive emotion and degree of dissociation. That is, as people engaged in greater amounts of dissociation, they also had more feelings of positive emotion. Better feelings and a more positive outlook were related to the use of dissociation. Traditional religion is a category of dissociative responding that, in general, carries mental health advantages. So we would expect religious dissociations to correlate with positive emotional experience. As we delve into the different psychopathologies, however, we will find that those *personal* modes of dissociation are typically correlated with negative emotional experience, most notably depression.

Richards's finding of a correlation between dissociation and positive emotion may be due to the fact that his subjects were part of an organization that allowed people to congregate periodically with like-minded individuals. Such a situation might safeguard these people from the feelings of deviance that would correspond to symptoms of a highly private nature, such as those falling into the category of clinical psychopathology. When participants in paranormal belief and ritual constitute an "autistic reality" (David Heise's term), as is often the case, then we might expect the emotional accompaniments of paranormal symptoms to be no better than those associated with clinical symptoms. Once the paranormal becomes *private* beyond a certain critical point, it is hard to fend off the judgment (both from without and within) that the behavior is *abnormal*. That is always a risk when dissociation and reality modifications are attempted alone, or with a group too small for purposes of normalization.

The relationship between paranormal belief/experience and dissociation was also studied by George Ganaway.[18] Specifically, Ganaway examined what he termed "close encounters of the dissociative kind" and demonstrated that UFO abductees have exceptionally high levels of hypnotic susceptibility, as well as a highly developed capacity for imaginative cognition. Ganaway helps us to understand the phenomenon of UFO abduction by describing it as a product of dissociation and suggestion. His analysis is especially enlightening, since he also specifies how the paranormal symptoms are the end result of alterations of memory. In our previous treatment of religion we saw that dissociation made it possible for certain memories to be suspended and subsequently replaced with false memories in relation to the religious suggestions made available to dissociated followers. Nonreligious paranormal misconstructions of reality appear to be achieved in a similar way, except that many paranormal beliefs and experiences lack the amount of social sanction existing within dominant cultural religions.

Ganaway also cites evidence to show that the beliefs and experiences of UFO abductees are formed in much the same way as the symptoms of multiple personality disorder and other clinical dissociative disorders. He therefore manages to bridge religion, psychopathology, and hypnosis while using the concept of dissociation as the common denominator. Ganaway introduces into his discussion the concept of *pseudomemories*, and argues that symptoms are made possible when dissociation enables a person to replace reality-based memories with false memories that are the result of suggestion.

Most of the alleged UFO abductees in his study had seen TV accounts or movies involving UFO abductions. In most cases, these sources of information became the building blocks for the autosuggestions that planted pseudomemories that were later "remembered." The fact that most UFO abductees did not even bother to report the abduction to authorities tells us that, as with religious pseudomemories, people also know the truth of the matter. That is, they both know and do not know, just as the religious believer both believes and does not believe. The *belle indifférence* of UFO abductees and religious believers closely parallels the indifference toward symptoms shown by victims of many clinical dissociative disorders. Dissociation, as we know, does not preclude awareness. The person remains aware at a level that does not have access to consciousness. When UFO abductees come down to earth, when religious people lose their "faith," when a "blind" person suffering from conversion disorder begins to see again—these are all instances of dissociative pseudomemories that have become loosened and replaced by more reality-based memories.

According to Ganaway, stories of reincarnation are also typically seen in people with superior dissociative capacities, as well as high degrees of fantasy-proneness. Their proneness toward fantasy is to be expected since research shows a strong correlation between fantasy-proneness and hypnotic responsiveness (i.e., dissociative capacity).[19] As with UFO abduction memories, the reincarnation memories are also *self-constructed* distortions of reality wherein these dissociation-gifted and fantasy-prone individuals create pseudomemories that are experienced as real. Again, as with the supposed UFO abductees, research shows that these individuals were exposed to various forms of media that became the basis for the self-directed suggestions structuring the reincarnation pseudomemories. Ganaway's work reveals that most instances of "age regression" can also be understood in relation to the processes of dissociation and suggestion as they combine to manufacture convincing pseudomemories.

Still another source of support for the dissociative nature of paranormal psychopathology comes from the research of Joseph Glicksohn.[20] Instead of measuring dissociative ability directly in relation to paranormal belief and experience, he assessed degree of *absorption*. We have already seen that absorption is a crucial element of the dissociation process, with several studies showing high levels of correlation between absorption and dissociation. Some of these correlations were found while investigating the relationship between absorption and dissociation as reflected in hypnotic susceptibility. With this in mind, one may predict that encounters with the paranormal will be associated with enhanced capabilities for absorption. And indeed, this is what Glicksohn found. Paranormal experiences are positively correlated with people's potential to become absorbed. It follows that this capacity makes possible the dissociative states necessary for "paranormal" reality transfiguration.

The entire range of paranormal beliefs and experiences should be conceptualized as dissociative exercises that have little or no cultural reality. For this reason, we can speak of these types of behavior as pathological. This is despite the fact that some paranormal symptoms have a small degree of social sanction which permits the person to remain marginally "normal" while participating in the paranormal. We might consider astrology and take the example of someone who studies an astrology guide every morning in order to obtain guidance for his or her actions. Research shows that approximately 5 percent of Americans change their behavior in relation to what they read in astrology reports.[21]

There exists a certain amount of tolerance for astrological beliefs, but this tolerance is very fragile since astrology as a vehicle for reality reconstruction is not sufficiently normalized. Therefore, even though many religiously starved Western people have turned to astrology in search of necessary falsehood, they are quickly identified as abnormal when they indulge themselves in that particular quasi-religion. If I failed to show up at our Monday staff meetings because certain stars were aligned in an ominous way, that behavior would be regarded as pathological or, at best, eccentric. If I began missing lectures because some other group of stars was out of kilter, I would soon lose my job and be given a recommendation to seek psychiatric help. By contrast, someone could quite easily remain normal if he or she failed to show up at a staff meeting or a lecture if their actions had some religious significance, even if the religious beliefs had no more foundation in reality than the astrological ones.

Other paranormal beliefs and their related behaviors have even less social currency than astrology. Some people, for example, have become devoted disciples of crystals. They sometimes sit facing a clump of crystals, using it as an absorption point for instilling in themselves a mild state of dissociation. Repetitive New Age music is sometimes used as an aid, as are other objects and paraphernalia with symbolic ("suggestive") significance. Throughout history, people in many cultures have attached magical powers to rocks and other ordinary elements of the natural world. However, their involvement with these materials was usually the result of culturally recognized religious belief systems. This allowed them to exploit rocks and other such objects without the fear of being isolated from the group on grounds of insanity. While crystals have a minimal amount of credibility among a tiny portion of the population, it is not sufficient to protect the person from a diagnosis of psychopathology.

Of course, nothing is stopping a person from doing whatever he or she likes with crystals behind closed doors. But if word got out that I was using the power of crystals to heal my child's acute appendicitis attack, the authorities would swoop down and take my child to a hospital. Spiritual healing has a long and colorful history, and ritualistic treatments with religious significance were once widely accepted. These practices continue in some parts of the non-Western world. In the West, however, there is not even much tolerance for people who prefer to turn to the divine in unconventional ways in order to accomplish healing. Faith healing in confined settings still enjoys some immunity from external regulating bodies, even though it is widely publicized as a form of deceit and quackery. With crystals, however, it should be clear that culture is not participating enough in order to make them a credible point of entry into an alternative construction of reality.

It is not necessary to labor over numerous examples of the paranormal as private and *unsanctioned* expressions of dissociation and suggestion. They all fall into this category of pathology that lies between religious and clinical pathology. But it is important to gain an understanding of the broad trend that they reflect in Western society. John Durant and Martin Bauer deal with this issue in their argument that the current proliferation of paranormal beliefs and practices must be understood as a problem of modernity, especially as modernity is associated with a deterioration of organized religion.[22] Durant and Bauer cite a large British research survey that casts some light on the cultural causes of paranormal belief. They found, for instance, that people with strong paranormal beliefs (e.g., in astrology) tend to have high levels of religious interest and yet to show low levels of integration into mainstream cultural religion. That is, they have become disconnected from organized religion and are attempting to compensate for religious deficits by engaging in culturally marginal paranormal beliefs and practices. Durant and Bauer make the perceptive observation that participation in the paranormal is fueled by *metaphysical unrest* that seeks to achieve transcendence as well as the personal integrity and social unity that is historically forthcoming from majority-sanctioned religion. Therefore, we have even more validation for the thesis that the paranormal is energized by the same natural inclinations that cause people in all cultures to indulge in religious renovations of primary reality. At the same time, social changes have made it exceedingly difficult for people to satisfy their religious needs. Again, the "dancers" have been driven into the street, where they are dancing to their own religious tune since the principal cultural religions are failing them.

Other research confirms that paranormal beliefs represent attempts to construct *functional alternatives* to mainstream religion. One study examined a sample of people with no affiliation to organized religion and found that they were significantly more likely than their religious counterparts to hold paranormal beliefs (e.g., in numerology, witches, clairvoyance, and astrology).[23] William Sims Bainbridge and Rodney Stark conducted studies revealing similar results.[24] We see again that people with deficits in terms of organized religion are significantly more likely to accept "deviant" (i.e., socially unsanctioned) supernatural and magical propositions.

Since our yearnings for reality distortion appear to remain constant regardless of secularization, the overall trend in Western culture is for people to seek *private* methods by which to achieve dissociation. This also means that people today have become much more reliant on procedures that allow them to *self*-administer their own reality-modifying suggestions once dissociation has been accomplished. This pursuit can take them in many other directions besides those types of compensatory paranormal beliefs we have already described.

DISSOCIATION AND PATHOLOGICAL DRUG USAGE

Self-forgetting and reality-forgetting are powerful drives, so much so that cultures themselves evolve in order to assist members toward these ends. As these goals are achieved, the self and reality generally take on new shape according to the cultural suggestions made available to people. We saw earlier that, in former ages, cultures made ready use of drugs in religious settings in order to promote in its members a dissociated state that would make them amenable to reality-modifying suggestions. Therefore, there was a convenient unity between drugs, dissociation, and suggestion. Furthermore, as Marlene Dobkin de Rios has shown, the traditional patterns of culturally sanctioned drug usage did not lead to the degrading and self-destructive addictions that are so much a part of society today. Rather than destroying the self and obliterating reality, traditional drug use creatively *reconstructed* the self as well as reality. But contemporary patterns of drug consumption require us to speak in terms of drug *abuse* rather than drug *use* for acceptable cultural purposes.

The relatively private drug abuse that is spreading like a plague in many parts of the industrialized world is the consequence of culture failure, and thus the eclipse of group-endorsed methods of coping. If we cut away all connotations and misconceptions, we arrive at a picture of drugs as the most basic and primitive form of religion. Drugs provide the first and most important ingredient for religion, namely, a dissociated state wherein a person's higher-order cognitive faculties are disengaged. Critical and analytic thought are suspended as people find a certain amount of refuge from reality. Some drugs act largely to dull the senses while producing only mild states of dissociation. Others, such as the hypnotics and hallucinogenics, promote deeper states of dissociation that are associated with hypersuggestibility. In most instances, the user can take advantage of the drug's ability to restrict and narrow the range of awareness. In a sense, the world becomes smaller as chunks of the person's former reality are eliminated from the field of consciousness. He or she then shifts from a generalized mode of attention to a more specific mode that temporarily neutralizes memory.

Drugs were once used to produce what Dobkin de Rios depicts as *culturally managed* altered states of consciousness.[25] The content of the altered reality was the result of suggestions that possessed social consensus. Now, as Dobkin de Rios points out, modern drug usage has become disconnected from a cultural context, thus giving the altered state a culturally *unmanaged* or undirected status. At that stage, there are as many altered personal realities as there are people using drugs to disrupt their critical faculties. We should not be misled by thoughts that drug abuse is merely the search for a "high." In truth, even the best of the euphoric drugs cannot compare to the ecstasy that religiously inspired "highs" have given people throughout the course of human history. Instead, they are more accurately understood as *self-medication* strategies deemed to be necessary in the context of a dysfunctional culture that no longer meets people's human needs, especially the need for reality transcendence. Modern drug taking is one of many unproductive exercises intended to fill what Philip Cushman has called the "empty self."[26] This emptiness now stands where once stood a culturally centered sense of identity, and people now must *go it alone*, so to speak. In other words, they are left increasingly to their own devices to make both sense and nonsense of the world.

Luigi Zoja echoes some of the above sentiments as he theorizes about current drug abuse in terms of the modern desperate search for ritual.[27] Zoja, like Dobkin de Rios, pinpoints deficiencies in Western culture as the reason that people turn to drugs for escape into a dissociated state. He makes the case that contemporary drug abuse should be regarded as a form of compensation for these deficiencies, i.e., that people are forced to become their own transcenders of reality. Zoja concentrates on the absence of ritualistic initiation rites that introduce and incorporate young people into the culture. It is almost as if people are left to their own devices in constructing a *personal*, or intrapsychic, "culture" that assists them in coping with the world. Drugs, of course, are a two-edged sword, with users paying a high psychological and social price for seeking reality deconstruction on a private basis. Even when other drug users make up a miniculture in which the individual may participate, this makeshift type of culture is still unable to offer much direction for the reshaping of the alternative reality.

States of dissociation accessed through drugs function similarly to dissociation that is produced by other techniques, whether they be traditional religion, formal hypnosis, or autodissociative psychopathologies. However, these drug-induced states differ from most other strategies in that they are not followed up by suggestions that are intended to reconstruct in some prescribed fashion the vacuous state resulting from the ingestion of the drug. We could again compare it to a situation in which a hypnotist went through the usual induction procedures that promoted dissociation as well as enhanced suggestibility, but then did not deliver any suggestions to give structure to the dissociation. It would also resemble a religion that had all the usual techniques for assisting people toward a dissociated state with heightened suggestibility, but without any religious suggestions.

Many drugs do, in fact, yield a state of hypersuggestibility as they act to generate cognitive dissociation. I recall a psychotherapy client who once told me about an "LSD trip" that he and some friends went on. They were driving in a car, but they pulled off the road once the drug began to exert its influence. They stopped under some large high-tension electrical pylons. For no apparent reason, my patient decided to "play with the minds" of his friends by describing strange happenings to them. He began by pointing out excitedly that the massive pylons were leaning to one side and in the process of falling. He claimed to me that, as a result of that suggestion, everyone in the car was able to see the pylons falling. Next my patient suggested that the trees were moving from the nearby forest into the road. By his account, everyone was then able to "see" the trees move in this way. He even said that the driver of the car became convinced that he could not proceed because of the trees.

Assuming that numerous classes of drugs can engender dissociative states, we are left to wonder how those dissociated states are managed in the absence of a recognized cultural pathway for reconstructing states of dissociation. In actuality, any reconstruction of these dissociated states is largely random and idiosyncratic in nature. At best, structure is given to these vacuous states by the microscopic subculture of people who participate in these activities. Granted, the strategic use of drugs can represent a formidable assault on memory as well as the person's ongoing capacity for critical awareness. In this way, one could argue that it has some adaptive value if certain memories or modes of awareness are problematic and the source of emotional distress. Yet, such an assault is indiscriminate, leaving users unable to function within reality as they employ their all-inclusive method of escape.

MUSICAL ADDICTIONS

Never before in human history have so many individuals spent so much time listening to music. Young people today in Westernized culture expose themselves to astonishing amounts of repetitive drumming that is embedded in most popular music. This far exceeds the drumming time of people in traditional non-Western cultures, both past and present. In traditional societies where music and formal trance are closely entwined, one observes that people listen to the drums only a small proportion of the time. Yet, when they do, it is very effective as a cultural source of dissociative trance. Furthermore, as we saw earlier, the musical dissociation is structured with socially relevant suggestions, usually of a spiritual nature.

With the exception of drugs, music is the age-old technique by which cultures have orchestrated dissociative trance as well as the reconstruction of reality. Gilbert Rouget went into this process in great detail as it has been used in traditional societies around the world. In extending Rouget's work to include contemporary Western society, we must assume that music is still used by people for purposes of dissociation. However, what we see now in modern industrialized society is music that has become detached from mainstream cultural significance. It is no longer part of a clear prescription for socially sanctioned trance and there are no obvious cultural suggestions to structure whatever dissociation is achieved. In this void, music is required in larger doses, just as ever more drugs are necessary when drugs for dissociation purposes are no longer connected to official reality-altering practices. The situation grows so acute that it is quite accurate to speak of *musical addictions* that coexist nowadays with other pathological addictions, including addiction to drugs.

Our heavy use of repetitive music cannot be dismissed on the grounds that musical equipment and sound recordings are now mass-produced and readily available. There must first be a *demand* for the music. The enormous demand that we see today is largely due to the mass recognition of music as a traditional avenue to dissociative trance. Instinctively, people continue to access dissociative states via music, but they are again "going it alone," in exactly the same way that the drug abuser is forced to contest reality alone. Portable headsets now let you take your dissociative trance with you wherever you go. Millions of people so equipped walk or drive about with glassy eyes and blank expressions that speak loudly of music as another form of ongoing self-medication. This is not unlike the drug abuser who is never far from his/her next "fix." Our excessive appetites for both drugs and monotonous music go some distance to "fix" reality by offering some escape into dissociative trance. But again they are no substitute for the more powerful reality "fixes" that come in the form of socially sanctioned religions that manage trance and escape at the collective level.

The passions aroused in these times by music are continual reminders of our fundamentally religious natures and the way in which that religious nature remains constant despite social change. I think again of our young people who are disenfranchised in so many ways, most notably with regard to cultural pathways for reality transcendence. For many of them, music and worship are experienced mutually. Anyone who can remain objective while attending a pop concert may sense the strongly religious quality of the gathering. The musicians are worshiped with an intensity and zeal that reflect their esteemed role as trance providers. Those in attendance are frequently seen to collapse from a combination of extreme agitation, hyperventilation, and exhaustion. Its only counterpart in traditional non-Western societies are the convulsive drug-induced or deprivation-induced fits that overcome youthful initiates during trance-fostering ceremonial rituals.

I do not intend to imply that all young people in the West are psychologically addicted to music. The same is the case with drug addiction. Even so, music can be understood, along with drugs, as a basic ingredient of the larger religious process through which people can achieve dissociation and some degree of necessary distance from reality and themselves. Certain individuals will undoubtedly rely more heavily than others on one or both of these strategies. Furthermore, musical dissociation is not limited to the younger age groups. We need only consider the beautiful and moving music of the Polish composer Henryk Górecki (Symphony No. 3, Opus 36). Recently a collection of Górecki's music was at the top of both the classical charts and the "pop" charts in Great Britain. Never before had a single piece of music topped both charts, suggesting that its appeal extended across all age groups.

Social analysts have speculated about the exact nature of Górecki's musical appeal. Most agree that it closely resembles some forms of church music. More specifically, it contains some of the same trance-fostering elements that made the compositions of the sixteenth-century English musician Thomas Tallis so potent within religious settings. Rather than drums and an acoustic-driving effect, Górecki's music makes use of extremely long and repetitive musical cycles. A high degree of obsessive monotony is generated and listeners are eased out of their general reality orientation. It is interesting that the lyrics are the prayers of children written on the walls of concentration camps during World War II. In a recent radio program I heard devoted to Górecki's music, the general consensus was that its popularity was due to the disappearance of traditional religious modes of transcendence. In the wake of this secularization, people of all ages continue to respond to their religious leanings by using whatever tools are available to them. The program's commentators referred to the larger musical trend toward "New Age" music, which they felt could also be understood in relation to people's unsatisfied spiritual needs.

Music's shortcoming as a modern weapon against reality is that it is only worthwhile in terms of reality deconstruction. That is, it assists the listener merely with regard to dissociation, while leaving unsolved the matter of suggestions that are useful toward the goal of reconstructing an alternative to reality. Consequently, music as it is employed today has an addictive appearance since, like a drug, it is only beneficial while in immediate use. While music may bring some temporary relief because of its soothing and restful meditative effects, it does not provide an ongoing alternative construction of reality. For that to happen, the culture must become involved in the management of the dissociated state.

In a closely related way, one could point to television viewing that has reached pathological proportions for millions of people in Western society. Studies have shown that large numbers of the population feel they could not cope with life without their televisions. Surely it is not the high quality of programing that has so many people visually addicted to their screens. More likely it is the prospect that people can escape into a vacuous dissociative trance by using the lit screen as a point of absorption. This is confirmed by the fact that many people, when interrupted, do not actually know what it is they are watching. Instead, the act of television viewing has become a sort of contentless meditation that affords benefits similar to those of other types of dissociative meditation.

We take our discussion next into the area of clinical psychology and psychiatry. Some of the specific types of private psychopathology that we will discuss next are more complicated than drugs, dissociative music, and television as mechanisms by which to combat, and better cope with, reality. One reason for this is that, like religion and formal hypnosis, many of them are not merely dissociative but utilize suggestions in order to reconstruct an alternative reality to the dissociated one.

PSYCHOPATHOLOGICAL DISSOCIATIONS

It has been shown that culturally orchestrated religion is the most common, and probably the most efficient, method by which our dissociative capabilities are tapped for reasons of coping via the creative regulation of reality. Psychopathological symptoms are also coping devices, except that they involve private dissociations and personalized attempts to regulate reality toward the goal of psychological survival, or coping. As shown earlier, both religion and psychopathology are "symptoms" in the sense that they function to somehow alter the perception and experience of reality, thereby removing the subject from reality as it would be recognized without those symptoms. In this respect, we could go further and speak of *symptom choice* as a process that must be undertaken by human beings. We could also say that, under optimal cultural conditions, religion usually provides people with an adequate *first* choice from the standpoint of symptoms. If we accept the position that religion is a socially patterned form of psychopathology, we may even venture the proposition that religion is the historical first choice for psychopathology.

Psychopathological symptoms as we know them today appear only when cultural religions have deteriorated to the extent that private symptom choices become necessary. The first cases of modern anorexia nervosa, for example, appeared around the same time that traditional religion began its gradual dissolution. In the view of Ernest Becker, psychopathological symptoms stem from the failure of absolute transcendence and the resultant attempt by people to fabricate their own religion.[28] One cannot understand psychological disturbance, according to Becker, unless one keeps in mind the fundamentally religious nature of psychological symptoms. As we pursue this seemingly unlikely proposition, we see that Becker is completely correct. For Becker, religion confers upon people a *social license* to act out madness, part of which entails the repeated psychological "vaccinations" that come in the form of abnormal rituals that are not deemed to be abnormal as a result of one's license. Thus, with religion, we are free to "fetishize," or narrow, or expand the world according to our own particular needs. Becker even speaks of religion's myth-ritual complex as "a social form for the channeling of obsessions . . . that places creative obsession within the reach of everyone."[29]

There is a growing sentiment that most, if not all, types of clinical psychopathology involve some degree of dissociation and concomitant autosuggestion. This case is argued very well by Colin Ross, who is well known for his work in the areas of dissociation and multiple personality disorder.[30] Based on his research with this and other pathological syndromes, Ross proposes that dissociation should be understood as operating along a *continuum*, from normal everyday dissociations at one end to highly dissociative pathological disorders (e.g., multiple personality disorder) at the other. In fact, Eve Bernstein and Frank Putnam have taken the first step in constructing such a dissociation continuum.[31] While utilizing research data in constructing this dissociative continuum, Bernstein and Putnam found modest levels of dissociation in "normals," with increasing amounts employed by alcohol abusers, phobics, post-traumatic stress disorder victims, and sufferers of multiple personality disorder (in that order). As research continues to be done in relation to the role of dissociation in psychopathology, we should be able to fill in further such a dissociative continuum.

Arnold Ludwig writes that, in cases of extreme conflict, including irreconcilable conflict, dissociation makes it possible to relegate one set of information to one state of consciousness and a conflicting set of information to another.[32] This, Ludwig says, prevents the subject from being suspended in, and paralyzed by, a conflict situation for which the subject has no apparent avenue of escape. In a very real way, human beings can use dissociation in order to distort reality in any number of ways, while also not sacrificing reality to such an extent that they would be incapacitated.

It has long been known that, under great emotional distress, people tend to go into a state of "spontaneous trance," or what also used to be known as "spontaneous hypnosis." These observations date back to the pioneering work of Jean-Martin Charcot, Pierre Janet, Josef Breuer, and Sigmund Freud. More recently, Michael Haberman has introduced the more theoretically accurate term "spontaneous dissociation" as this adaptive mechanism initiates itself in order to prevent possible overarousal and eventual breakdown.[33] Haberman emphasizes the autonomous nature of this process, an observation that was also made by Charcot over a century ago. That is, defensive dissociations are not the consequence of a conscious choice, but rather the result of a "decision" taken at the level of preintellectual or unconscious awareness. Eugene Bliss compares and contrasts formal hypnosis and the type of "spontaneous self-hypnosis" characteristic of dissociative psychopathology. Like Ernest Hilgard, he depicts formal hypnosis as a type of autohypnosis that is assisted by an external agent. As part of this process, the subject makes some sort of conscious decision to participate in the trance induction procedure. However, Bliss emphasizes the nonvolitional and largely unconscious nature of psychopathological conditions that employ extensive amounts of dissociation:

> The spontaneous self-hypnosis which these patients demonstrate is quite different. It is a rapid, unpremeditated withdrawal into a trance, a dissociation, a primitive defensive reflex which they experience when anxious or fearful in response to some psychological or physical threat. . . . Emotions may be concealed or an amnesia may be created.[34]

As a mechanism for manufacturing defensive symptoms, auto-dissociation offers enormous versatility with the potential for symptoms of almost any appearance, design, and function. This point is made by Bliss, who compares the dissociative symptom formation process to formal hypnosis, arguing that any behavior that can be created during hypnosis should also be capable of appearing as a symptom. Since hypnosis can produce limitless behavioral variations, it follows that the range of psychological symptoms should also be limitless. Bliss was also aware of the fact that dissociative trance has played a key role in religion. He mentions the self-hypnotic, or autodissociative, capabilities of shamans and other spiritual healers, while also attributing religious visions, ecstasies, and frenzies to the dissociation process. Bliss adds that "early medical therapies—the Cult of Aesculapius and the 'Royal Touch,' the tactics of Agrippa, Cardan, Van Helmont, Kircher . . . and Greatraks (1666), and the cures at Lourdes, all probably reflected spontaneous self-hypnosis."[35]

RESEARCH ON DISSOCIATION AND PSYCHOPATHOLOGY

The only disorders currently categorized as dissociative disorders are multiple personality disorder (now called dissociative identity disorder in the *DSM-IV*), dissociative fugue, dissociative amnesia, and depersonalization disorder. Some types of psychopathology clearly involve extensive use of dissociation in order to achieve *indiscriminate* erasures of memory. Hilgard offers *psychogenic fugue* as an example. Here people dissociate from previous memories to such an extent that they lose much or all of the former sense of identity. This state coincides with autosuggestion, enabling the person to assume a new identity, whether that be partial or complete. Wilfred Abse adds to our understanding of fugue as a dissociative process in stating that "fugues are one of many kinds of *hypnoid states* and are characterized by distinctive alterations of consciousness . . . precipitated by a need to escape from intolerable pressure."[36] As one reads about the preconditions in fugue, one is reminded of the personal and situational conditions that often precede religious conversion. In both cases, defensive dissociation and suggestion are able to achieve radical alterations in identity.

Dissociative amnesia also takes advantage of dissociation in order to cordon off large blocks of memory. Usually these targeted memories are "toxic" ones whose availability to conscious awareness could prove to be the source of severe emotional distress. Dissociative amnesia is usually precipitated by traumatic events and, according to Colin Ross, consists of "the dissociation of a limited aspect of a single cortical function: one forgets only a limited amount of psychic material."[37]

Depersonalization is unquestionably another disorder whose symptoms must be understood as dissociative in nature. People with depersonalization disorder experience the feeling that they are somehow detached from either their body or their own mental processes. Their descriptions of their condition often bear an uncanny resemblance to those of people who report out-of-body experiences, such as astral projection, or even near-death experience when the subject has the sense of being physically removed from the body. Another depersonalization symptom is the experience of being an *automaton*, or of being in a dream. Again, we are tempted to draw comparisons between this dissociative disorder and the "symptoms" of various types of paranormal experiences and encounters.

As with the above dissociative syndromes, very few people would argue that multiple personality disorder is the result of dissociation that is used defensively in order to escape certain harsh realities in the person's life. Of concern, however, is the very small number of mental disorders presently recognized and classified as dissociative in nature. Colin Ross argues the case that *most*, if not all, forms of mental disturbance have a significant dissociative component.[38] The growing body of research in this area demonstrates quite clearly that Ross is justified in his claim that dissociation is a *common* factor in psychopathology of virtually all types.

The four dissociative disorders officially acknowledged in the *DSM-IV* are remarkable for their use of dissociation in order to alter a person's reality via manipulations of memory and/or identity. Yet

Ross deduces that dissociation should be capable of altering a person's reality in any number of ways in addition to making alterations to memory. He states:

> There is no particular reason why dissociation should be limited to the areas of the cortex responsible for memory and identity. It is more likely that dissociation can occur in any area of the brain. If this is the case, then dissociation of any given psychic function will result in a monosymptomatic dissociative disorder, or occur as a component of a complex, chronic dissociative disorder.[39]

Ross's thinking is a logical extension of Braun's "BASK" model of dissociation wherein Braun maintains that the process of dissociation can function to alter behavior, affect (i.e., emotion), sensation, and knowledge.[40] In fact, Ross uses the BASK model in outlining the multiple effects of dissociation in a case of *conversion paralysis.* He begins by pointing to the characteristic calm indifference that seems to contradict the fact that the person has lost the use of a major limb. This tells us that, like the religious individual who is able simultaneously to believe and not believe, the conversion paralysis victim knows that he or she is not *actually* (in the physical sense) paralyzed. Beyond that, dissociation has influenced: (a) *behavior,* since the person's actions become restricted; (b) *affect,* as revealed in a flattening of emotions, including the *belle indifférence* phenomenon; (c) *sensation,* since *anesthesia* is produced in the paralyzed limb; and (d) *knowledge,* since the person comes consciously to "know" that the limb is paralyzed, even though the truth remains intact in the dissociated material existing at the level of unconscious awareness.

In light of the multifaceted dissociations that take place in conversion disorders of this sort, it is difficult to understand why conversion disorder is not classified formally as a dissociative disorder. As Ross would agree, there needs to be a complete overhaul of our present diagnostic system based on our improved understanding of dissociation, as well as the part played by autosuggestion in reconstructing the dissociated state. Support for a much broader role of dissociation comes when one considers the wide range of mental disorders that have been shown to be associated with cognitive dissociation. As with research in the area of religion, some of these studies have employed measures of hypnotic susceptibility, while others have used the more recently developed specific measures of dissociation. Since hypnotic responsivity is essentially dissociative responsivity, we should again assume that tests measuring hypnotic ability are also measuring dissociative ability.

We might follow through on our discussion of conversion disorder by pointing out research that implicates dissociation in its symptom formation. Fernando Bendefeldt and his colleagues administered three tests of hypnotic suggestibility to seventeen individuals who had been hospitalized for various types of conversion disorder. In addition, the researchers gave a battery of memory tests as well as tests of attentional ability, since they hypothesized that these dissociative symptoms would involve a certain cost to these areas of cognition. Bendefeldt et al. found that the conversion disorder subjects, when compared to a control group, were considerably more hypnotically responsive. Bendefeldt's team also found that deficits of memory and attention were associated with the conversion symptoms. This latter finding is consistent with etiological theories that regard the goal of conversion symptoms to be a diversion of attention (as well as memories) away from perceived sources of conflict and threat. The same goal is apparent in many dissociation-based psychopathologies. We must also remember that the ultimate goal of religious symptomatology, as it similarly relies on a combination of dissociation and suggestion, is to divert attention in such a manner that followers are rendered consciously ignorant (i.e., no longer attentive) of large chunks of reality.

Richard Bryant and Kevin McConkey studied processes of attention by using hypnosis in order to produce artificial cases of conversion disorder. Specifically, they were able to produce in their hypnotic subjects the same form of "hysterical blindness" seen in conversion disorder. A series of subsequent tests of attention led the researchers to conclude that "attention may have been allocated by subjects to maintain blindness to information."[41]

This particular finding becomes exceedingly important when we consider the relationship between attention and all expressions of psychopathological symptomatology. This is because the actual symptoms produced by the dissociation-suggestion mechanism serve the function of deflecting attention away from other sources and refocusing them on a safer source. For instance, the person who develops a genuine case of conversion blindness usually does so as a reaction to life events or experiences that generate emotional distress *when attended to*. Once "blind," however, dissociation (and autosuggestion) enables the individual to create an overriding focus of attention in the form of the blindness, yet one that does not generate distress since the person is unconsciously aware that the blindness is not real. Even so, an adaptive *reallocation of attention* produces a psychological diversion for the individual, and attention is diverted from the true source of distress.

Eugene Bliss likewise cites research showing that conversion disorders involve greater than usual utilizations of dissociation. He summarizes studies showing that many diverse patterns of psychological and social disturbance are autohypnotic, or autodissociative, in nature. Research is presented in which significantly higher levels of cognitive dissociation are found in people with multiple personality disorder, Briquet's syndrome (multiple physical complaints without an organic basis), phobias, anorexia nervosa, sociopathy, criminality, and even some cases of extreme obesity caused by compulsive eating.[42]

Bulimia Nervosa

A number of studies conducted by Helen Pettinati and her associates have demonstrated that higher levels of hypnotizability can be seen in individuals displaying bulimia nervosa.[43] Using the more recent specialized tests of dissociation, a group of Dutch researchers also found bulimia nervosa to be associated with high levels of dissociation.[44] Binge eaters were studied by Shirley Sanders, who measured dissociation using the *Perceptual Alteration Scale*.[45] Significantly higher dissociation scores were found among the binge eaters when compared to a control group. Sanders found moderate levels of dissociation in her "normal" subjects and explained this in terms of the workings of dissociation in the everyday lives of people. However, in many forms of psychopathology, the person relies more heavily on this cognitive capacity, thus explaining the consistent finding of elevated dissociation in "abnormal" behavior. In essence, one is dealing with *abnormally* extensive usages of dissociation.

The above findings strongly suggest that bulimia nervosa, like conversion disorder, should be classified formally as a dissociative disorder. Further evidence for this comes from research showing that 75 percent of bulimics experience dissociative symptoms of depersonalization or derealization.[46] Additionally, bulimic individuals frequently claim that their episodes of bingeing and purging take place *automatically*, as if they were operating beyond conscious control. It is not even uncommon for a bulimic to describe the onset of these episodes exactly as one would describe the onset of trance. They even sometimes use the actual word "trance" as they attempt to convey the uncontrolled nature of their inexplicable actions.

Anorexia Nervosa

Anorexia nervosa is also a dissociative disorder, and some research shows that the use of dissociation is higher in anorexic individuals than control groups. This seems to follow logically from the bulimia nervosa research, especially since approximately 50 percent of anorexics likewise suffer symptoms of bulimia nervosa. However, the actual research relating dissociation to anorexia nervosa is somewhat confusing. Some colleagues and I recently conducted research on anorexic and bulimic inpatients at an eating disorders unit of a large public hospital in Australia.[47] Using the *Questionnaire of Experiences of Dissociation Scale*, we found that both anorexics and bulimics engaged in significantly greater dissociation than control subjects. Additionally, the anorexics scored slightly higher than bulimics. Yet this contrasts with other research showing that bulimics have higher dissociation levels than anorexics. Different clinical populations, with varying severity and duration of symptoms, were used in the research in this area. Therefore, until additional studies are conducted, the exact similarities and differences in these two partially related dissociative disorders will remain a mystery. Even so, the dissociative features of anorexia nervosa have been mentioned frequently in the clinical literature. For instance, Lydia Temoshok and C. Clifford Attkisson theorized that anorexia nervosa exists along the same "hysterical" continuum as the other disorders whose symptoms appear to be constructed on the basis of the dissociative process.[48]

Multiple Personality Disorder

Numerous studies have demonstrated conclusively that dissociation is at the heart of multiple personality disorder. This has been confirmed using specialized tests of dissociation as well as numerous measures of hypnotic susceptibility. People with multiple personality disorder have been labeled *hypnotic virtuosos*. We might follow our present line of theory by stating more precisely that they are *dissociative virtuosos*. For a convincing overview of research linking dissociation with multiple personality disorder, the reader may be referred to Colin Ross's book *Multiple Personality Disorder*.

Theoretical and experimental work also provides compelling evidence that several other types of psychopathological symptoms are the results of dissociation. These include paranoia,[49] hypochondriasis,[50] phobias,[51] and post-traumatic stress disorder.[52] The post-traumatic symptoms of sexual abuse survivors have also been shown to be the result of dissociations taking place in response to that particular type of trauma.[53]

There is little doubt that future investigations will confirm Ross's visionary conclusion that most manifestations of clinical psychopathology have in common the human capacity to dissociate "toxic" information onto information pathways that bypass conscious awareness. We will then be left to answer other questions dealing with the specific workings of dissociation as it functions to provide adaptive escapes from problematic realities. Another question concerns the events and/or emotional experiences that precipitate pathological dissociations. Still another has to do with the manner in which dissociation is accomplished without the assistance of culturally managed dissociation techniques, such as those found in religion. There is also the matter of suggestion and how it is self-delivered in order to construct highly specific symptoms once dissociation has been achieved.

FACTORS TRIGGERING DISSOCIATIVE REACTIONS

More than a century ago, Pierre Janet recognized that dissociation was a cerebral function that was continuously available in order to regulate the amount of stress placed on the nervous system. I described earlier how dissociation is an essential aspect of culturally constituted reality distortions that involve large enough segments of the population to be seen as normal. But Janet was especially interested in the extreme types of dissociation that are sometimes necessary when these "normal" symptoms cannot provide the degree of reality departure required for coping purposes. In this regard, Janet theorized that pathological magnitudes of dissociation were adopted by people who were facing a *breakdown of adaptation*.[54] Intense emotionality was seen by Janet as the potential cause of a collapse of adaptation, or a failure of coping. He emphasized psychological trauma as one obvious source of excessive emotionality, and spoke of instances wherein dissociation was resorted to in order to eliminate memory of the trauma. A brilliant researcher and theoretician, Janet even used the term "a phobia of memory" to describe how dissociation can split off traumatic memories and prevent them from being integrated into consciousness.[55] He also realized that this could be accomplished outside of conscious awareness, thereby postulating the existence of innate monitors that can make decisions about material that needs elimination or distortion.

Modifying and elaborating on Janet's theory, Ernest Hilgard

speculated that the "hidden observer" orchestrates our adaptive dissociations (including psychopathological ones) in making possible "deflection in advance of awareness."[56] That is, there exists within the human brain a censoring function by which the person makes decisions prior to conscious awareness. This is very similar to the previously mentioned concept of "reification" presented by sociobiologist E. O. Wilson. It is postulated, therefore, that we have the ability to deflect preconscious information in such a way that it is already distorted by the time it reaches consciousness.

Hilgard's neodissociation theory even allows for the possibility that memory can operate outside of consciousness: "it is possible to have an experience registered, processed, and stored in memory in a recoverable form, *even though it has never been consciously felt or reported.*"[57] Likewise, dissociation allows for conscious memories to be extracted from consciousness while still remaining in recoverable form. Such dissociated memories frequently emerge over the course of psychotherapy as the subject resolves the conflicts that made the defensive dissociations necessary in the first place.

Research confirms that trauma is one way that dissociative symptoms are triggered. Yvonne Dolan offers numerous examples of dissociations that stem directly from traumatic sexual abuse.[58] These memories are so painful and repugnant that one can safely say that the subject develops the phobia of memory to which Pierre Janet referred. In some cases, this dissociation is a reflexive response on the part of the internal monitor, thus preventing the memory from ever reaching consciousness. Quite a bit of variation can be seen in the use of dissociation as a coping device following sexual trauma. Dolan states:

> The adult survivor of sexual abuse is likely to be highly skilled at dissociation. . . . In the attempt to survive an overwhelming and potentially psychologically destructive event such as sexual or physical abuse, the victim is likely spontaneously to resort to a variety of unconscious dissociative devices. . . . Memory disturbances among sexual abuse victims have been well documented . . . particularly in reference to partial or even complete amnesia. In more extreme cases, the result of the client's attempt to defend herself from devastating memories of abuse memories is a complete lack of memories for extended periods of childhood. Given the pain and trauma inherent in memories of sexual abuse, this amnesia can be understood as an unconscious attempt to defend against reexperiencing the victimization through memories. In some cases, it seems apparent that amnesia was the victim's only alternative for psychological survival.[59]

Similarly, Anne Marie Paley describes the *frozen watchfulness* of traumatized people who respond to the previously mentioned "phobia of memory" with dissociative strategies to erase the reality of the trauma. She writes:

> It seems that the traumatized child constricts his or her own emotionality . . . these children have dissociated their feelings of terror and helplessness because it is only by dissociating these feelings that they can focus their attention on avoiding repeated trauma. . . . Dissociation is adaptive: it allows relatively normal functioning for the duration of the traumatic event and leaves a large part of the personality unaffected by the emotional effects of the trauma.[60]

While it is true that dissociation operates to cordon off from consciousness the information that would prove toxic to the individual, it must be added that there are emotional and cognitive costs to be paid for such psychological dissociative strategies. Depression is a residual factor in many such defensive maneuvers, even when the dissociative reaction is working in order to falsify reality, and to give it positive bias. As Pierre Janet was able to observe, even though unwanted material is dissociated, it continues to exert an influence on emotion, perception, and behavior. The actual content of the material remains outside of conscious awareness, but partial side effects of the dissociation are still experienced at the level of consciousness. Yet we must assume that these would be far less severe compared to the emotional consequences of a full exposure to the toxic information (i.e., if dissociation were not employed at all).

When, for some reason, dissociated memories become dislodged and invade consciousness, we see the symptoms of what has been labeled post-traumatic stress disorder. This tells us that post-traumatic stress disorder is another example of a dissociative disorder that is wrongly classified by our current system of diagnosis. Its symptoms vary somewhat depending on the nature and severity of the traumatic memories that have been dissociated. The periodic lifting of the dissociative barrier causes the traumatic event to be reexperienced in a number of possible ways. Frequently there is a breakthrough of actual recollections into consciousness. In children, this is sometimes expressed in highly repetitive play involving themes related to the original traumatic event. At other times, the traumatic event is reexperienced in distressing dreams. Certain individuals are overcome with a sudden sensation that the traumatic event is actually occurring in real life. They also can have illusions, hallucinations, dissociative flashback episodes, and the experience of reliving the event.

Factors Triggering Multiple Personality Disorder and Its Relation to Religious Dissociation

A large body of literature exists implicating early childhood trauma in the dissociative reaction underlying multiple personality disorder (MPD). A history of severe physical, sexual, or emotional abuse is seen in over 95 percent of cases of multiple personality disorder.[61] This is combined with a literal helplessness and absence of control over their environment. As David Spiegel states:

> MPD is the victim's use of dissociation as a defense mechanism to control emotions in a dangerous situation and manage the subsequent pain and fear. . . . Thus dissociation buys a certain temporary peace and perhaps survival . . . at the price of an internal sense that the real self is a hidden one.[62]

Our traditional models of consciousness do not allow us to explain MPD with any degree of satisfaction. For the most part, they assume a single integrated "self" that has internal consistency and a unified "mind." Such models fall apart, however, when we notice the dissociation-based splitting that occurs in MPD, leaving one to the task of explaining a multiple self with considerable independence associated with each "self." And this becomes even more problematic when we understand that dissociation is an ongoing aspect of normal, as well as abnormal, behavior.

A knowledge of MPD can even help us to better comprehend the dynamics of religion. When I previously described the workings of religion in relation to dissociation and suggestion, I explained why we must assume that distortive religious beliefs are held and also not held by the so-called believer. The reason for this is again that distortions of reality such as those seen in religion are the direct consequence of "data" (including memories) that are partitioned off and dissociated onto an information processing channel that does not have access to consciousness. Yet we also know that dissociation does not preclude awareness, even though the information is not located on pathways that have entry to consciousness. Thus religious belief is the result of cognitive processing wherein certain segments of data have been subtracted from the person's total pool of reality-based information. If this type of dissociation were not possible, it would also be impossible to believe the otherwise unbelievable.

We might now consider the dissociative model of religion in relation to a dissociative disorder such as MPD. Then we may ask about the religious beliefs of the different personalities that exist within any one person with this disorder. As we do this, we should recognize that MPD is only a large-scale exaggeration of the normal nonpathological dissociation process employed by all human beings. The main difference is that, in MPD, the deployment of dissociation in response to trauma is so extensive that actual "identities" crystallize along the parallel information-processing channels. This is different from normal dissociations, in which a central organizing function remains intact and capable of retaining the impression of a unified self despite the dissociations that exist for the usual purposes of coping and adaptation.

Continuing this logic, we would predict that many cases of MPD involve religious belief by one or more of the secondary or alter identities, and unbelief by other identities. In other words, in the single individual afflicted with MPD, there should exist the possibility that one identity has relatively more contact with reality-based data than another channel, or identity. Therefore, the same physical person, depending on the alter personality that is at the fore, would be seen to manifest both religious belief and unbelief. And, in fact, this is exactly what one finds. Different alter personalities frequently hold widely differing God images, and it is not uncommon for some personalities to be strongly religious while others are completely irreligious.

Elizabeth Bowman presents some fascinating case material on this subject, while distinguishing between the primary (i.e., core) personality and secondary personalities.[63] She reports the consistent finding that the primary personality of someone with MPD is more religious than the dissociated secondary or alter personalities. Bowman even presents case descriptions in which the primary personality was religious, but the secondary personalities were openly antagonistic toward the notion of God. Of the secondary personalities that believed in God, some regarded that being as malevolent or sadistic. This difference between primary and secondary personalities is reflected in actual religious practices. Bowman discusses a study of seven cases of MPD. Six of the seven primary personalities prayed and claimed that prayer was a meaningful exercise. By contrast, only one of the many secondary personalities prayed, and "most scoffed at the idea that God would respond."[64] Similarly, six of the seven primary personalities attended church and three of those had close and highly supportive relationships with their church pastors. But only one secondary personality had ever attended church, and even this lone attendee had done so only on a sporadic basis. None of the secondary personalities had any sort of relationship with their pastors.

Bowman attempts to explain these remarkable findings on the basis of the primary personality probably having had more exposure to religious training and formal worship practices than the secondary personalities. Yet I feel that a more satisfying explanation can be arrived at if we think about religiosity as it is dependent upon the dissociation of reality-based information. From this perspective, our reasoning tells us that secondary personalities probably consist of dissociated chunks of data that were dissociated in order to enhance the coping prospects of the primary personality. If religious beliefs are, in fact, made possible by using dissociation in order to place this reality data (and memories) onto another information-processing channel, and if MPD represents the "coming alive" as separate identities of these independent channels—then we are forced to assume that at least some of the dissociated channels or identities know something about reality that is no longer known by the primary personality. It follows directly that, since the secondary personalities have more reality contact than the primary personality, the secondary personalities would be considerably less religious. This is precisely what we see when comparing the religiosity of primary and secondary personalities in cases of MPD.

The above line of evidence corroborates once again the theoretical formulations viewing both religion and psychopathology as expressions of dissociation. Furthermore, in both instances, we must conclude that, regardless of the self-deception involved, people displaying both types of behavior simultaneously know and do not know the actual nature of the reality from which they are fleeing. With MPD, I have been showing the obvious role of early life traumas as the triggering factors in the formation of the disorder.

As research shows, not all dissociative reactions, whether "normal" or "abnormal," entail the degree of dissociation seen in MPD. This is true even of people who are intensely religious. Comparisons of their scores on measures of dissociation and hypnotizability show that they score in the same range as those with mental disorders of moderate severity. With clinical disorders in this middle range, one sees various personal and/or situational conflicts that trigger the unconscious decision to utilize defensive dissociation for purposes of additional coping. I am familiar with some of these as they relate to eating disorders, which happen to be a special research interest of mine.

Possible Causative Factors behind Eating Disorders

In bulimia nervosa, some research has found a history of abuse, but not to the extent usually seen in an extreme clinical syndrome such as multiple personality disorder. Additionally, a history of trauma is not seen in a high proportion of people with anorexia nervosa. Research shows that trauma is as frequent in bulimia nervosa as it is in the general psychiatric population.[65] Many people point to the overlapping causative factors in bulimia nervosa and anorexia nervosa while trying to explain the two disorders in somewhat similar ways.

Eating disorders are frequently conceptualized in terms of the issue of personal control. It is thought that those who are predisposed to dissociative disorders like anorexia nervosa and bulimia nervosa have been deprived of developmental experiences that lead to a clear-cut sense of self, or autonomy. Consequently, in terms of coping ability and availability of personal resources, they are disadvantaged and find themselves overly reliant for direction on external sources of control. As this theoretical logic would dictate, such individuals encounter serious problems as they attempt to make the transition from childhood to adulthood since they lack the coping capabilities to meet the new demands and responsibilities of adulthood. They become overwhelmed and resort to dissociative strategies that make possible distortions of reality aimed at *reducing* their world to a size that is perceived as manageable and within their control. The actual *content* of their reality distortions will also make sense as we take our discussion of dissociative symptom formation into the domain of suggestion and, in particular, cultural suggestion.

It is impossible to specify the exact situation triggering dissociative reactions in the different types of psychopathology. Even in the same disorder, there will be considerable variation with regard to the *breakdown of adaptation* that led the subject to that particular set of reality-transforming symptoms. We could draw the same general conclusion with regard to religion and say that an almost infinite number of factors could explain why one person would partake of dissociation more than another for the purpose of developing religious "symptoms" for reasons of coping. However, despite different triggering factors across the range of psychopathological disorders, there are some factors that these sets of symptoms have in common with regard to the cognitive mechanics involved in creating and maintaining the symptoms.

THE COGNITIVE WORKINGS OF PSYCHOPATHOLOGY

Of crucial importance is the observation by Eugene Bliss that "hypnotic" (i.e., dissociative) defensive reactions usually have one of two effects on the cognitive world of the person employing these strategies.[66] One is the ability to *fixate intensely upon something, thus magnifying the experience.* Or, in a somewhat reversed way, it enables the person to *focus away from an object or event, thus diminishing it or eliminating it altogether.* A further exploration of the dissociation/suggestion process as the common denominator of symptom formation will show that one of these two goals is usually achieved for defensive reasons. In each case, the individual is able to distort internal and/or external reality and thereby escape from sources of conflict or perceived threat. As in religion, private dissociations and autosuggestions make possible myths (i.e., delusions) that are supported by the enactment of certain rituals in connection with those myths. Whether the pathological symptoms are aimed at expansion or constriction of reality, subjects are able to diminish their conscious exposure to the source of the conflict. Sometimes this is selective, in which case one can speak of "targets of amnesia" (Ernest Hilgard's term), whereas in other cases there is a diminishing of general reality orientation or even a total loss of identity under exceptional circumstances.

Although I have been describing dissociative psychopathology as private reality regulation by contrast to collective reality regulation (e.g., religion), it should be said that the symptoms of individual mental disorders do bear some relationship to the culture of the afflicted. They are constructed in relation to cultural conditioning, or the cultural suggestion process. Cultural suggestion is typically involved in a person's symptom choice, even if that choice is made completely outside of conscious awareness.

David Phillips gives us a feel for this process with his theory of suggestion that sees psychological symptoms as the mimicking of social suggestions.[67] For example, Phillips reports that the national suicide level jumped 12 percent following newspaper and television reports of Marilyn Monroe's supposed suicide. Apparently this is a very common occurrence and has been labeled the "Werther effect," after Goethe's literary character whose suicide was imitated by others. Those who kill themselves after receiving a media suggestion may be assumed to have serious psychological problems from which they want desperately to escape. There are many possible ways to seek such escape. All one can surmise is that the media suggestion gave *direction* to their escape. Phillips offers other examples of cultural suggestions that can serve as mediators in symptom formation:

. . . [A]fter Mrs. Nelson Rockefeller and Mrs. Gerald Ford discovered that they had breast cancer, breast cancer became a more
salient problem for women across the United States. Similarly, after
a fictional individual in a television commercial becomes aware of
"bad breath," this problem may become salient for many viewers.
Thus suggestion and modeling may function as a kind of mediating
mechanism, a kind of "mental switch" which leads an individual
to become preoccupied with one problem rather than another.[68]

When religion was the overriding and dominant cultural suggestion, people's symptoms were almost always of a religious flavor.
The situation is much different today, with a broad diversity of
cultural suggestions influencing our choice of symptoms. The subtle-
ties of this process become clear when one considers some of the
different ways in which psychopathology presents itself within our
current cultural climate.

Psychopathology and Reality Transformation

A large percentage of psychopathological symptoms *work* because
they are able to *reduce the size* of the subject's world. In the process,
the actual source of the conflict or threat is thereby diverted away
from the main field of conscious awareness. In a real sense, the
value of the symptoms lie in their ability to *monopolize* our understandings of the world and ourselves. As cognitive techniques by
which to avoid emotional and psychological incapacitation, they
provide a focused preoccupation that enables a fading of the general
reality orientation. They deploy cognitive dissociation in the course
of yielding a smaller, and therefore less threatening, perceptual set.

The idea that reduced cognitive scope serves prophylactic
purposes has a considerable history. It dates back at least as far
as Kierkegaard who, in *The Sickness unto Death*, wrote about people's
ability to "tranquilize themselves with the trivial."[69] The symptoms
of autodissociative disorders are "trivial" in the sense that their main
purpose is to be the focus for a dissociated state. Of much greater
importance is the final achievement which comes in the form of
self-forgetting and a detachment from potentially devastating aspects of perceived reality. This is true even in disorders where, on
one level, the symptoms appear to be of utmost concern to the
victim.

Paradoxically, the reality-constriction procedure typically involves the highly unrealistic *expansion* of a small segment of the
person's world. Dissociation and suggestion are required in order

to accomplish both reality constriction and expansion. We might start with a case illustrative of these psychopathological techniques.

Allow me to mention briefly an actual case that I had several years ago. For our purposes, let us call him Mike. He is noteworthy since his behavior reflects a very simple use of reality constriction and expansion, without the culture-specific features that complicate slightly our understanding of mental disorders. Mike was a 24-year-old man who had been under stress from several fronts. His turbulent marriage of two years was on the verge of collapse, and a six-month-old baby was fueling the emotional impact of the breakup. Mike's patchy work history aroused the wrath of his in-laws who lived nearby and made no secret of their dislike of him. Prior to Mike's arrival at our mental health center, he was holding down an unsatisfying job as a men's clothing salesman in a department store. Business was poor and Mike was apparently singled out by the manager as a likely candidate for dismissal.

The cumulative psychological effect of these and other problems were weighing heavily on Mike until something "very weird," as he described it, happened to him. For several days, he had been taking inventory at the store, spending hours at a stretch counting ties, socks, shoes, shirts, and so forth. As he recalled the incident to me, Mike felt a gradual breakthrough of extremely intense anxiety as he worked that day. It was of a quality and magnitude that he had never experienced before. Mike told me that he had the distinct sense that he was "going crazy." This persisted and his unexplained anxiety was made worse by his fear and anxiety about going completely insane.

Finally, Mike could stand it no longer. He rushed out of the store and began to walk quickly down the streets lined with shops. As he passed each shop, however, he felt an irresistible urge to count whatever was in the store windows. Since he was walking at a fast pace, he did not get beyond the number four or five for any one store window, but then began counting all over again when he reached the next window. When he had exhausted himself from walking, Mike stopped at a single store window and found that he could satisfy his new drive by counting the same objects over and over. In that particular instance, he was looking at a display of nine appliances. Mike counted from one to nine, moving his eyes from one object to the other as he did so. This he did over and over again as quickly as possible. When he stopped or even slowed down, he felt an upsurge of anxiety that propelled him back to his counting. Mike was only able to leave the shop window by counting whatever he saw as he made his way home. Once home, he continued in this manner, counting continuously in the firm belief that terrible consequences would befall him if he stopped.

By the time Mike sought psychotherapy, his entire reality seemed to revolve around his compulsion to count things. While he sat in my office at our first meeting, I noticed that his attention and concentration seemed to be affected. I asked him if he was counting as we talked and he replied that he had targeted three flower pictures that hung from the wall immediately behind my head. Interspersed among any comments he made to me was a continuous succession of "one-two-three" self-statements. Mike said that he could never muster the courage to stop counting and considered seriously the daunting prospect that he would have to count for the rest of his life. In his mind, not to do so would be to invite hellish repercussions.

There was a time in my life when I spent hours at a time repeating the names "Jesus, Mary, Joseph" in an attempt to reduce my Purgatory sentence. Obvious similarities exist between Mike's "one-two-three" symptoms and my "Jesus, Mary, Joseph" symptoms. Both were myth-ritual complexes that redefined reality through the employment of self-generated dissociative trance procedures. There were also some significant differences, however, one being that I was more able than Mike to initiate and terminate my mental actions. That is, the lesser severity of my symptoms still enabled me to employ *selectively* my religious symptoms. Mike's circumstances were more acute, requiring him to make continual use of these symptoms in preventing a breakdown of adaptation. In this regard, there was a *preventive* element to my use of the symptoms that came with my religion. Mike's symptoms were attempting to deal with emotional distress that had already taken Mike close to his absolute limits of adaptive capability. As it happened, Mike was not at all religious at the point of onset of his symptoms. In fact, he had been raised in a family with no formal connections with organized religion. Even if Mike had had religion at his disposal, it is likely that he would have needed "clinical" symptoms in addition to those he could have adopted that were "normal" within the religious myth-ritual complex.

We will recall the three essential ingredients for hypnosis as described by Etzel Cardeña: absorption, dissociation, and suggestibility. Not only are they requisite aspects of hypnotic induction and suggestive responding under hypnosis, but these same three processes have been seen to be responsible for religious belief and behavior as well. Now to that we can add that Mike's symptoms, and a great many psychopathological symptoms, are also the result of these three ingredients listed by Cardeña. In Mike's case, the final product looks a bit different from religion and/or the behaviors typically enacted under formal hypnosis. But in our quest for an integrated theory, we find that there are more similarities than differences.

The workings of absorption, dissociation, and suggestion must be understood in relation to delusional myths and supportive rituals. We saw that these were the cornerstones of all religious symptoms and the same can be said of our so-called psychopathological symptoms. Even given Mike's sketchy background information, it should be apparent that he was experiencing nervous system overload requiring him to engage in protective measures. He needed to create distance between himself and the source of his hyperarousal. This could be phrased according to Thomas Scheff's previously mentioned theory about the value of ritual. Thus it could be said that Mike was in a precarious psychological situation compelling him to distance himself from his emotions.

After making an unconscious decision to this effect, Mike sought an *absorption point*, functionally not unlike a church candle or a tack on the hypnotist's ceiling. What he did was to target articles of clothing and eventually other objects and to allow those to be the focus for *obsessive monotony* that came via his repetitive counting of those objects. At that early stage, Mike had the equivalent of a drum beat or a relentless chant or the repetitive and monotonous words of the "hypnotist." In a makeshift fashion, Mike would use self-talk in the form of numbers to drum himself into a modest dissociative trance. As he became more and more absorbed by this obsessive counting, his critical and analytical thinking faculties would diminish. Then Mike would have taken the first step in reducing the size of his world and therefore distancing himself from his sources of conflict and overarousal.

Konrad Lorenz defines neurosis as "a process allowing particular ideas to become overvalued until they finally assume control of the entire personality of the person and force silence upon all other motivations . . . the personality is gradually consumed to the extent that he is no longer interested in anything else. . . ."[70] Lorenz correctly refers to this process as an extension of the human instinct to impose order upon chaos and confusion, and to convert dissonance into harmony, even if this means actively restructuring reality by substituting automatism for open awareness. And this is exactly what Mike was doing as he pursued his symptoms in the unknowing wish to restore a sense of order to his world, however illusory that order might be.

Almost every psychopathological syndrome has a different *over-*

valued (i.e., delusional) idea that, once magnified out of all reality, reduces the scope of the person's cognitive and perceptual world. Throughout the history of clinical psychology and psychiatry, theorists have been tempted to exaggerate the actual meaning of the overvalued idea. If a person became phobic of dirt or germs, for example, it was often thought that the dirt or germs made a great deal of sense in terms of the subject's unique history or his/ her personality dynamics. More often than not, however, this is not the case.

We see in Mike an illustration of symptom choice that is largely random and meaningful only because he had been counting for several days while taking stock inventory. One could even say that Mike's choice of symptom, or absorption point, was no more or less meaningful than the "choice" between a drum or choral chant for purposes of obsessive monotony and subsequent dissociation. The main goal, regardless of the targeted absorption point, is for the person to somehow monopolize his/her resources for attention until a dissociative trance is established. David Spiegel and his colleagues discuss "hypnotic focal experience" and compare hypnotic focal points to those used in dissociative pathological disorders. Accordingly, these serve as the basis for a *polarization* of consciousness that, through intense hypnotic absorption, permits the subject to escape sources of emotional overarousal.[71]

Rather than attach unwarranted significance to Mike's counting, we must regard it only as a convenient and available form of *admission* into a dissociative state that might meet his need for increased adaptation through symptom formation. Once Mike managed that initial phase of the operation, he was then in a position to construct something out of the dissociated state that he had generated by repetitive self-directed counting. This does not differ from a religious situation in which the priest or minister fills people's dissociative voids once he has produced a dissociative state with the usual religious induction techniques. This is what we have been describing as the process of suggestion. We saw how it worked in formal hypnosis and religion, but now we need to examine suggestion in the context of psychopathology. It works somewhat differently since the "patient" must be his or her own hypnotist or priest, so to speak. This was also true in terms of Mike's *self-induction* of dissociative trance. He was reliant upon a variation of self-hypnosis, or even a variation on the induction procedure that prepares people for religious conversion.

In numerous mental disorders, including Mike's compulsion to count, the suggestion process is a mere continuation of the behaviors that give rise to the desired state of dissociation. With Mike, his arbitrarily selected counting symptom translated into self-suggestions to the effect that he had to continue counting if he wanted to avoid catastrophe. His myth, or delusion, was that the counting was of great and vital importance, and even a dire necessity. Of course, he was in error in relation to counting, per se. Counting was only of value as a method of "drum beating," and fostering a needed state of dissociation. The ritual component of this peculiar myth-ritual complex was the actual repetitive act of counting, thus making the myth and the ritual almost one and the same.

Obsessive-compulsive disorder is one that usually wraps itself in fear or some other unpleasant emotion in order to ensure the undivided attention of the person selecting these symptoms. It takes advantage of a psychological "devil," except that it is invented at the private level. Fear has the desired effect of sustaining the dissociated state of consciousness. Guilt also works quite well and is common in Western obsessive-compulsive disorders. Obsessions are usually the mythic portion of the myth-ritual complex, whereas the associated compulsions are the sustaining rituals. In a high proportion of cases, the subject concocts a specific myth making the subject himself or herself the devil, or more precisely the potential devil. In this sort of myth, people become convinced that they will be the cause of injury and pain to others if the rituals are not carried out according to plan.

Mike's dissociative reaction began as a vague sense that he would lose his mind unless he counted, but then this eventually became a better defined pattern of autosuggestion with more clearly specified consequences. Within a few days of the onset of the dissociative strategy, Mike had come to believe the myth that his six-month-old child would die if the counting stopped for any length of time. We are reminded here of the Aztecs who held the religious myth that the sun would not rise without the ritualistic removal of human hearts. One of the main differences between Mike and the Aztecs is that between collective and private myth-ritual complexes. Another difference is that, no matter how morbid the feared consequences, people with private obsessive-compulsive symptoms almost never act those out against other people. The same is not historically true regarding religion as it carries these out as a group, since personal responsibility tends to diminish when one's delusions are endorsed by the masses.

I also once worked in therapy with a woman who devoted most of her waking hours to boiling her husband's food in pressure cookers. Let us call her Denise. Her delusional myth was that her husband would become contaminated and die if she did not purify the food in this never-ending manner. The ritual component was the highly repetitive act of boiling and reboiling the food. But the food was never pure enough to Denise's satisfaction. It was as if it needed to be *infinitely* pure, which also reflected her departure from reality-based constructions of the world, including food. In Denise's case as well, she had generated attention-grabbing emotion by manufacturing a "devil," namely herself, if she failed to follow the simple commandments of her private reality-skewing religion. Her *real* problem (i.e., the trigger for her dissociative disorder) had very little to do with food or worries about contamination in the same way that Mike had no real investment in counting. Both were symptoms of convenience and the choice of those symptoms was made on the basis of availability. Denise spent much of her time cooking for her husband and her four children, and her choice of symptom was therefore consistent with the contents of her environment. The service that these symptoms provided, however, had much more to do with pressing problems and frustrations that had been building for months and even years. As such, Denise's symptoms were more pervasive and uncontrolled than religious types of obsessions and compulsions that revolve around food contamination.

Obsessive-compulsive disorder is but one of many pathological syndromes that, like religion, equip a person with a method for reality transcendence. While Mike and Denise lacked the religious ecstasy that comes when this is conducted properly and normalized by the group, they nonetheless had *transcended* the constraints of their former reality. They had managed to defend themselves psychologically by using dissociative symptoms to *specialize* their world, making it far smaller and simpler than would be perceived without their specialization techniques. Instead of dissociation and suggestion deriving from external sources as in religion, both were executed by the individual with the end result being a constellation of poorly organized and only marginally effective symptoms.

Many disorders have the same general themes with regard to myth-ritual complexes, the personalized usage of dissociation and suggestion, and the transformation of reality aimed at the defensive interception of imminent failure of adaptation. Therefore, before we examine other specific types of mental disorders, it would benefit us to examine more closely the actual dynamics of dissociative symptom formation. Then it will become possible to understand a wider range of psychopathology and to explain the symptom choice in the context of the *cultural* suggestions that influence autosuggestion in these dissociative disorders. It is only by viewing this class of psychopathology in terms of the dissociative process that we can arrive at any accurate determination of their etiology and purpose, as well as their eventual treatment. So let us take one additional step and ask ourselves about the exact manner in which the symptoms of autodissociative disorders are accomplished by people who need to resort to these additional modifications to perceived reality.

AUTODISSOCIATION VIA MONOIDEISTIC COGNITION

I believe that the concept of *monoideism* can form the basis for a new appreciation of autodissociative mental disturbance. Although the construct of a monoideism is not new, it has never found its way into the common thinking or vocabulary of the psychological community. In his pioneering work in this area, James Braid argued that the word "monoideism" would be the most suitable term to describe hypnosis and related phenomena.[72]

In recent years some members of the psychiatric community have reminded us of the potential usefulness of Braid's concept of monoideistic cognition. Among them is the Israeli psychiatrist Mordecai Kaffman, who feels that monoideistic cognition can explain several forms of mental disturbance.[73] Kaffman, like Braid before him, defines a monoideism as an *altered* state of consciousness involving total concentration on a single dominant idea or cognition. Moreover, in order to form the basis for an effective altered or dissociated state, the thematic content of the thought must be extremely restricted but well emphasized in nature. Then, the person is easily able to *detach* himself or herself from extraneous unwanted cognitions in favor of the *microscopic* world of the monoideism. People are able to sustain a dissociation from generalized reality through a *monotonous repetition* to themselves of the highly focused idea or image making up the monoideism itself.

There are many similarities between monoideistic thought and hypnotic trance. As we saw earlier, many hypnotists have their subjects concentrate their attention in similarly highly restricted ways. But if we are to compare monoideistic thought to hypnosis, the comparison should be made to *self*-hypnosis. In fact, Kaffman views monoideistic disorders as an autosuggestive process very much like self-hypnosis. The repetitive idea or thought upon which the person concentrates attention during monoideistic thinking could be likened to the trance-facilitating sound of a metronome. We know that repetition of certain sounds, words, or actions has the power to send the listener or viewer into dissociative trance.

Kaffman believes that self-directed verbalizations are an integral part of monoideistic syndromes. But this raises an important question: How can a single brain talk to itself? Also, who/what is talking to whom/what? Still more fundamentally, can the brain make noises or sounds or talk that it can hear? These questions must have an affirmative answer if we are to support a theory of self-induced dissociative techniques.

In a description of self-hypnotic methods for achieving dissociated states, Ernest Hilgard refers to a "pseudo-dyadic relation of speaker to listener" which can replace "heterohypnosis" (i.e., trance dissociation aided by another person).[74] In Hilgard's view, the brain is able to act as both a speaker and a listener. That is consistent with his neo-dissociation theory, as well as his famous concept of the "hidden observer." Hilgard's ideas on "self-hypnotic" dissociation can clarify the mechanism that might underlie the one-way communication which Kaffman deems essential to the construction of monoideistic syndromes. There are many parallels between Hilgard's concept of "pseudo-dyadic relation of speaker to listener" and the "closed one-way communication" that Kaffman deems to underlie monoideistic syndromes. They both describe the central function of self-hypnotic or autodissociative techniques, which is to neutralize toxic information.

In order to illustrate this, Hilgard gives the example of people trying to put themselves to sleep by counting sheep.[75] That is actually a very good example, as that simple act resembles very closely what takes place when someone retreats into autodissociative syndromes. When counting sheep, the person does two things in order to achieve sleep. The goal of sheep counting is to escape from certain intrusive cognitions that could interfere with relaxation and subsequent sleep. In all likelihood, these thoughts are more benign than those from which the autodissociative trance is designed to escape. In any case, sheep counting involves the same two processes that allow a person to dissociate via "clinical" (or "monoideistic") syndromes. First, the scope of the thought process is severely restricted, in this case to the size and form of sheep. Second, the person employs repetition which is a universal feature of all forms of trance dissociation. The same soporific effect would not be achieved by focusing on a single motionless sheep. Although still poorly understood, the mere process of repetition fosters a hypnogogic, i.e., sleep-inducing, mental state. Hypersuggestibility is produced which can be used to autosuggest a modified reality that remains at a safe distance from the person's underlying sources of conflict and anxiety.

In the previous case of Mike and his counting, we saw that he was able to restrict his cognitive focus to the size of clothes counting. In so doing, he involved himself in a ceaseless circle of *self-talk*, thus achieving a vehicle for repetition in the form of the "sounds" of his own words. Mike managed to construct a monoideism that fulfills Kaffman's criterion of highly restricted thematic content in conjunction with repetition in the form of circular inner dialogue. In line with Kaffman's thinking, Mike's monoideism probably gained strength as it was repeated. The final syndrome was a problematic, but partially effective, version of sheep counting. He was able to fashion for himself a revised reality that was manageable in its greatly diminished size. The toxic part of reality was rendered temporarily harmless. The problems with which Mike was unable to cope were effectively *ignored* during the entire course of his singular preoccupation with counting. Regardless of the content and mode of expression of the symptom, all autodissociative disorders have *ignorance* as a goal; that is, they seek to ignore certain components of reality that threaten to impinge on them and thereby diminish their capacity for survival.

ADDITIONAL DISSOCIATIVE DISORDERS

A thorough discussion of all facets of psychopathological disorders lies well beyond the scope of this book. Yet it is possible to look at a number of disorders while concentrating on their commonalities regarding the use of dissociation and suggestion, as well as their close relationships to religion and other "hypnotic" behaviors.

Fred Frankel makes an excellent point that dissociative trance is "the superordinate concept used to refer to states of mind characterized by the relative unawareness and nonfunctioning of the generalized reality orientation."[76] For Frankel, trance unites behaviors that are "hypnotic" as well as "psychopathological" in appearance. In order to elucidate trance as a strategic coping mechanism, he goes to considerable lengths to outline the similarities between phobias* and dissociative trance. Frankel's theoretical work in this area is backed up by his quantitative research showing that nearly 60 percent of phobic people have exceptionally developed dissociative capabilities as measured by tests of hypnotic susceptibility.[77] This

---

*Phobias, at their root, are almost identical in structure to the obsessive-compulsive symptoms mentioned above in relation to the cases of Mike and Denise. In fact, one would have to say that Mike and Denise were also phobic since both were extremely and *unrealistically* fearful of certain consequences that would take place if the compulsive rituals were not acted out.

is consistent with two additional studies that found nearly 50 percent of phobics to have very high levels of dissociative capacity, again as measured by their ability both to succumb to formal hypnotic induction procedures and to respond to suggestion.[78]

Frankel observes that "the frequency of depersonalization and other evidence of distorted perception associated with phobic behavior means that dissociation is frequently part of the mechanism involved."[79] Frankel notes that, in an odd way, this is a maladaptive defense that is used for adaptive purposes. This convoluted situation arises from the fact that one state of anxiety, tied to an unrealistic situation or object, is created in order to compete with the anxiety flowing from an actual or real source. Evidence is offered by Frankel demonstrating that phobias are frequently precipitated by feelings of panic, leading him to conclude that

> phobic behavior appears to involve spontaneous dissociation that could be part of a defense against overwhelming anxiety [but] we will have considerable difficulty trying to differentiate this specific dissociation from that attained under the conditions created by a hypnotic induction procedure.[80]

As with obsessive-compulsive disorder, the symptom often represents little more than a convenient absorption point for repetitive self-directed cognitions that can generate a state of dissociation and therefore a point of departure from toxic elements of the person's reality.

Kenneth Bowers and Donald Meichenbaum recount one of Morton Prince's clinical cases as Prince, a pioneer of dissociation theory, attempted to explain psychopathology, including phobias, in terms of the processes of dissociation and suggestion.[81] It is worth discussing here since it illustrates how dissociative symptom formation seeks to manufacture monoideisms that function to compete with portions of reality deemed to be troublesome from the standpoint of effective coping.

The case is that of a woman who had an intense phobia of church towers and church steeples. Initially, the symptoms made no sense to her and she remembered very little about their genesis except that the phobia began when she was about fifteen years of age. The woman was largely incapacitated by her symptoms, devoting much of her mental and physical activity to the task of avoiding these dreaded objects. Under hypnosis, however, she was able to reveal more information. It turned out that the phobic symptoms began shortly after the prolonged illness and eventual death of her mother. During the course of her mother's illness, the young woman channeled her stress and anxiety over her mother into religious symptoms in the form of praying rituals performed in the local church. As it happened, the bells in the steeple of that church rang every fifteen minutes, an event that meant very little to the woman at the time. But when her mother died as a result of the illness, the woman became profoundly disturbed. It was after this that the phobia of church towers and steeples developed.

I feel that Bowers and Meichenbaum are theoretically correct in attributing the evolution of this particular phobia to an accidental association that had been formed between the woman's memory of her mother's death and her memory of the church bells. They state:

> [T]owers and church steeples had come to represent the full emotional charge of those painful events, with the result that the patient's memory of her mother's actual death was pale, emotionless, and without importance to her. Thus focused and localized, the experiencing of these painful emotions could be escaped by avoiding the towers to which they had become attached—or, in clinical terms, the patient had developed a phobic neurosis. . . . Initially the emotional charge associated with the mother's death was *displaced* to a small, insignificant fragment of the totality of the imagery of the painful event itself; it was shifted from the naturally painful memory of the mother's death to the memory of the church tower bells, which in and by themselves alone had no inherent meaning or capacity to arouse feeling. Secondly, the emotional charge was *projected outward* from the mental imagery of towers to actual towers in the external environment. . . . The patient was thereby enabled to avoid painful memories by a final defensive maneuver of *avoiding* any form of contact with the towers in her environment.[82]

The woman's symptom choice was clearly made in order to afford her the basis for a dissociative reaction against the memory of her mother's death. The symptoms themselves allowed her to monopolize or *specialize* all of her attention around the relatively safe steeples and towers. Through the endless repetition of certain steeple-related cognitions, the woman was able to promote an autodissociative state that further permitted her to self-direct suggestions concerning the steeples and towers. This, in turn, led to a blatantly *overvalued* idea that would absorb her attention and distract her from the reality of her mother's death.

Ernest Becker, in *Escape from Evil*, seeks to bridge psychopathology and religion in claiming that neurosis must be comprehended as the incapacity to transcend ourselves to an adequate extent. He adds the illuminating statement that one of the most common "techniques of madness" is "to make the body the referent for the whole cosmos."[83] In actuality, we see this madness technique, as Becker calls it, in several types of psychopathology. One that comes to mind immediately is hypochondriasis, a dissociative disorder categorized as a *somatoform disorder*. The term "somatoform" refers to disorders involving physical complaints that have an exclusively psychological basis. The hypochondriacal person possesses the unwarranted belief that he or she is afflicted by an illness of some sort. No amount of reassurance to the contrary will be able to change this belief. This resembles the futility encountered by someone attempting to challenge a person's religious beliefs. But hypochondriacal individuals also know that they do not have the disease. That is, they both believe and do not believe, a sure sign that dissociation is at the core of this syndrome. When asked, many people with hypochondriasis will openly acknowledge that they are probably not ill in reality. This phenomenon reveals itself in the fearless "fears" about having even the most dreaded of diseases, such as cancer. Their emotional flatness in relation to their delusional illness beliefs reveals that the disorder is one of *preoccupation* rather than actual fear. In fact, there are many case reports of hypochondriacs expressing *relief* and a paradoxical relaxation when told that they are suffering from a disease. They then have full reign to remain preoccupied by their imaginary symptoms.

In true dissociative fashion, these hypochondriacal preoccupations serve to focus the individual's attention in a highly specific manner. Again as with the tack on the hypnotist's ceiling or the mesmerizing flicker of a church candle, these people become completely absorbed by such things as the beating of their hearts, the amount of sweat on their skin, miniscule sores or skin irregularities, slight sensations in the throat that could signal the coming of a cold, and so forth. Arnold Ludwig discusses hypochondriasis in the context of dissociation and describes the manner in which all hypochondriacs' attention becomes "locked" on to their symptoms in order to grossly *overvalue* some aspect of bodily function. As a result, they can effectively "gate," or shut out, external stimuli, thus providing them with an adaptive mechanism for distraction.[84]

Taking the obvious example of someone with a delusional belief that his heart has an irregular beat, we can readily see how the person can expose himself to highly repetitive stimuli in order to engender a state of dissociative trance. For hours each day, he listens to his heartbeat, letting the general reality orientation give way to the obsessive monotony of that particular fixation, or absorption point. Even if there is no actual beat, as in the case of the delusional heart problem, the person can just as easily derive obsessive monotony from continual examination of a tiny bump on the surface of the skin or a faint tingle in the tip of a toe.

The "something wrong" in hypochondriasis functions like the devils in religion since it adds an emotive element to the whole procedure that assists in maintaining the subject's fixation of attention. This works to some extent despite the fact that the truth of the matter is also known by one part of the information-processing system. The dissociated state made possible by the repetitive actions and the monotonous cognitions put the subject in a position to self-direct suggestions that can bring "reality" to the nonexistent disease or affliction. Once this is accomplished, the subject has again managed to constrict reality to the size of the symptoms. The motivational source of the dissociative reaction (i.e., the "real" problem) is distanced from the subject. Even though the disorder is associated with some emotional distress, those "calculated" emotions are probably less taxing than would be the emotions stemming from unmitigated contact with toxic information that requires dissociation.

The other somatoform disorders are also myth-ritual complexes that involve the dual processes of dissocation and suggestion. They, too, as Becker saw, enable the person to transcend and transform reality by making the body the sole referent for an altered and much reduced reality.

Body dysmorphic disorder is a type of dissociative syndrome involving an extreme preoccupation with an imaginary physical defect. Someone with this disorder might concentrate his or her attention on facial hair, or the curvature of the nose, or the shape of the mouth. Frequent consultations with plastic surgeons or dermatologists consume much of the person's time once this pattern of dissociation and suggestion is fully established. We can see how this type of symptom would function in a way very similar to hypochondriasis in terms of a "specialization" that derives from the auto-induction of dissociative trance and the self-administration of suggestions. As with hypochondriasis, these suggestions become firm beliefs that are held in defiance of all evidence to the contrary.

Conversion disorder, which is also classified as a somatoform disorder, has been discussed already as a dissociative syndrome in which the patient avoids conflict situations by locking on to an actual bodily dysfunction produced via dissociation. This might be "blindness" or "paralysis" or any one of numerous other physical symptoms. While conversion disorder's symptoms vary somewhat in appearance from those of hypochondriasis or body dysmorphic disorder, it is again quite clear that this represents a dissociative avoidance response that is accomplished by an extreme narrowing of attentional focus combined with an overvaluing of the illusory "problem." Thanks to the workings of dissociation and autosuggestion, a benign monoideistic problem is forged and substituted for ones that have been unconsciously diagnosed as problematic, thus affording patients escape into the modified and constricted reality of their creation.

Somatoform pain disorder (also called psychogenic pain disorder) is another clear example of the use of dissociation and suggestion toward the goal of monoideistic "specialization," thus enabling the patient to become completely absorbed into an extremely narrow focus of the world. The patient's attention is highly focused and concentrated around some specific "pain" that has no physical basis. Prior to the onset of the actual syndrome, the patient is usually under considerable stress of some sort or in a conflict situation from which she cannot see an avenue of escape. An improvised escape is made when the patient targets some part of the body and concentrates on it to the exclusion of all other stimuli. Obsessive monotony is thereby achieved and over time the patient finds herself able to produce a state of dissociation with that particular bodily absorption point. At this stage, the patient can autosuggest that certain "pains" are emanating from that part of the body. She can produce an illusory sensation of pain just as it can be done through the use of formal hypnosis, or self-hypnosis. Somatoform pain disorder, like the dissociative syndromes already described, should be seen as a "self-hypnotic" or autodissociative procedure. Thus, somatization disorders and factitious disorders have the same essential ingredients of absorption, dissociation, and suggestion, as well as the same goal of functional escape through reality constriction and overvaluing. Likewise, all these disorders have rituals that follow from the delusional beliefs, which in turn serve to perpetuate the symptoms.

Paranoid disorders might seem superficially different from the types of psychopathology so far discussed in this section. Yet, as Mordecai Kaffman describes so well, these, too, must be regarded as auto-hypnotic monoideisms that focus the person's attention onto fictional mental constructions.[85] In Kaffman's view, the patient enters into a hypnotic (i.e., dissociative) trance through the repetition of rigid and inflexible cognitions. This is done in an ongoing and highly monotonous way until the patient's critical thinking capacity wanes and he becomes tolerant of logical inconsistencies. The same messages that the patient uses to "drum" himself into a state of dissociation become the suggestions that bring to life the paranoid ideation that will preoccupy the patient and be the vehicle for escape.

This does not differ too much from the religious example I gave in the last chapter in which a religious leader's words are both the "drum" *and* the suggestion structuring the dissociative state once the "drum" has done its job. Unlike religion, however, pathological states such as paranoia are a self-created myth, rather than one that is readily offered by culture. Inevitably, one sees repetitive rituals that sustain the paranoid myth. Again these are largely private, as in the case of a person who develops a fanatical ritualistic lifestyle of building dugout shelters in order to protect himself or herself from an imminent nuclear holocaust.

Kaffman is aware of the fact that many autohypnotic, or auto-dissociative, monoideistic psychopathologies can function as a religion. Not only do they give the patient a mode of escape from personal and situational problems, but they can fill his or her person with a sense of life's meaning and purpose. With specific reference to paranoid delusions, Kaffman states:

> In most cases the monoideistic paranoid belief provides an absorbing cause to work for, a goal and a direction in life to a person whose neurotic personality had hitherto been plagued by feelings of doubt, failure, and insecurity in a world lacking sufficient guidelines for one's behavior. The patient's tenacious clinging to his monoideistic belief gives him an illusory escape from his fear to a life perceived to be full of existential threats.[86]

As Kaffman describes the person who is predisposed to absorption into paranoid beliefs, we are reminded once more of those lost souls who are ripe for religious conversion. Many of the same needs get met by religion and psychopathology. One of the main differences in these two systems of illusion, however, is that religions are usually made up of both positive and negative illusions, whereas the pathological disorders under discussion here tend to rely almost exclusively on negative illusion. Religions are more likely to have benevolent gods (plus some devils), while devils tend to dominate in the psychopathologies. Even so, dissociative psychopathology and its many illusory "devils" provide needed escape as well as a means by which to add structure to one's cognitive world. Another distinction that can be made between religion and psychopathology has to do with the nature of the emotions that are generated in each.

As one would expect, positive illusions such as those seen in most religions tend to yield positive emotions. This generalization holds true despite the strategic fear and/or guilt that is sometimes exploited by religions to rivet attention and ensure compliance. Furthermore, positive emotions are generally forthcoming from the cooperative and interactional nature of religion as it is acted out at the collective level. By contrast, psychopathology is almost entirely dependent upon negative illusions. We have already given many examples, including phobias, conversion disorders, factitious disorders, paranoia, hypochondriasis and the full range of psychosomatic disorders, obsessions and compulsions. Beyond this, the person who is forced to rely on psychopathology is largely deprived of the positive emotions that come from participation in the *group* dissociation and suggestion methods that do a better and more sociable job of modifying reality.

The same could be said about certain quasireligions, such as some radical militant anti-abortion groups. Although slightly more advantageous than entirely private psychopathology, they are largely negative obsessions revolving around a "devil" who has been magnified out of all proportion. The "lost souls" who abandon themselves to these movements derive some sense of spiritual purpose and a limited experience of belongingness. But it is not ideal as a symptom choice and a strategy for reality transcendence since it fosters emotions and social conflicts that are themselves pathological, or at best unpleasant. This again contrasts with traditional religious symptoms that are sanctioned at the wider level of culture.

PSYCHOPATHOLOGICAL SYMPTOMS AND CULTURE

Psychiatric historians have noted that, prior to the twentieth century, the symptoms of schizophrenia tended to be of a religious nature much more frequently than today. This is despite the fact that schizophrenia itself is a biochemical disorder with a large genetic component independent of time or culture. Even when the mental disorder is mostly physiological in origin, it still shows the close connection between symptoms and culture. Granted, some of the "neurotic" disorders mentioned previously were relatively private in their construction when compared to the symptom constellations associated with public religious endeavors. Yet, with some exceptions, those, too, bear the signature of the culture and/or subculture of origin. We might reconsider the paranoid individual whose symptoms include the delusional belief that the world is about to be destroyed by a nuclear holocaust. That particular symptom could not have existed prior to the advent of nuclear technology. Therefore, it would not, prior to 1945, have been an effective foundation to use in order to monopolize one's understandings of the world. Conversely, in Western society today, paranoia almost never centers on the singular fear that syphilis is being deliberately spread with the intention of killing all human beings, as it once might have when syphilis was an incurable affliction. Today, however, it is not uncommon for paranoia to revolve around the monoideistic delusion that AIDS is being spread in the same devilish fashion.

From Juris Draguns comes a challenging analysis of the relationships between personality, psychopathology, and culture. He presents a credible theoretical model that views psychopathology as an *exaggeration* of personality that manifests itself as a "caricature of culture."[87] This assumes that psychopathological disorders are often extensions of the "normal" elements of the culture and that abnormal people differ only in terms of the *magnitude* of the cultural elements that find their way into pathological disorders. A considerable amount of clinical evidence supports this model. We might continue our coverage of some specific types of dissociative disorders in relation to this theory.

Alfonso Martínez-Taboas has written about multiple personality disorder as an example of dissociative symptoms whose content and structure are the result of *social constructionism*. He introduces his theoretical position by describing culture as the framework for reality perception, as well as the blueprint for inner conflict and the symptoms that are mobilized as a response to these conflicts. Furthermore, he states that "dissociation is a mechanism that is exquisitely and always mediated by cultural expectations [that] influence the patient's perception, experience, expressions, and pattern of coping with stressors."[88] Martínez-Taboas's particular approach allows for the likely possibility that dissociation is a constant factor in all human beings, while also being able to explain the endlessly different expressions of the dissociation mechanisms in different cultures of the world. These variations are seen in terms both of normal and abnormal usages of dissociation. Thus, by letting his theory revolve around the common denominator of dissociation as it interacts with cultural suggestion, Martínez-Taboas takes us beyond a simplistic type of cultural relativism that does not attempt to anchor cultural variation to a unifying process such as dissociation.

There can be little doubt that the symptoms of multiple personality disorder have a close relationship to the prevailing cultural suggestions that surround the person who is constructing the disorder. In this respect, Martínez-Taboas would be correct in his argument that there is a large amount of *local* content in virtually all forms of psychopathology, including multiple personality disorder. After all, the actual behaviors of the alter personalities are restrained by the reach of the person's cultural experience. We see this with regard to religious beliefs among multiple personality victims. Even though the dissociated "selves" profess varying degrees of religious belief and sometimes even beliefs that cross religious denominations, all these can be traced to contact that has been made by the person with this dimension of his or her culture. Sometimes this might also involve contact that the individual has had with other cultures.

Eating disorders such as anorexia nervosa and bulimia nervosa provide an even better illustration of dissociative symptoms that are simultaneously "private" and the product of the patient's cultural milieu. Why do young people, particularly young women, develop this disorder in our culture? Moreover, why is it the case that young people in other cultures who are similarly predisposed *do not* develop anorexia nervosa? We know, for example, that the types of eating disorders so familiar to us in the West are virtually nonexistent in other societies.[89]

In light of our theory, we may safely surmise that would-be anorexics "diagnose" themselves as incapable of coping with their situation. An unconscious "decision" is made to employ dissociation in order to construct a symptomatic reality much smaller in scope than the actual reality. This is still another example of adaptive dissociative specialization aimed at locking on to highly focused elements of reality in order to construct an alternative reality that can be more easily managed and controlled. As part of this, it is not difficult to imagine how the patient facilitates autodissociation by way of a relentless concentration on tiny areas of imaginary body fat. I once had an anorexic student who sat in class for the full hour pinching the same area of skin on her forearm and studying it for signs of fat. In an analysis of anorexia nervosa and bulimia nervosa as a social epidemic, Richard Gordon explains why victims of these disorders choose that particular pattern of delusion. From the broad perspective of culture, he states:

> Anorexics and bulimics draw upon the common cultural vocabulary of their time, through latching onto the contemporary mania about dieting, thinness, and food control that have become endemic to the advanced industrial societies. They utilize these cultural preoccupations as defenses that enable them to escape from—and achieve some sense of control over—unmanageable personal distress, most of which revolves around issues of identity.[90]

According to Gordon, each culture contains different belief systems, values, and attitudes that individuals draw upon as they construct symptoms offering escape and the illusion of control. In

Malaysia, where anorexia nervosa is rare, there is a culture-bound disorder known as *amok*. Afflicted individuals run through the streets lashing out violently at people, sometimes inflicting serious physical injury as they continue on the rampage and avoid all attempts at capture. While this syndrome might seem completely unrelated to anorexia nervosa, its main difference lies in the way that dissociated states are constructed by culturally based suggestion. In looking at the events preceding the onset of amok, one also sees a conflicted person who is under high levels of stress and pressure. As in anorexia nervosa, there is an unconscious decision that defensive dissociation is needed in order to safeguard the integrity of the nervous system and to maintain some degree of survival capacity. But "be thin" does not exist in Malaysia as a dominant cultural suggestion, making it unlikely that the person will make that particular symptom choice. This does not change the fact that the individual still needs a foundation for the dissociative reaction.

The actual symptoms of amok make sense in terms of certain historical aspects of Malaysian culture. Gordon even demonstrates that these symptoms are modeled after patterns of behavior that are highly esteemed in Malaysian society. This apparently dates to a point in the country's past when aggressive acting out was deemed a heroic reaction to the abuses of authority by the political rulers of the time. In this regard, amok has the symbolic quality of self-sacrifice even though the bulk of the Malaysian population would dread the prospect of falling prey to this affliction. Therefore, amok is patterned into the consciousness of Malaysian culture in a way that could not be understood by an outsider. It represents one of many possible symptom "choices" for someone experiencing the need to embark on a course of defensive dissociation.

The culture-bound *windigo* syndrome affords us another illustration of cultural suggestions that can find their way into the overt symptoms of dissociative reactions. This is a dissociative disorder affecting certain Native American cultures (e.g., the Cree and Algonquin) in parts of the northern United States and southern Canada. Curiously, it is an eating disorder, but of a much different kind than anorexia nervosa or bulimia nervosa. Those who develop windigo are overcome by the urge to engage in cannibalistic bingeing. It typically remains a cognitive preoccupation wherein they are locked on to the fearful prospect that they might actually give in to the impulse. This becomes a monoideism by which patients become totally absorbed. Their internal world is reduced to the size of this preoccupation, and they can therefore achieve distance from the conflicts and painful emotions that gave birth to the need for such drastic defensive tactics.

Explaining windigo requires us to explore the inner structure of the Native American cultures involved. When we do this, we gain insight into the origins of the beliefs and taboos that play a part in the genesis of windigo. Groups of native North Americans endured prolonged periods of starvation and semi-starvation around the time that large trading companies, such as the Hudson Bay Company, began to invade their territory and strip their land of its food supply. Starvation combined with long northern winters to create a situation so acute that the eating of other humans became an issue related to basic survival. It remains unclear how much cannibalism actually occurred, and some anthropologists argue that all Native American cultures suffering from this disorder did not need to endure famine directly.[91] But it is clear that, as a measure for resisting this tendency, a powerful taboo evolved in these cultures to the effect that *one must not eat other people.* Severe consequences were built into this taboo which instilled intense fear in anyone entertaining cannibalistic notions.

In most Western societies, the cultural suggestion heard more loudly than almost any other by young women is that *one must not be fat.* Consequently, extreme measures to avoid that cultural taboo are an understandable symptom choice for those people. The same underlying or predisposing emotional factors may be in place for the individual Cree who needs to "specialize" into an altered reality of more manageable and controllable size. It also follows, however, that a fearful obsession about becoming cannibalistic would be a possible symptom choice for the Cree, whereas the dissociative symptoms of the young Western woman would probably be consistent with those cultural beliefs to which she has been exposed.

It is necessary to stress once more that mental health professionals must not restrict their attention to the actual symptoms of psychopathology, whose primary importance lies in their value as vehicles by which to monopolize these patients' cognitive faculties and their subsequent perception of the world and themselves. What lies behind the surface of the symptoms themselves is often only remotely related to the symptoms adopted. We saw this to be operative in anorexia nervosa, which can be traced to problems of transition into adulthood. In another culture, those same predisposing factors will often lead to psychological symptoms with a completely different appearance. I have described elsewhere the "culture-bound" syndrome of *koro* as the *etiological equivalent* of anorexia nervosa.[92] That is, many of the same preonset personality traits and situational factors produce the "decision" to make a defensive dissociative reaction, except that the different cultures in which they emerge shape the specific symptoms much differently. With koro, which affects young men in parts of Southeast Asia, Indonesia, Malaysia, and southern China, the patient becomes completely absorbed into the delusional belief that his penis is shrinking. This is accompanied by body image distortion similar to that witnessed in anorexia nervosa. The fact that the anorexic sees her body as larger than it is while the koro victim sees his penis as smaller does not change the fundamentally identical forces underlying these two disorders.

The presenting symptoms of mental disorders vary across cultures even though the motivations that exist at the individual level are frequently the same. Raymond Prince helps us toward an improved understanding of this process as he discusses anorexia nervosa in relation to *brain fag*, a culture-bound disorder affecting considerable numbers of people in Nigeria and other West African cultures.[93] Brain fag is clearly a dissociative disorder as revealed by symptoms including alterations of sensations, visual distortions, feelings of "vacancy," memory depletion, and loss of ability to understand spoken and written words. Prince noted a high prevalence of this dissociative reaction in secondary school students who were not performing up to the standards set for them. In all likelihood, brain fag is a response to prolonged periods of stress and anxiety, whose symptoms enable the patient to escape into a smaller world of "impaired" cognitive efficiency. As Prince realizes, the symptoms of brain fag must be viewed in light of cultural beliefs that are propagated in these parts of Africa, just as anorexia nervosa is tied to cultural suggestions in the West.

An analogous conclusion is made by Hildred Geertz, who analyzes the cultural dynamics of another culture-bound dissociative disorder, namely *latah*.[94] Writing about latah as it manifests itself in Java (Indonesia), she summarizes the most common symptoms. Among these are a compulsive involuntary tendency to blurt out obscene words or phrases and/or to imitate in a highly compulsive way the actions or speech of other people. Also common is a hypersuggestibility that inclines those with latah to obey unquestioningly whatever orders are given to them, no matter how ridiculous or offensive these might be. Geertz outlines similarities between latah and other culture-bound disorders, but notes that each has a symptom set directly related to culture-specific beliefs, attitudes, and conditions. She details the inner workings of Javanese society and shows how latah is a logical symptom choice for those who find themselves in need of "magical immunization" from pressing conflict situations.

Without going into great detail on this fascinating syndrome, suffice it to say that latah has at its heart a strong taboo regarding the importance of social etiquette. As Geertz writes, in Javanese society social etiquette has deep religious and ethical significance. Conversely, obscenity in any form is considered to be highly immoral and reproachable. This makes it quite simple to lock on, both cognitively and emotionally, to the taboo associated with the violation of socially prescribed laws of morality and etiquette. In turn, people can become *all-absorbed* by their potential to commit the violation, leading eventually to a "specialized" inner world reduced to the size of their new preoccupation or obsession. Yet, even though latah symptoms are undeniably shaped by unique characteristics of Javanese culture, we cannot assume that the disorder is *etiologically* unique. Geertz recognizes the need to separate our understanding of symptoms and etiology when she writes that "latah may, in fact, be only one rather extreme manifestation of a more general fact: the involvement of culture in the process of symptom formation and symptom choice."[95] Beyond this, Geertz reiterates that the *same* underlying factors that result in latah in one culture can result in a different set of symptoms in another cultural context:

> . . . [I]t appears that latah is an unusually clearcut example of how the form of a set of symptoms may be determined primarily by a cultural tradition, a tradition which persists because of its congruity with basic themes in the wider culture. It may be that here is a case in which the culture presents to a certain—as yet unspecifiable—category of disturbed persons, a coherent set of culturally meaningful behavior patterns, through which they find it possible to express their personal conflicts. It is reasonable to expect that when enough individual latah subjects have been adequately studied, the dynamics of their disease will be found to be similar to certain disorders of the Western world. . . . It almost seems as though these individuals—who probably would be sick in any culture—instead of creating their own idiosyncratic symptoms, found a satisfying solution to their conflicts in the preexisting cultural pattern of latah.[96]

We are again presented with a picture of people who, regardless of their place of origin, find themselves with a need to participate in dissociative procedures designed to escape irreconcilable conflicts through the manufacture of delusional reality-constricting "solutions." Instead of embarking on this process of monopolization in a completely idiosyncratic or private way, they often let their symptoms become extreme variations of already existing cultural constructions of reality. Stated differently, dissociative symptoms often contain a certain amount of cultural "truth." The unconsciously calculated use of dissociation and suggestion permits the person to stretch or magnify certain cultural "facts," thereby adding an element of credibility to otherwise incredible formulations of reality.

As another example, there is a certain amount of truth, or at least conceivable truth, to the paranoid's visions of the world as resting on the brink of a nuclear cataclysm. Some "truth" is also contained in a phobia of heights, cars, germs, and so forth. The anorexic is also upholding some "truths" by devoting himself or herself to the pursuit of thinness. Being thin carries a number of advantages from the point of view of Western culture. On behalf of those who participate in psychopathology, it must be said that anorexics are merely taking generally accepted cultural truths and using them as a springboard for an altered reality that substitutes for a problematic personal reality. The same thing occurs when someone develops religious symptoms in relation to culturally meaningful religious "truths," thereby allowing reality distortion to ride on the back of socially sanctioned mental constructions.

Some mental disorders draw on culture more than others for purposes of symptom formation. Furthermore, even within one category of disorder, some individuals will rely on preexisting cultural constructions more than others with the same affliction. Consider phobias and the person who develops a morbid fear of pine needles or blue automobiles. For the most part, these particular symptom choices would not be tied to the collective beliefs found in Western culture. On the other hand, someone with an unremitting phobia about going to hell or becoming fat has made a symptom choice that pushes cultural "truths" to the point that these truths are revealed to others as forms of deviance. As we saw, it is sometimes very difficult to diagnose people as mentally ill when their choice of symptoms involves cultural truths.

Religion as a Cultural Distortive Mechanism

We may bring matters full circle by reintroducing religion into our treatise on psychopathology. We saw that culture is essentially a *coping* process that modifies reality for reasons of improved functioning and enhanced adaptation. It was also seen that, until recently, religion was culture's main strategy for delivering to its members a "normal" distortive mechanism that could be utilized to whatever extent was deemed necessary. Most of what we now label "neurosis" did not exist in premodern times, since religion was sufficiently viable to normalize those religious symptoms.

In pursuing this logic, we are forced to regard modern Western psychopathology as a cluster of dissociative religious responses that no longer enjoy an intact normalizing religious system. It is even possible to describe as *private* religions those neurotic symptoms that are almost totally idiosyncratic in nature, such as the phobia of pine needles. Anorexia nervosa would be an example of a failed public religious activity, in which the core delusional belief is not recognized as a legitimate religious belief. Anorexia nervosa is on the religious borderline. Yet, if Western culture went much further in terms of worshiping thinness, it is conceivable that anorexic individuals would be viewed as disciples of a *holy cause*. This has actually happened already with regard to the symptom of unrestrained materialism. In the West, the obsessive and compulsive acquisition of money and possessions, as well as the delusional beliefs involved, have become normalized in the same way that religion was once able to normalize almost any degree of insanity. It is even normal today for the materialistically insane operating in this "religious" climate to work themselves to death in the pursuit of *more*.

A number of contemporary scholars have written specifically about anorexia nervosa as a religious response, even though its connection to religion is no longer obvious. As Rudolph Bell states in his book *Holy Anorexia*, food refusal in the medieval period has close links with prevalent religious beliefs.[97] Caroline Banks, who also theorizes about the fundamentally religious nature of anorexia nervosa, observes that fasting and other extreme forms of dietary restriction had become common features in Christianity by as early as the mid-fifth century.[98]

As part of her thesis, Banks cites clinical research showing that modern anorexics are more traditionally religious than their non-anorexic counterparts.[99] It is almost as if the anorexic symptoms were an extension of their already existing religious leanings. This comes through in some of the actual case histories presented by Banks wherein food refusal is expressed through religious symbol and idiom. Banks concludes that, in anorexia nervosa, self-starvation and its effects are frequently interpreted in religious ways, or at least with distinct religious intimations. Clinicians, sociologists, and others concerned with anorexia nervosa have observed how the self-denial of this disorder bears close resemblance to the asceticism that has featured in Western religious behavior throughout the ages. Some of the classic works of Hilda Bruch contain excerpts from conversations with anorexic individuals. In her book *The Golden Cage*, Bruch discusses a fifteen-year-old anorexic girl who makes the following statement in relation to the onset of her disorder: "My body became the visual symbol of pure ascetic and aesthetics, of being sort of untouchable in terms of criticism. . . . Everything became very intense and very intellectual, but absolutely untouchable.[100]

This patient thus makes clear the "holy" quality of her particular anorexic experience. Anorexia nervosa stands out as an exceptionally good illustration of psychopathology as an aberrant expression of religion, and I have dwelled on it for that reason. As a set of symptoms, it involves the same processes of dissociation and suggestion as those seen in religion. But with anorexia nervosa, the patient is giving herself over to the god of thinness, a god who does not yet have full cultural endorsement as a deity. The same is true regarding the rituals associated with this disorder. As much as we applaud devotees of thinness, we stop short of praising them all the way to their graves. At times in the past, their symptoms might have had full religious recognition, thereby protecting the symptoms from a diagnosis of psychopathology.

Although "holy anorexia" stands out in terms of its parallels to religion, we must realize that almost all forms of psychopathology are likewise *religious responses* at heart. Many commonalities unite religion and psychopathology, and these are further linked by the common denominator they have in terms of dissociative and suggestive responding. Religion has a larger representation of mainstream culture built in to its symptoms, but culture is often a partial guiding light for psychopathological symptoms as well. Both religion and psychopathology have their own version of "music" that generates obsessive monotony and a subsequent dissociative state that can be reconstructed with suggestions. What we have come to label as mental disorders typically entail a greater use of *self*-orchestrated dissociation techniques, as well as *auto*suggestion. In this sense, it could be argued that psychopathology is more difficult to establish and maintain, in the same way that many scholars speak of the superiority of heterohypnosis to self-hypnosis.

This entire model of psychopathology opens to question our usual methods by which to differentiate "normal" and "abnormal" behavior. A great deal of confusion arises when we extend this model into the domain of religion. New questions arise which may seem superficially absurd but which take on increasing importance as they are scrutinized more closely. These questions are made even more important within the current climate of religious decline since the overlap between religion and psychopathology is becoming greater. More and more, psychopathology is seeking to substitute for religion. As religion loses its social currency, many religious symptoms are beginning to be viewed as pathological. So, at what point do we begin treating religion? Should psychopathology be treated as one treats dysfunctional religion? Is it time to intervene at the level of culture and begin to design new religions that will replace the collapsing ones? Furthermore, given the indispensability of reality-altering "symptoms," should we be trying to devise new cultural sources of these delusional symptoms in the broader context of the needs of our threatened species? If so, what should be the "music" of the future, and what should be the new suggestions once that music has its effect? Let us approach the final chapter with these unlikely questions in mind.

6 Treating the Individual and Society

A number of implications may be derived from what we have discussed in previous chapters. Some of these relate directly to the many individuals who suffer from one or more of the mental disturbances that have befallen people in our "insane" society. Our improved understanding of the processes underlying most forms of psychopathology should be able to direct us toward more effective psychotherapy techniques. Other implications have relevance at the cultural level when we ask what, if anything, can be done to cure a sick society. If our knowledge of the dynamics of culture can enable us to revitalize the culture itself, then many positive benefits should follow for individual members of that culture. Let us begin by placing psychotherapy in a broad perspective while considering ways in which better methods could be developed.

Psychotherapy as we know it is a Western invention with few counterparts in traditional societies. Like "hypnosis," another Western invention, psychotherapy made its debut in a climate of religious decline. Since secularization is largely restricted to industrialized Western societies, it is not unexpected that modern psychotherapy methods have not made many inroads into non-Western cultures. While the situation is changing rapidly in some newly developing societies, traditional healing methods are still common in many parts of the world. Where this is the case, therapeutic healing is usually intimately bound up with the religious beliefs and practices of the people.

The spiritual healing strategies of the traditional healer vary enormously from one culture to the next. These differences are a direct result of the equally great variations in the religious systems of different cultures. Yet traditional healing approaches continue to attract the attention of cross-cultural psychologists and psychiatrists because of one important aspect that is shared by all of these traditional methods. This is the frequently reported finding that their

217

success rates are often higher than those enjoyed by Western psychotherapists. Consequently, in recent years there have been increasing calls for Western mental health professionals to take heed of traditional therapies and to develop new techniques that incorporate some of their effective ingredients.

We have been slow to learn from traditional healers even though the potential benefits could improve the lives of many people in need of help. In some instances, there has been open resistance to any move in the direction of traditional healing methods. To understand this, we must recognize that the Western mental health professions have evolved in irreligious and countercultural directions. Studies reveal that mental health professionals tend to be significantly less religious than the general population.[1] An almost opposite situation exists with regard to the bulk of traditional non-Western methods, which tend to be closely linked to both religion and culture. The gap is so wide that most Western psychotherapists find it difficult to relate to the radically different "spiritual" strategies existing in traditional cultures.

There are other reasons as well for our inability to take advantage of the generally more effective techniques of the traditional healer. With few exceptions, Western therapies have developed into highly self-conscious and intellectual exercises that fail to actively engage the client on a deep emotional level. The sessions themselves are quite subdued and usually include only the identified patient. If additional people are involved, these are usually limited to a spouse or the immediate family. In Western psychotherapy, there is no music, no dancing, no fire, no dissociative trance (except when "hypnosis" is used), no pageantry, no drama, no costumes, no community, and no magic other than the weak sense of mystery surrounding some of the therapist's comments or techniques. On all these counts, the Western therapist is at complete odds with the more powerful methods used by non-Western agents of change. All considered, Western therapy is a rather dead affair by contrast to non-Western healing practices. This situation mirrors the comparative death of religion in the West.

Our therapeutic industry has been built around the goals, aspirations, and lifestyles of people living in a competitive capitalistic society. This is still another factor accounting for the industry's relative inflexibility and its reluctance to change. For instance, it is far too impractical for most people today to leave free an entire day or even several whole days in order to be healed. Many traditional spiritual healing methods take this long, and even longer in some cases. Most of us live complex lives that force us to squeeze our psychotherapy into already tight schedules. Even though adherence to these schedules may be the source of many of our problems, that is part of our cultural reality. It is a fundamental principle that, in order to be effective, therapies must operate within the prevailing culture. This is even the case in the West where psychotherapy functions somewhere along the cultural periphery.

On this latter point, a number of religious scholars and others have suggested that contemporary psychotherapy functions as a substitute for religion in our secular society.[2] It is said that the therapist now steps in where there was once a priest or minister, or group spiritual healing techniques that were orchestrated by someone with religious authority. There can be little doubt that psychotherapy in its present form emerged as a response to secular forces. However, the question of its viability as a religious surrogate is quite another matter. For the most part, contemporary psychotherapy does not begin to provide the healing power and potential that was historically contained within socially sanctioned religious frameworks. But there are notable exceptions. We may even point to a subtle trend in which increasing numbers of psychotherapists are experimenting with more "spiritual" approaches to treatment. Some of these even bear a slight resemblance to the techniques typically associated with non-Western cultures. While these new methods still stand against the background of a conservative and pragmatic psychotherapy industry, their results have been quite impressive. As a consequence, it is conceivable that they will exert an ever greater influence on the insipid and unimaginative strategies that dominate psychotherapy in the West.

TOWARD THE SPIRITUALIZATION OF PSYCHOTHERAPY

The rationale for a basically "religious" approach to psychotherapy should be quite clear in terms of the central themes of this book. Hopefully, I was able to show the accuracy of Freud's insight that psychopathology is a pathological counterpart of religion, or what he termed "individual religiosity."[3] Collective religion works in relation to the interaction of myth and ritual. In fact, religion is dependent upon myth and ritual. This fact extends into the domain of "individual religion," or psychopathology. Patrick Vandermeersch develops this theme while criticizing much of Western psychotherapy as ritual that lacks myth.[4] He adds that, for psychotherapy to be effective against "individual religion," it, too, should possess a *mythology* that gives contextual meaning to the use of rituals. However,

Western therapy usually lacks the myths that could compete with those contained within the actual disorder.

Some have argued that psychotherapy does feature the implicit myth that the therapist is psychologically superior to the client and that life would improve if the client became more like the therapist. Yet that is a feeble myth that is exploited less and less by therapists. If anything, the trend by therapists is to dispel that myth by broadcasting that they have weaknesses of their own and that the client is their equal in all respects. Even if therapists did seek to maintain a mystique about themselves, as was done by some of the pioneering psychologists, that alone would prove insufficient as a mythological foundation for behavior change.

Some Feminist Approaches

Certain feminist movements within psychology have led the way in the creation of new therapies that take advantage of creative myth and ritual toward the goal of therapeutic healing. Different names have been attached to some of these movements, including the Women's Spirituality Movement, The Goddess Movement, and the Movement for Feminism and Theology.[5] One specific therapy technique, namely the lesbian fire ceremony, might serve as a useful illustration. It constitutes a therapeutic strategy that improves considerably on the usual modes of psychotherapy that are devoid of myth and ritual.

As described by Eva Ouwehand, the lesbian fire ceremony is employed with lesbians who, for obvious reasons, feel angry and depressed by the ridicule and discrimination they encounter as a result of their particular sexual preference.[6] Ouwehand describes this ritual, noting that many of these women had felt the need to remain "invisible" from the world, something that was a constant source of fear and anguish. She presents this therapy approach within the larger context of the inadequacy of modern religion, which finds people "just sitting quietly on the bench listening to what the preacher has to say."[7] In the same vein, most psychotherapy clients today just sit on the bench, so to speak, without actively participating in the therapeutic process, including its myths and rituals.

Both myth and ritual are an aspect of the lesbian fire ceremony. The clients congregate around an actual open fire which is crucial in terms of the healing rituals. Before the physical rituals are performed, each participant acknowledges the goddess by saying aloud, "I welcome the goddess in the shape of my friend. . . ." This statement is completed as each client states her own name as the "friend." By doing this, the client recognizes the beauty, strength, and goodness of the goddess, while attesting to the same attributes by equating herself with the goddess. Already at this early point, as Ouwehand states, "one can feel the power of this ceremony, as if every woman is worthy to bear the name of the divine."[8]

Once the goddess has been addressed, each woman singly takes a branch and throws it into the fire. When the symbolic branch enters the fire, the woman expresses what is bothering her. In this context, it usually involves feelings she has about being a lesbian, but related issues can also be addressed. The clients understand that these problems will be burned away and transformed along with the branch as it burns. The atmosphere of this small congregation becomes very intimate as more and more elements of the women's misery are destroyed and purified by the healing fire and the guiding hand of the goddess.

The religious quality of the therapeutic lesbian fire ceremony should be quite apparent. We know from Anthony Giddens that collective ritual is the defining feature of all religions.[9] Certainly the lesbian fire ceremony qualifies on that count. There is also an obvious myth involved, i.e., the goddess, that provides the foundation for ritual enactment. But a question arises in this latter regard. Do these women really believe in the illusory goddess? After all, the goddess in that therapeutic strategy is not featured in any of the popular Western religions. Furthermore, prior to their entry into this form of therapy, these women have virtually no *practice* at believing in this particular deity. On the surface, it seems unlikely that any genuine belief could arise in the short span of time encompassed by the period of treatment.

Before we reject the prospect that the beneficial effects of the ceremony were tied to a belief in the goddess, we must first determine if the technique was designed with dissociation in mind. That is, were people provided the necessary technical means for them to achieve the minimal degree of dissociation required for the adoption of distortive suggestions? To answer this, we may look at a number of elements of the lesbian fire ceremony. First, it involves group participation which we know to be facilitative to dissociative trance. The groups are usually small in size, but we can still speak of a group effect that could make dissociation easier. Second, there is the fire which offers an excellent point of absorption. Continued staring into the flickering flames could readily promote trance entry, just as has been the case throughout much of human history.

The lesbian fire ceremony also involves a small amount of monotony in terms of the ritualistic group repetition of the names of the group members. This occurs when the whole group echoes the name of the group member after she fills in the goddess welcoming address with her own name. One could even regard the ritualistic throwing of branches into the fire as another monotonous element that could focus attention and foster absorption. Certainly, the above techniques are not ideal when contrasted with the far more efficacious trance-induction techniques seen in the socially sanctioned spiritual healing techniques of many non-Western societies. Yet they offer much more in this regard than the typical "sitting on the bench" therapies. Furthermore, we are tempted to speculate that they have the potential to foster the minimal dissociative reaction needed to make people override their critical faculties and to adopt distortive suggestions. Thus it is not inconceivable that, during these ceremonies, the lesbian clients actually believe in the goddess.

A somewhat different goddess-centered feminist healing ceremony is described by Janet Jacobs.[10] The clients are mostly victims of rape and physical assault, and the ceremony revolves around the catharsis of shared hostility. In addition to the goddess myth, a key aspect of the therapy process is the group ritual of egg throwing. Jacobs recounts the words of a rape victim who, with the help of the goddess and the other participants, was able to resolve some of her anger and pain. The following is a description given by the client:

> When we threw the eggs and shouted I felt my own anger come to the surface so strongly, so immediately there, and I was crying and I could see it there, coming with the other women too, and it felt like something you could reach out and touch, a really charged atmosphere. I could see this other woman's pain and feel the similarity between her pain and mine. . . . I guess there were two elements there, feeling the anger, feeling it come to the surface so quickly, and feeling in the larger sense that this is something all women have, that we all need to get out. . . .[11]

From this, we get the sense of someone overcome by more than a simple sense of catharsis. We also recognize in the woman's words the experience of ecstasy and oneness usually reserved for avid disciples of religion. The advantage of goddess therapies and other emerging spiritual therapies is that they draw on elements of religion in promoting the therapeutic process. The logic of such an approach is commendable in light of a theory that unites psychopathology and the workings of religion. Any disadvantages come from the fact that this type of religion-therapy does not fall within a clearly defined cultural context. The goddess belief, if it can be instilled, is not supported and reinforced by the culture at large. The therapy disciples remain deviant by virtue of their minority status and the healing effects are limited by whatever experience of deviance filters through from any source. In short, the spiritual therapies mentioned so far cannot be expected to compare favorably to therapeutic healing carried out within the context of a culture's dominant religion and its associated beliefs and rituals. This is despite the laudable efforts to build a therapeutic strategy on a foundation of myth and group ritual.

Ritualistic Healing Ceremonies

Additional trends in the direction of the spiritualization of psycho-therapy are discussed by Joyce Vespers.[12] She concentrates on the recently conceived ritualistic healing ceremonies that are sometimes used with people suffering from multiple personality disorder. This involves not only the primary personality but all the secondary, or alter, personalities as well. The aim, as stated by Vespers, is to cleanse the patient of the dissociated traumatic memories responsible for the original formation of the defensive dissociative symptoms. According to Vespers, the ceremony is usually devised on an individual basis, depending on the dynamics involved in each case.

As an illustration, Vespers cites the case of a multiple personality client whose disorder could be traced to her earlier involvement with a druidic cult called the Keltoi. While part of that cult, the client witnessed the horrific ritualistic murders of several male infants. The memories of these murders threatened to incapacitate her emotionally, which explains the adaptive dissociative splitting process that took the form of multiple personality disorder.

According to Vespers, the client chose to participate in the healing ceremony in hopes of breaking free of the memories of the cult. All the various secondary personalities became involved in the ceremonial procedure. Some secondary personalities had musical ability and were therefore instructed to select music for the ceremony. The core or "host" personality had poetic talent and agreed to prepare poetry readings for the ceremony. One of the personalities was religious, so it was given the task of writing an introduction that would be read at the opening of the ceremony. The personalities involved in the cult murders (and in possession of those memories) were instructed to bring to the ceremony all remaining objects and materials that related to the former cult practices. In this regard, while in those different personalities, the client was able to assemble a collection of stones, pine cones, wood, strings, and even some braids of hair from her deceased mother and grandmother who had also been Keltoi cult members.

The spiritual healing ceremony took place not in the therapist's office, but rather in a nearby park. Ralph Vaughan Williams's Symphony No. 5 was played on a tape. I feel that this was a good choice because sections of the symphony are deeply meditative and even "hypnotic," with a musical structure that can be compared in places to Thomas Tallis's famously dissociative music. A fire pit had been prepared ahead of time and all relevant objects were placed in the pit upon the arrival of the client and therapist. At that stage, the fire remained unlit. When all preparations were in order, the client began to speak in her "religious" personality. Part of the introduction included the following words:

> I want to separate myself from those people and their acts in a ceremony of cleansing. A small fire will burn, representing the burning away of evil that lingers within me. I want to burn mesquite, which represents cleanliness. . . . I will break a stone, definite action of my own free will, breaking all connection with the Keltoi . . . asking forgiveness, wholeness, guidance. I will become a new child, a spiritual infant, will experience spiritual birth. . . . I will become one with the moment, with the earth, with my feelings, and with God.[13]

As the client continued to speak, the therapist lit the ceremonial fire and the symbols of her traumatic past were incinerated. From Vespers's account, this use of ceremonial healing proved highly beneficial to the client and she continued on a course of personality integration allowing her to function more effectively and even to gain admission to a university with a full academic scholarship. Vespers states that the use of ceremony need not be as elaborate as the one described here. Even when they are simple in their construction, she says, they can be very helpful in resolving traumatic memories. More generally:

> Ceremony is effective because it is the vehicle by which the individual actively demonstrates an acknowledgement of past trauma and proclaims a willingness to seize health. . . . Each rite allows the person to take leave of the traumatic past while permitting the movement toward personal growth and freedom. . . . The use of ceremony and the understanding of the personal myth assist the client in reclaiming him/herself from a frightening, unsafe world.[14]

The therapies described above would strike many as poorly conceptualized and somewhat arbitrary in their use of spiritual elements. Despite their potential merits as psychotherapy strategies, it is true that they lack many essential components of their traditional non-Western counterparts. Yet I would not deny that these types of therapies could some day become the nucleus of a new class of psychotherapy responding to the religious nature of psychopathology. Such a trend could be fueled by the growing number of research findings showing that psychotherapy is more effective if it has a spiritual or religious component. This is especially the case when the client holds religious beliefs that can be exploited for therapeutic purposes.

In one of the best designed studies of its kind, L. Rebecca Propst and her colleagues analyzed the effectiveness of a group of religious psychotherapy clients.[15] She was especially interested in the popular therapy strategy known as cognitive-behavioral therapy. This technique concentrates on clients' cognitions (i.e., thoughts, or "self-talk") and attempts to bring about positive change by helping them to substitute a new set of cognitions for the original faulty set. Many cognitive-behavioral therapists prefer to view this technique as a process of replacing irrational beliefs with rational ones. An example would be Albert Ellis's Rational Emotive Therapy, a widely used form of cognitive-behavioral therapy.[16] It is worth mentioning here that Ellis himself is one of the most outspoken of therapists on the need to view religion as just another expression of irrational thinking that can lead to psychological problems.[17] As a result, it is not uncommon for therapists using this approach to openly challenge clients' religious beliefs and to actively encourage them to abandon those in favor of more rational and reality-based ones.

Propst gave a unique twist to cognitive-behavioral therapy by devising a version of it that incorporated a large amount of religious, or what we could also call *irrational*, content. This runs entirely counter to Ellis's cognitive-behavioral therapy, which views religion as an irrational mode of mental activity promoting psychopathology. In Propst's study, the effectiveness of the newly developed religious version of cognitive-behavioral therapy was compared to that of the ordinary approach that does not employ religious content. She found that the religious version significantly outperformed the standard one as measured by two tests of depression, and by measures of social adjustment and overall symptomatology.

The research investigation by Propst also involved religious as well as nonreligious therapists. The very worst therapy outcome was achieved by nonreligious therapists using the nonreligious version of cognitive-behavioral therapy. One major drawback of this particular piece of research is that it did not include a group of nonreligious psychotherapy clients. This would have permitted a comparison between religious and nonreligious clients. However, it must be remembered that the vast majority of people in a place like the United States (where Propst's study was conducted) do hold religious beliefs. This suggests that religiously imbued therapies like that of Propst should not be offensive to a great many clients. Of course, the deeper issue is that of the strength of these people's religious conviction. Another question to be asked is whether the particular religion still has enough social currency for its "magic" to be effective in a healing context. The answer in most cases is probably no. But, in theory at least, the inclusion of religious content makes a good deal of sense in light of the present argument that psychopathology itself is "individual religion" that falls outside of a cultural context. It follows quite clearly, then, that the client could benefit from a therapeutic exercise that sought to promote coping by tapping the resources of mainstream cultural religion. In this manner, many clients could relinquish their irrational private symptoms in favor of those that are irrational but outside the domain of psychopathology.

Let us consider further the Propst investigation and specifically the finding that the religious version of cognitive-behavioral therapy was more effective than the nonreligious in reducing depression. In the first chapter of this book I discussed the sizable body of research showing that depressed people tend to be more *in touch* with reality than nondepressed people. In fact, Propst's clients were selected for treatment on the basis of evidence of depression. Her religiously oriented therapy permitted the clients to entertain irrational constructions of the world and themselves. If out-of-touchness with reality is a defense against depression, then we would expect irrational interventions to promote a lifting of depression. This is exactly what was found in the Propst investigation and similar studies.[18] Also, this is perfectly consistent with the full range of research mentioned earlier in relation to Shelley Taylor's book *Positive Illusions*.[19] There she demonstrated unequivocally that the healthy mind is a *self-deceptive* one that thrives on illusion and misconstructions of reality.

Therapies that work toward the goal of adaptive self-deception should be much more effective than those seeking somehow to put people more in touch with reality. Herein lies the fundamental flaw with most modern therapies, especially those that openly espouse rational modes of cognition. The relatively superior performance of most traditional non-Western therapies is due to their basically irrational structure, which helps advantageously to remove people from reality. After all, reality is the usual culprit in emotional and psychological disturbance, as we know from research on this subject. One does not try to put out fires by throwing flammable liquids on them. Neither does one treat clients' personalized attempts to escape reality by throwing more reality at them.

In my estimation, therapists in the near future will take ever greater heed of the paradoxical foundations of mental health and mental disturbance. As this occurs, we will witness continued efforts to spiritualize psychotherapy, and regain part of the therapeutic magic that we have lost. More and more people will see the merits of introducing irrational methods into the therapy process. Again, the major obstacle will be the way in which religion has become marginalized in Western society. Traditional spiritual therapies work so well because the myths and rituals employed are still at the forefront of the culture. We may have on our hands more than a lot of sick people in Western culture. The culture itself may be sick and in desperate need of rejuvenation. Ultimately, this may prove more valuable than a search for better therapies for the individual client.

THE RELUCTANT RESURGENCE OF HYPNOTIC THERAPIES

As more and more forms of psychopathology are shown to be the result of the dissociation process, hypnosis is being prescribed as the treatment of choice. This is because of the close relationship between dissociation and hypnosis. We know from our previous discussion that formal "hypnotic" induction and suggestion techniques are but one of an endless number of ways in which dissociated states can be promoted and structured. In the previous chapter, research was discussed demonstrating that the symptoms of many types of mental disorders are constructed as a person embarks on a course of autodissociation and autosuggestion. In almost all cases, the researchers who have connected psychopathology with dissociation have gone on to hypothesize that hypnotherapy should hold advantages over conventional nontrance therapies.

The logic appears indisputable in terms of calls to employ hypnosis for disorders that are "hypnotic" or dissociative at heart. Furthermore, if Colin Ross is correct in his well-supported claim that most or all types of psychopathology are dissociative in nature, then we should continue to tout hypnosis as the best chance for bringing about positive behavior change.[20] Yet hypnosis has not lived up to its growing reputation as the treatment modality that should be able to compete with the psychopathologies that now appear to be dissociative in their design. Despite modest success rates using hypnosis, the clinical literature is littered with reports of "resistance" coming from psychotherapy clients. It is as if the therapeutic "hypnotic" trance cannot compete easily with the deeply ingrained autodissociative trance underpinning the pathological symptoms.

On one level, it seems surprising that a client should resist the well-intentioned efforts of the psychotherapist. The therapist is there to alleviate the client's suffering and to promote better coping. Yet resistance is frequently encountered by therapists, including those who make use of formal hypnosis. One explanation for this resistance is pertinent to all therapies and almost all forms of psychopathology. This has to do with the purpose and value of the symptoms themselves. I have given numerous examples of symptom patterns that function to constrict a person's awareness and thereby distort reality in such a way that other problems and issues are pushed out of immediate awareness. Dissociation plays a crucial role in this process as otherwise trivial matters or objects become overvalued and magnified in importance. The person comes to believe the unbelievable as the symptoms dominate his or her entire experience of reality. As painful and debilitating as these symptoms can be, they are strategic personalized attempts to cope with perceived threats.

Removing the symptoms can be as threatening to the individual as the actual factors that led to the original formation of the symptoms. Competent therapists are continually alert to this fact. On this subject, Mordecai Kaffman discusses the potential hazards of "successful" therapy.[21] In referring to the adaptive value of paranoid symptoms, Kaffman describes the dangerous personal and existential vacuum that can result when the paranoid delusions are taken away. It would be nearly comparable to a situation in which someone stripped away someone's religious beliefs and rituals without consideration for alternative mental constructions that could supplant the void. Therefore, it is understandable that many clients in therapy feel an inexplicable urge to defend their psychopathology. I have seen this many times in working with clients with eating disorders and I am confident that most therapists would report similar experiences. Indeed, this would be expected regardless of the type of psychotherapy employed.

In explaining further the surprisingly mediocre results obtained from the therapeutic use of hypnosis, we must take into account the actual structure of the symptoms. The reason that research shows higher levels of dissociation to be associated with many disorders is that these patients have manufactured their symptoms through the use of dissociative trance and autosuggestion. This means that they are *already* in a state very closely resembling the dissociative states that are facilitated through formal hypnotic procedures. Their dissociative capabilities and suggestibility are already bound up in the form of the pattern of defensive symptoms. Consequently, even though clients may be demonstrating a greater capacity for dissociation, the hypnotherapist finds him/herself unable to exploit it for therapeutic purposes. If we may compare this predicament to religion, it would be as if you were attempting to convert to one religion someone who had recently been converted to an entirely different religion. Superficially, it might seem that you had a good chance of success since the person already has large amounts of religious capacity. Yet the reality would be that the already converted would be inaccessible, their religious capabilities being already bound up in an existing set of religious constructions. In the same way, many psychotherapy clients are inaccessible to hypnotic techniques even though they are themselves indulging in dissociative or "hypnotic" practices.

Still another reason for the limited therapeutic value of hypnosis has to do with the previously mentioned fact that hypnosis as a trance device lacks a recognizable cultural context. The void to which Mordecai Kaffman alluded has little chance of being filled if the person's culture does not feature in treatment offering alternative constructions (or misconstructions) of reality. Also, we saw that the specific techniques themselves are inadequate to instill in most people the depth of dissociative trance needed when attempting to eliminate psychopathology. In *Wings of Illusion*, I made the case that Western psychotherapy is in urgent need of a new set of treatment strategies that are far more powerful than hypnosis in its present form.[22] Only then can we hope to successfully compete with the dissociative trances that the clients themselves are maintaining of their own accord. But I also mentioned the need for any new dissociation-based therapies to fall within some sort of cultural context. As I noted, there is no obvious way to do this in our current climate of secularization. Hypnosis, both as an induction technique and a method for delivering suggestions, stands outside the realm of cultural meaning. The same problem would be present if a more amplified version of this method were developed. A partial solution is to locate already existing areas of cultural meaning and attempt to build the techniques around those.

Salish Spirit Dancing

An interesting example is given by anthropologist Wolfgang Jilek,[23] who describes the traditional "spirit dancing" of the Salish-speaking Indians of the Pacific Coast of North America. In past ages, this ritualistic healing procedure was used successfully in the restoration of the mental, physical, and social health of the Salish people. In more recent times, much of Salish culture underwent a process of deterioration. But the spirit dancing technique was kept alive by some of the elders. In 1967, amidst renewed interest in preserving Salish culture, spirit dancing was actively revived and reinstated as an accepted therapeutic technique. As Jilek observes, its use has been extended well beyond its former boundaries and can now be used to treat some "modern" afflictions such as alcoholism and "anomic depression." Spirit dancing is also employed for a wide range of other psychological disorders.

The effectiveness of spirit dancing is probably due to the fact that it still has a basis within the larger culture, even though considerable cultural erosion has occurred. The technique itself would have to be classified as "religious," since it is founded on beliefs in traditional spirits and since the rituals correspond to these religious beliefs. Spirit dancing revolves around a death-rebirth myth. As Jilek points out, the suggestions offered to dissociated patients have death and rebirth as their central theme. Supernatural powers are understood by the participants to be responsible for the "death" and spiritual/psychological "rebirth" that transpires as a consequence of treatment.

As a nativistic method of psychotherapy, spirit dancing contains most elements that should ensure a high degree of success. First, it includes a mechanism which allows patients to enter a deep dissociative trance. As we know, this is vital in order for the critical and analytic thought processes to become suspended. If this is done correctly, patients will become susceptible to suggestions even if their own psychopathology is the result of trance. That is, much stronger dissociative trance can eventually override patients' private trance. The way the Salish healer forces upon patients a deep state of dissociation is by isolating them in a dark "smokehouse tent" for a period of between four and ten days, and sometimes even longer. We saw earlier that sensory deprivation of this sort is a trance-instilling technique seen in vast numbers of healing practices throughout the non-Western world.

The prolonged sensory deprivation is interrupted occasionally as patients are required to engage in very strenuous exercise. Physical exhaustion of this sort is also known to be useful toward the goal of dissociative trance. In Salish theory, this portion of the treatment process is viewed as a form of "torture" that serves to "depattern" patients, thereby making them amenable to subsequent reorientation or reindoctrination. Jilek quotes one Salish participant who comments:

> It is an Indian treatment, it is a kind of brainwashing. . . . Through this torture they soften up, their brains get soft. During that time you're the weakest and *your brain is back to nil,* anything you're taught during those ten days is going to stick with you, you'll never forget it.[24]

Some of the "torture" exercises that are imposed on patients during the depatterning phase would strike many people as extreme and even cruel by contrast to conservative Western therapies. These may even include starvation and fluid restriction, immobilization with physical constraints, blindfolding, tickling and hitting, teasing, and intensive acoustic stimulation. In this last strategy, loud repetitive drumming and rattling music is played in rapid rhythms for long periods of time. This is usually combined with howling and singing close to patients' ears. Eight so-called workers continue to depattern patients in this way, only terminating the procedure when the patient has been "grabbed." Once grabbed, patients have usually entered a deep dissociative trance.

Cultural therapeutics take over at this stage. Patients begin to hallucinate and the vacuous dissociated state is filled with their own "song" and "dance." In "a state between sleep-dream and wakefulness," as Jilek puts it, patients are even able to hallucinate unique face paintings that will be reserved for them alone. A guardian spirit also appears to them in the dark cubicle and helps each "get his song straight."[25] The "song" that comes to patients is certainly a *cultural* song in the respect that their culture has made available certain expectations giving structure to the dissociative state. This is very different from the Western hypnotic subject who lacks clear culturally transmitted expectations that help to reconstruct the dissociated state. Patients typically break into spontaneous dance and song and these, too, are culturally patterned.

As a healing procedure, spirit dancing operates in a manner similar to its original role as a method of initiation into Salish culture. Patients who find for the first time the "song" and the "dance" are regarded as "babies" who need to be filled with knowledge. Therefore, intense indoctrination is a major part of this healing technique. This includes the teaching of the rules of spirit power, the giving of examples of the magical works of spirit power, and the telling of traditional folk lore. The newly emerged "dancers" are instilled with a strong sense of responsibility and respect for tribal elders. If drug addiction has been a major reason for the spirit dancing procedure, the indoctrination phase would include suggestions to the effect that the reborn individual will no longer indulge in the problematic drug or drugs. Indoctrinating suggestions can also be tailored to whatever other problems or disorders are affecting patients. Jilek writes that, as a result of this "therapeutic brainwashing," each patient "sheds the last vestiges of his old personality as the snake sloughs off its old skin."[26] Culturally meaningful suggestions then permit a transformation that includes personality reconstruction and different motivations consistent with culturally defined goals. The technique is so powerful that any private dissociative reactions in the form of psychopathology give way to the well-conceived strategies making up the spirit dancing technique.

We see in the above description an example of culture as a coping mechanism that plays an important role in the therapeutic process. However, it is a unique situation in many respects since there is considerable tradition attached to the myths and rituals allowing for successful "brainwashing" and reconstruction of reality. We know that Western psychotherapy is largely devoid of myth and that it flounders terribly in its application of healing rituals. Such a situation is a mirror image of the depletion of myth and ritual in general in the West. Throughout much of human history, socially sanctioned healing systems have intervened in order to give positive bias to those in need. This has been done by taking advantage of recognized myth-ritual complexes that are embedded into the culture. When members of these societies fell prey to the need for more reality distortion, they could be treated by the myths and rituals that were there for the purpose of misconstruing reality in *normal* ways. Usually this was all done within the broad context of religion. Through this procedure, people could be prevented from becoming isolated in private psychopathological maneuvers. Or, they could be brought back from private psychopathology, as was illustrated by the Salish spirit dancing.

Charisma as a Therapeutic Tool

Looking objectively at Western psychotherapy, one sees that, instead of culturally intact myth-ritual complexes, there is only *charisma* to serve as a basis for therapeutic change. Usually this is the charisma of the therapist, and often there is only very little of that. Thus there is additional emphasis placed on the dubious and frequently alien therapy techniques themselves. Max Weber has defined charisma as "a certain quality of an individual personality by virtue of which he is considered extraordinary and treated as endowed with supernatural, superhuman or at least specifically exceptional powers or qualities."[27] It is well known that the effectiveness of "faith healing" is often the result of the charisma of the religious leader. In this respect, it may be said that charisma can sometimes substitute partially for the absence of preexisting religious myths, or myths that have undergone some erosion of credibility.

As Charles Lindholm has observed, personal charisma is sometimes capable of permitting subjects to enter into altered states of consciousness that involve a total neutralization of the general reality orientation.[28] They may become capable of believing and acting in accordance with even the most irrational and nonsensical of messages or ideas that spring forth from the charismatic leader. Without much in the way of credible myths, Western psychotherapists are more reliant than they sometimes realize on their own charisma. Moreover, they are deluding themselves when they think that their specific therapy techniques are the driving force behind the change process.

According to Max Weber, charisma emerges within a society when traditions have been lost and when people are no longer inspired to follow old patterns. Today, we are surrounded by the signs of the breakdown of tradition, including religion. Our contemporary Western world is thus a fertile environment for the appearance of charismatic figures. However, most of these have earned their charisma because of their status as celebrities, or as the products of an industry of consumption. Being part of a somewhat closed system, psychotherapists typically do not have the type of exposure that allows them to muster substantial amounts of charisma. Therefore, with some exceptions, a realistic appraisal of our current situation reveals that most psychotherapists do not enjoy a degree of charisma that can compensate for the dearth of myths in modern psychotherapy.

It is no wonder that studies occasionally surface showing that completely untrained people are as effective (and sometimes more effective) than fully qualified and experienced psychotherapists. Contemporary psychotherapy is so impoverished in all crucial areas that we must ask if modern society has any real system of healing available to it. The enormous proliferation of ill-conceived therapies is cause for further concern in this regard. Estimates of the number of different psychotherapies that now exist go as high as 450, with that number increasing all the time. Behind this rush of largely experimental therapies lies, unfortunately, the same ineffectiveness pervading current psychotherapeutic methods. This again stands in stark contrast to traditional cultures in which there is one and only one cure—where everyone knows about the cure since it is usually embodied as an aspect of religious belief, and where everyone knows that it works. Therefore, since no one ever doubts the potency of the treatment, it rarely fails to deliver relief. Regrettably, our current psychotherapeutic methods have drifted away from the dominant cultural belief systems and their associated rituals, leaving a great deal of doubt and suspicion in their place. Understandably, clients frequently continue to resist therapeutic efforts, since nothing awaits them in the form of cultural coping that could replace their maladaptive improvised coping attempts.

HEALING A SICK SOCIETY

Earlier I discussed Joseph Campbell's astute observation that the modern Western world has fallen out of "form," especially with regard to its inability to respond to the spiritual and transcendental needs of the populace. Campbell is not alone in this view. Anthropologist Raoul Naroll has also written about the concept of the "sick society," tracing this in part to the breakdown of traditional myth and ritual systems.[29] This matter is also taken up in Erich Fromm's classic work *The Sane Society*, which depicts Western culture as so sick that its members are figuratively dead and suffering from a *normal* type of pathology."[30] Fromm elaborates on the preeminent role played by culture in determining the health or illness of individual members of the culture:

> Mental health cannot be defined in terms of the "adjustment" of the individual to his society, but, on the other hand, that it must be defined in terms of the adjustment of the society to the needs of man, of its role in furthering or hindering the development of mental health. Whether or not the individual is healthy, is primarily not an individual matter, but depends on the structure of his society.[31]

Fromm informs us that one main reason for our present state of collective and individual "insanity" is that the old myths and gods have been replaced with spiritually barren quests for possessions: "in the nineteenth century the problem was that *God is dead*; in the twentieth century the problem is that *man is dead*."[32]

The "death of God" phenomenon has been blamed, with good reason, for many of the social and psychological ills afflicting people today. It appears that the majority cannot live without myth and reality distortion. The events in the former Soviet Union attest to the tenacity and strength of the human drive for a translated version of reality. After decades of active suppression of religious belief and practice, citizens of the former Soviet states were finally given free rein to indulge their religious yearnings. When this happened, it became highly apparent that the government had been largely unsuccessful in eradicating religion. Undoubtedly a certain number of atheists were produced by antireligious propaganda. In many instances, however, the all-powerful State itself, along with its ideologies or myths, satisfied some religious needs. Even so, we see today in the former Soviet Union a dramatic return to conventional religion. Beyond that, we also see there an unprecedented gravitation toward every conceivable category of paranormal belief and practice. Many of the new devotees of the paranormal and quasireligious are young people whose needs for transcendence had not been quelled by political indoctrination. Deprived of orthodox religious outlets, they are clearly seeking expression of these needs as they embrace aspects of the paranormal now flourishing in the former USSR.

Even renowned skeptic Paul Kurtz expresses doubts about the majority of humanity's ability to live without irrational and distortive constrictions of reality. In seeking to answer the important question of whether or not we can live without myths, Kurtz concedes that he has been struck by "the dogged persistence of human irrationality. . . . I have found that irrational beliefs are not necessarily deviant aberrations but perhaps the norm inasmuch as they are so widely held."[33] Most of human history has witnessed irrationality as the norm, with religion as a total way of life. Through the workings of our capacity for dissociation, the unreal has been able to coexist with the real, and thereby provide many social and intrapersonal benefits.

Never before in our history have so many been sorely deprived of an avenue to dissociated consciousness and the cultural dissemination of culturally patterned distortive suggestions that construct reality. Entire societies can be seen groping for more in the way of activities and practices that offer the opportunity to exploit their natural reality-biasing capabilities. This need has spilled over into religion, where we see an understandable migration toward religious-induction procedures with technically more sophisticated dissociative trance-induction methods. Some striking examples of this may be observed in Brazil, where large numbers of people are abandoning

Catholicism and gravitating toward some of the many high-energy charismatic religions that continue to spring up there. This same trend can be seen within other Western societies where membership is shifting toward revivalistic and Pentecostal types of religion.

Despite people's attempts to satisfy their basic cravings for the fruits of cognitive dissociation and distortive suggestions, we are left with the sad truth that Western culture is "sick," lacking in "form," and thus unable to respond like other cultures in former ages. As E. O. Wilson points out in *On Human Nature*, post-ideological societies such as our own tend to regress steadily toward *inward self-indulgence*.[34] This is the result of the rapid dissolution of *transcendent* goals around which entire cultures can organize their energies. Wilson discusses the prospect of establishing a "new morality based on a more truthful definition of man," one that would require us to retrace our evolutionary history.[35] Since many of our social and individual problems are the consequence of the collapse of transcendent ideology, I have often wondered whether it would be possible somehow to repair the damage. Culture has always been the intended architect of reality. Therefore, the act of revitalizing a sick and insane society would need to be one that exerted its influence at the level of society.

We know from Erich Fromm's theory of *cultural patterning* that even the most ludicrous and blatantly erroneous ideas can become accepted as unquestionably true.[36] Not only that, this phenomenon causes those who are not deviant to experience themselves as such if they do not accept the deviant proposition of the majority. Thus there is continual social pressure on individual members of the group to adopt the socially patterned beliefs regardless of their validity. Obviously, this helps to explain the dominance of religion, as well as the many secular forms of madness that have swayed entire societies of people. What Hitler did by brainwashing his countrymen is not unlike the persuasive "hypnotic" methods employed by certain great religious leaders in the past. Hitler's message was evil, but few observers would disagree that his methods were effective. In fact, he has often been referred to as an exceptionally gifted group hypnotist. One is left to ask if equally impressive amounts of good could be achieved by similar deployments of mass dissociation and suggestion techniques. We might pose the question: Is it possible to create a new religion superior in most respects to the current weak religions that fail to meet our needs for transcendence?

In *The Sane Society*, Erich Fromm explores the possibile development of a new religion in the foreseeable future that could help to rehabilitate our currently insane and godless society. He states that "it is not too far-fetched to believe that a new religion will develop . . . which corresponds to the development of the human race."[37] In Fromm's mind, cultural insanity exists in the form of "idolatry"— in our case, the worship of the modern idols of consumerism and entertainment. This is consistent with the previously mentioned view of E. O. Wilson, who also understands our mindless self-indulgence and overconsumption in light of the loss of ideology in the West.

Fromm regards contemporary idolatry as a major cause of the alienation and anomie pervading the "insane" masses in Western society. But Fromm does not concern himself with the truth or falsity of the religious systems that could restore our ability to meet our basic need for reality transcendence. The main consideration is whether or not religion *works* in order to combat our current cultural lapse into insanity. In this respect, Fromm does not discount the potential value of revitalizing "humanistic" religions such as Christianity and Judaism in hopes of countering our insidious idolatry. At the same time, he speculates that theistic religions are becoming obsolete under prevailing social conditions. Yet Fromm in no way suggests that religion or people's quest for transcendence will ever disappear; he merely theorizes that the theistic forms of religion will give way to those with a different structure and complexion.

On the topic of a new religion, Fromm makes the following comments:

> . . . The most important feature of such a religion would be its universalistic character, corresponding to the unification of mankind which is taking place in this epoch; it would embrace the humanistic teachings common to all great religions of the East and of the West; its doctrines would not contradict the rational insight of mankind today, and its emphasis would be on the practice of life, rather than on doctrinal beliefs. Such a religion would create new rituals and artistic forms of expression, conducive to the spirit of reverence toward life and the solidarity of man.[38]

Unlike some social philosophers who also deal with the issue of a new religion, Fromm maintains that religions are not readily invented. Instead, people must wait until "the time is ripe" and also until a great teacher acts as the cornerstone for the foundation of the new religion.[39] This is where I feel that Fromm's ideas are outdated in terms of present-day methods of mass persuasion, including techniques that could greatly facilitate dissociation and suggestibility while paving the way for the adoption of new beliefs. Also, there is plenty of evidence that new religions are not difficult to concoct and that followers are not difficult to find. Anthony Wallace has written about religion as a revitalization process while observing how new religions appear in abundance when the culture has become disorganized.[40] As illustrations, he cites the many novel religions that sprang up so frequently in "primitive" societies once those societies became fractured as a result of contact with European civilization.

In Wallace's words, new religious beliefs and practices

> always originate in situations of social and cultural stress and are, in fact, an effort on the part of the stress-laden to construct systems of dogma, myth, and ritual which are internally coherent as well as true descriptions of a world system and which thus will serve as guides to efficient action.[41]

When a culture is under stress, new religions can arise quite readily with only a modicum of effort. To illustrate this point, Wallace offers the example of a religion begun in 1799 by the Iroquois Indians of New York State. The initiative for composing the myths and rituals of the religion was taken by Handsome Lake, an Iroquois chief whose life was dominated by excessive alcohol consumption. Social and personal problems were common among the Iroquois culture of that period. The culture itself had experienced great stress as a result of several factors, including the British victory in the French and Indian War. Also, the American Revolution had resulted in the burning of Iroquois villages and considerable dispersion of their people. Their lands were confiscated and they themselves were confined to various types of small slumlike reservations. The situation continued to deteriorate until Handsome Lake made public the revelations of the word of God, known to this day as the *Code of Handsome Lake*.

Describing the history of this new religion, Wallace states that Handsome Lake's revelations "sped like a golden arrow, dispelling darkness and gloom."[42] This is despite the fact that the sacred message had some highly threatening elements. For example, Handsome Lake told his would-be disciples that heavenly messengers had warned him of complete world annihilation if the Iroquois did not become new people. This required them to forego alcohol and interpersonal antagonism, as well as the witchcraft beliefs and practices that had become prevalent in that spiritually bankrupt environment. Handsome Lake claimed to have a succession of visions, each prescribing a new code of living. Some featured new rituals that must be followed, while others contained theological content that eventually forged new religious beliefs. A number of heavenly messages were highly practical, specifying, for example, that the Iroquois should adopt European methods of agriculture, that they should learn to read and write English, and that marriages should be kept intact. In summarizing Handsome Lake's visionary prescriptions, Wallace states:

> His code was a blueprint of a culture that would be socially and technologically more effective in the new circumstances of reservation life than the old culture could ever have been.[43]

The new religion set up by the Iroquois chief met with great success. The Code of Handsome Lake became the focal point for a church that sought to perpetuate the beliefs and ritualistic practices that had their roots in Handsome Lake's original revelations. Many of these have undergone further evolution and continue to be practiced to this day. Some have even become the rationale for formal religious holidays, an example being the Strawberry Rite. At one point in the early formation of the religion, Handsome Lake identified strawberry juice as a substance possessing strong spiritual powers. He said that the sacred juice of the strawberry could bring about miraculous physical and emotional healing. This "revealed truth" came to be celebrated during the annual Strawberry Rite, with buckets of strawberry juice handed around to the members of the congregation. The ceremony, which also persists to this day, includes the recitation of words that are attributed to Handsome Lake. At one stage, a sacred meal was incorporated into the ceremony, which identified certain foods as supernatural and virtuous in nature. Other foods were deemed to be profane and in need of purifying by a blessing ritual. This illustrates how religions become increasingly elaborated and embellished over time. Frequently this happens to the extent of obscuring their humble origins. The Iroquois religion introduced by Handsome Lake has become elaborated in many impressive ways, including the introduction of public confession as a mechanism for encouraging self-control.

The many other developments in this religion are beyond the scope of the present discussion. The main reason for highlighting it here is to describe the relative ease with which new religions can be established when cultures are stressed and in need of revitalization. In this regard, one must again question Fromm's view that religions cannot be invented in calculated ways. In actuality, this happens with remarkable regularity in our pressurized and "insane" society. Furthermore, the reason it does happen so often is exactly because society is under great strain. For evidence of this we need only consider the worrisome increase in violence and social ills of all sorts, as well as the mental health crisis in which we currently find ourselves.

Ernest Becker is one of the few concerned scholars who has projected his imagination sufficiently in order to foresee new spiritual directions for modern society. He acknowledges that many of our current myths are destructive ones that are in immediate need of revision. Becker's ideas rest on the well-reasoned premise that most human beings will continue to succumb to the irrational. This can be seen when he observes that "man must live in a lie to live at all."[44] Yet, for Becker, this does not mean that we must remain passive with regard to the myths and rituals that we embrace. He even refers to the importance of choosing intelligent and well-conceived myths as we strive to improve our sick society. In Becker's view, this can be done without relinquishing the bias and reality distortion that allows us to operate within reality. Becker even alludes to an ideal religion when he asks "What is the nature of the obsessive denials of reality that a utopian society will provide to keep men from going mad?"[45] In *Escape from Evil*, he adds:

> If illusions are needed, how can we have those that are capable of correction, and how can we have those that will not deteriorate into delusions? If men live in myths and not absolutes, there is nothing we can do or say about that. But we can argue for non-destructive myths; this is the task of what would be a *general science of society*.[46]

In Becker's revolutionary and exciting general science of society, citizens would allow themselves to analyze the requirements of the individual and society and then prescribe a beneficial blend of fact and fiction. Recalling what has been said already about dissociation theory, it does not matter that we know the truth about our myths, or "lies." As we saw, even the most staunch believer in distortive constructs of reality is also privy to the information that precludes such belief. Myths become possible as errant information is temporarily allocated to cognitive pathways that bypass consciousness. Thus we are not aware that we *are* aware of the falsity of our truths. In this light, the door is open to take seriously Becker's general science of society, even though its pursuit treads on many delicate areas, including people's present religious beliefs.

Mary Maxwell has written about religion as a cultural universal. She observes that, in this century, communism has been the most conspicuous religion phenomenon. This is despite the fact that communism is usually thought of as a political rather than a religious movement. Yet, Maxwell argues:

> . . . an ideology such as communism calls upon the same psychological and social underpinnings and predispositions as does religion. The list of features . . . includes: reification, commitment, myth, blind faith, indoctrinability, sacralization, obedience to authority, masochism, righteousness, superiority, prophetism, tribalism, identification of evils and outside threats, and demands for doctrinal purity.[47]

Maxwell is certainly correct in describing communism as a religious movement in many crucial respects. But recent historical events have exposed some of the fundamental weaknesses in that particular system of beliefs and practices. Also, its many destructive elements have shown it to be less than an ideal vehicle for reality transcendence, as well as less than an ideal prescription for social and psychological health. Ernest Becker, in his bold work *The Revolution in Psychiatry*, envisioned a "post-psychiatric" age when neurosis would be conquered by intelligent adjustments at the level of cultural reality. Some of Becker's ideas in that book went far astray as he exaggerated the powers of love, not unlike the core mistake in the otherwise brilliant theoretical career of Erich Fromm. For example, Becker agrees with Fromm's definition of love as "the other path to knowing the secret" while he himself takes the highly romantic position that "love is superbly counter-fictional."[48] In that, Becker seems to be saying that love reduces the need for reality transcendence, a theoretical stance lacking substantiation at all levels. That aside, Becker is able to show us that the optimal cultural situation exists when the right type and content of "symbolic fiction" is infused with reality.[49] When this is not achieved, tension will manifest in psychopathology, social ills, and a pathetic appetite for whatever reality transcendence can be managed by the individual.

Some Prescriptions for the Future

The playwright Eugene O'Neill, despite his own unbelief, was intrigued by the possible social directions that might be taken in response to "the death of the old God and the failure of science and materialism to give any satisfying new one for the surviving primitive religious instinct."[50] O'Neill went on to describe the extreme importance of dealing with this issue by artists such as himself: "It seems to me that anyone trying to do big work nowadays must have this subject behind all the little subjects . . . or he is simply scribbling around the surface of things."[51] The same challenge could be given to social scientists who profess a desire to make a real difference in these times of social and personal trouble. Becker's call for a *general science of society* requires that we take some responsibility for the manufacture of new myths and rituals that can counteract what O'Neill saw as "the death of the old God." Psychotherapy has failed dismally toward this end and shows no signs of filling the void.

Naturally, ethical and moral issues arise when one suggests the manufacture and marketing of a new and more functional *obsessive denial of reality*, as Becker termed it. At the same time, Theodore Roszak states in *Unfinished Animal*, there is an urgent need for *new centers of consensus* that could function as religions once did in former ages.[52] He points out that, as we survey our current religious status, "we have a terrible measure of how degraded the spiritual life of modern Western society has become."[53] This situation, according to Roszak, stands in contrast to former human cultures that were rooted deeply in transcendent myth and magic and thus capable of fostering a "higher sanity."

Roszak's thinking is overly influenced by the potential for psychotherapy to assume some of the previous roles of religion. This is unlikely to occur given the scattered, disunified, and directionless character of psychotherapy today. But Roszak must be commended for his courageous attempt to specify the founding elements of a new cultural religion, and what he terms our "next reality."[54] Furthermore, some of these elements appear to be well-reasoned and worthwhile aspects of any emerging religion in replacing current religions that have undergone decay. For instance, Roszak speaks on behalf of the need to construct a new religion that is eclectic, generic, and *universal*. Such a religion should, he argues, take into account "the many means that the visionary genius of our species has invented to achieve transcendence," and then strive for "planetary consensus," or what he also calls a convergent "symposium of the whole."[55]

There seems to be considerable value in another proposed attribute of Roszak's new religion and "next reality," namely, the *illumination of the commonplace*.[56] This particular suggestion should cause us to realize that the reality generated by our myths and illusions does not need to be destructive. It has an equal potential to operate in positive and adaptive ways. But our existing myths threaten us from all sides. Possibly the most dangerous of all is the nearly ubiquitous modern myth that accelerating production and ever-increasing consumption will transform life for the better. In *The Triumph of the Therapeutic*, Phillip Reiff exposes this as a mutant new religious motivation that seeks to answer all questions with the answer "more."[57] Like Fromm, who depicts the West as filled with disciples of the religion of *Having*, Reiff goes on to say that this destructive type of religion is difficult to oppose since it stands for nothing. Those faithful followers of "more," according to Reiff, are nothing other than islands of private religion. Competition and greed are the backbone of this religion, and these are among the small number of contact points between these islands of dysfunctional faith. On these islands, says Reiff, any regard for quality has been overshadowed by the myth of quantity. Magical properties have been associated with people who excel at acquisition and consumption.

Our sickly religion of Having is understandable as we analyze the social structure of modern identity. Philip Cushman, recounting recent historical developments, concludes with the emergence in the West of what he calls the "empty self."[58] The self, as Cushman defines it, is an artifact of a person's culture. On this, he writes in the spirit of Martin Heidegger:

> Human beings are incomplete and therefore unable to function adequately unless embedded in a specific cultural matrix. Culture "completes" humans by explaining and interpreting the world, helping them to focus their attention on or ignore certain aspects of their environment, and instructing and forbidding them to think and act in certain ways. . . . Culture is not indigenous clothing that covers the universal human; it infuses individuals, fundamentally shaping and forming them and how they conceive of themselves and the world, how they see others, how they engage in structures of mutual obligation, and how they make choices in the everyday world. . . . Cultural artifacts . . . shape and mold the community's general reality orientation in subtle and unseen ways.[59]

In particular, the self is sculpted from the *shared understandings* that materialize as a consequence of various historical factors. In premodern times, culture "completed" the self through the weaving of shared understandings into a collective religion that preoccupied the mental world of its members. More recently in the West, however, the locus of meaning has shifted more and more to the individual. Cushman theorizes that people born into our current impoverished cultural climate have the experience of being an "empty self" that needs filling. But culture is no longer there to "fill" us and to create an identity within the context of the *shared* understandings of the group. Thus, in their inner emptiness, people are constantly hungry for anything that can help to fill the self. This filling process is never completed and people are inclined to engage compulsively in a process of consumption.

In its quest to be "filled up," Cushman continues, the self becomes

> . . . aggressively, sometimes desperately, acquisitive. It must consume in order to be soothed and integrated; it must "take in" and merge with a self-object celebrity, an ideology, or a drug, or it will be in danger of fragmenting into feelings of worthlessness and confusion. . . . The individual has become a consumer who seeks, desperately, to buy. . . . It is a kind of mimicry of traditional culture for a society that has lost its own—a pseudoculture that promises an instant, illusory cure, a "transformation."[60]

Yet we know that any and all transformation emanating from the pseudoculture and pseudoreligion of consumption is fruitless and destructive. It is disorienting and alienating at the level of the individual and counterproductive at the planetary level. So we can return to Roszak's recommendation that a well-designed new religion should contain the myth that simplicity and the ordinary are ultimately important and worthy of worship. A strategically introduced new religion of tomorrow would need to actively combat and reverse the social phenomenon that witnesses our sad efforts to fill the empty self. As part of this, the *opposite* of mindless acquisition and indiscriminate consumption would need to be heralded as a great virtue whose meaning *transcends* any meaning that could be comprehended in earthly reality.

If we accept that a new and technologically sound religion can correct many of our present ills, then there seems good reason to push ahead with such a venture despite the outrage that might be incurred. We might even be surprised at how little resistance is encountered as we proceed. The desperate situation in the West may resemble the conditions among the Iroquois that enabled Handsome Lake to pull a new religion out of a hat and have it received with open arms. While the prospect of concocting a new religion is understandably offensive to many, it may also be true that a great opportunity exists to exploit our religious instincts to great advantage.

Standing back to survey our global circumstances, we are faced with some terrifying realities, which may or may not be correctable. All indications suggest that humankind is racing toward an ecological cul-de-sac. We may exercise awesome intelligence on small-scale levels, but we exhibit almost no intelligence at the species level.

If we think of our entire species as a single organism, it appears to be a blind and brainless one with no ability to reverse direction from its current collision course with extinction.

Maybe this is where my own madness reveals itself, but let me follow this line of thought a bit further. Scientists have estimated that, given our present levels of technology, the planet can tolerate only one and a half billion human beings. With numbers greater than that, we accelerate our relentless assault on the delicate ecological subsystems keeping us alive. Yet the human population continues to soar, with scientists further predicting that the world population will plateau in one hundred years or so at an Earth-killing eighteen billion people. If we could snap our collective fingers and reach zero population growth today, our current six billion human beings would still prove too much of a burden for the planet. Simple logic tells us that something far-reaching must be done soon if we are to safeguard the future of our species. The measures must be so potent and effective that we significantly *reduce* the population from its present level.

We hear daily stories about rising ocean levels, tornadoes in places where they should not occur, overradiated sheep wearing sunglasses in southern Chile, and entire species of frogs disappearing almost overnight. A large number of *individuals* have become aware of the impending disaster. At the same time, no evidence of species-level intelligence has manifested itself and we blunder ahead inflexibly, continuing to promote with enthusiasm the same values and goals that represent our doom. Developing countries all over the world are clamoring to become more industrialized, and the health of entire economies are still evaluated in relation to their ability to "grow." People are encouraged as much as ever, and maybe even more so, to consume and to value enterprises that push us even closer to our collective grave. While the planet-saving efforts by individuals and small groups are certainly commendable, they are regrettably insignificant when judged against the enormous momentum pulling us ever closer to the edge of extinction. Rational considerations of our drastic plight seem to make very little difference. Irrational forces, on the other hand, seem to have more capacity to sway human behavior.

In this latter regard, we could look at religion's influence on human population. Catholicism comes to mind as one of several possible examples of religions containing dictates that affect people's motivation to reproduce. Worldwide, hundreds of millions of human beings (including myself) have been produced as a direct result of the Catholic belief that it is a punishable offense against God to use effective contraception. Over time, those millions will themselves reproduce and become billions, thus jeopardizing even more our collective fate.

Phillip Adams, a well-known Australian columnist and radio broadcaster, as well as a high-profile atheist, recently commented on the destruction caused by religion over the ages. God, he states:

> is the starting point for the biggest, cruellest bureaucracies on earth, not to mention thousands of years of pogroms, wars, cruelties and inquisitions. . . . All things considered, it is really an enormous relief to be an atheist.[61]

While Adams is correct with regard to these accusations, it would be misleading to think that religion could not be steered toward desired outcomes. If a religion can succeed in indoctrinating people in such a way that they are compelled to have children, it should also be capable of inducing people not to have children. Doing without children could quite easily be molded into a religious virtue. Ritualistic ceremonies revolving around the celebration of God's will in the form of population control could make abundant use of well-planned religious dissociation and suggestion techniques, including repetitive arrhythmic drumming, absorption, eye tracking, dance, and other monotony-inducing devices. If that sounds insane, let us remind ourselves that religious insanity is the historical hallmark of our species. Moreover, these beliefs and any related rituals would cease to be bizarre once they became codified as religion.

The beauty of a religious belief discouraging its followers from further populating the planet is that the belief would be aligned with the actual reality in which we find ourselves. More than anything else, we must immediately initiate measures to reduce the population of human beings living on this planet. A new religion might be the best way to do this. To treat a person as holy for sacrificing the chance to have children is to make that individual holy for acting in accordance with earthly reality. Furthermore, unlike traditional religious beliefs, which are false by definition, this particular belief would be *true*.

We might ask ourselves at this stage if a true religious belief could survive. If not, then we can forget about the lofty prospect of constructing a religion that could save us from ourselves while also providing the social and mental health benefits generally forthcoming from viable religions. Most of what I said earlier would lead to the conclusion that religious beliefs become operational only if they are able to distort reality with a positive bias. Following this logic, one could predict that a reality-based religion would get a very poor reception indeed.

I am reminded here of a passage from Graham Greene's *The End of the Affair*, in which the character Mrs. Smythe states:

> People are longing for a message of hope . . . can't you see what hope there'd be if everybody in the world knew that there was nothing else but what we have here? No future compensations, rewards, punishments. . . . Then we'd begin to make this world like heaven.[62]

More than a few concerned thinkers have wondered if we could somehow meet our religious needs within the confines of this world, while knowing that nothing of benefit to us existed beyond ourselves. Some have concluded, rather like Graham Greene's Mrs. Smythe, that people could eventually come to regard this world as both the beginning and the end of ourselves. Their reasoning is usually that we would begin to view our world and ourselves as sacred if we did not allow ourselves to transcend (and thereby discredit) this world. But however convincing they might be in arguing this sort of case, I do not feel that human beings will ever abandon their natural yearnings for *transcendent* mental constructions. Robert Bellah states this point most explicitly in speaking about the steep psychological price of becoming captives of

> a literal and circumscribed reality . . . which is precisely and classically to be trapped in hell . . . without transcendence, without manner, and without the devastating power of the sacred.[63]

Religion has been from the beginning a major part of the human scene since it offers *unreasonable* understandings of the world and ourselves. These are meant to compete with, and neutralize, the many hellish aspects of this-world reality. Still again in this regard, research not unexpectedly shows reality *distortion* to be associated with emotional adjustment and a sense of well-being. As we look broadly at ourselves, it seems clear that strategic cognitive error is invaluable to us as it blends so neatly with our awesome ability to perceive reality accurately. Only dissociation theory can explain this paradoxical juxtaposition of illusion and fact.

It might seem like science fiction to speak of the creation of a new religion to rescue us from ourselves. Yet I can imagine a need at one point soon to do just that. This would be for survival purposes, and not simply fanciful utopian folly. Religion is by far the best way to motivate the masses with a deeper sense of conviction, far better than can be done by appealing to their rational sensibilities. Therefore, the question would become one of coming up with a reality-embracing religion that simultaneously provided people with effective escape from that same reality. In a sense, we would be searching for a religion both true and deliberately false, but false in harmless or even beneficial ways.

A possible solution to this puzzle might be found in the form of Paul Kurtz's challenging system of belief known as *eupraxophy* (from two Greek words meaning "good practice"). Kurtz uses this term "to designate nonreligious belief systems that present a naturalistic cosmic outlook and a humanistic life stance."[64] More specifically, this would be a system of beliefs born of critical awareness, reflective judgment, and skeptical inquiry. In turn, these beliefs would empower people to gain reliable knowledge and wisdom that could guide our earthly actions in self-serving and life-serving directions. Kurtz does not present eupraxophy as a new religion. In fact, he develops the case that people can live without the destructive traditional religions that have existed for so long. However, the strength of Kurtz's proposed system of beliefs lies in his willingness to accept the possibility that a strictly empirical mode of understanding could undermine motivation and sap vitality. Thus one cannot dismiss Kurtz's system as the work of a naive skeptic who overestimates the average person's tolerance for *this-world* constructions of reality.

Kurtz shows his sensitivity toward people's natural quest for transcendence in arguing that a new system of beliefs must have more than cognitive appeal. It must also be able to arouse emotions in an intense and profound manner, while permitting some contest between accurate belief and "deceptive passion." Consistent with his overall thesis, Kurtz maintains that reliable knowledge should be the desired goal of such a body of beliefs. He also speaks on behalf of the need for people to retain an underlying optimism that somehow exceeds the limits of purely rationalistic beliefs. This is where he introduces the term "natural piety," stating that naturalistic mental constructions do not preclude the sense of piety usually associated with the more obviously transcendent systems of religious belief. Kurtz even discusses piety within the framework of atheism, quoting the philosopher George Santayana, who depicted his own atheism as a "true piety towards the universe."[65]

There is little doubt that, for our own survival, our beliefs and rituals must move us closer to ourselves and this world. Yet we have developed sophisticated brain mechanisms enabling us to maintain gross distortions of reality at this precarious point in time.

My initial pessimism tells me that this will continue to be the case. In the end, it will probably be reality transcendence that gets etched on our collective gravestone as the main reason for our demise. For all its merits, an alternative belief system such as eupraxophy lacks much of what people crave in terms of understandings that defy reality. I fear it is only a small minority who could experience spiritual piety within a set of largely rational beliefs. Creation is certainly magnificent and can fill us all with a sense of awe and mystery. But creation is also horrific in its design, consisting mostly of mobile intestinal tracts eager to consume other intestinal tracts. We happen to be an intestinal tract with a massive brain resting atop it, which makes us uniquely able to perceive the grotesque as well as the splendid. This world, in and of itself, can never be heaven. Furthermore, it is always at risk of being perceived as the hell that it is in many respects.

As has been demonstrated throughout this book, human beings are endowed with a strong predisposition toward an "insanity" that puts us *out of touch* with reality. We do this in small and large ways while usually (but not always) benefiting from our misperceptions, or our "positive illusions." We saw that the processes of dissociation and suggestion lie at the heart of our misconstructions of reality. Both religious and psychopathological beliefs employ the same mechanisms, with the main difference being that religious techniques are orchestrated at the level of culture. It has also been shown that, for the most part, modern forms of psychopathology must be understood within the context of the breakdown of dominant systems of religious belief and ritual.

So can we treat a sick society? In assessing the tattered state of religious beliefs in the West, it is tempting to conclude that we have entered a secular age from which there is no turning back. This would mean that people are destined to grope in private and improvised ways for the dissociation and suggestion that can satisfy their need for illusion and self-deception. In all likelihood, they will continue on their present course increasingly as worshipers of things and disciples of Having. One could leave it there and assume that we will never again come together as a culture of true believers in a health-giving form of reality transcendence. Still, I am captivated by Ernest Becker's notion of a general science of society that strives intentionally to establish ideal obsessions and ideal denials of reality that can carry us into the future. Again, this would be done in relation to our short-term and long-term needs. I have no doubt that huge numbers of people would eventually come to follow a new religion planned and promoted as part of such a science of society. Modern communication systems have made the world into a small place where intensive mass media campaigns can readily program millions at once.

On the surface, it seems an impossible task to decide what we should believe. A situation might arise resembling B. F. Skinner's famous claim in *Walden Two*, that society could be much improved if operant conditioning techniques were employed to program people on a large scale.[66] The question on everyone's lips had to do with *who* would actually make the decisions about the specific nature of people's programing. More important, who would control the controller? Critics of Skinner's Walden Two society decried what they regarded as a nightmare scenario wherein a mischievous and unscrupulous programer controlled the entire population without any checks on his or her behavior. Nothing so sinister comes to mind as I attempt to envision the potential workings of a general science of society such as that put forward by Ernest Becker.

Facing us is the fact that Western culture is seriously "unfit" and in the grips of a spiritual crisis that has people struggling to fill the "empty self," often in degrading and maladaptive ways. This coincides with a frequently cited mental health crisis in which psychopathology and psychotherapy attempt unsuccessfully to supplant a workable cultural religion. Although this is a regrettable situation, it may also represent an unprecedented chance to help us fill our empty selves with the sort of material that could make a difference to our chances of survival. It is not beyond the realm of possibility that we could put into action our knowledge of dissociation and suggestion. We could even do so by adding a transcendent dimension to a system of beliefs such as those contained in Kurtz's eupraxophy.

I hope that I have been able to show that the actual *content* of both religion and psychopathology is not of primary importance. What does matter is that people have some alternative to strictly this-world constructions of reality. As Joseph Conrad put it in his tale *Victory*, even the strongest of people tend to have as their motto: "Anything but this!"[67] In this regard, anything and everything by way of reality-distorting beliefs have been held by people, both past and present. The same is true of the rituals that foster dissociation and hypersuggestibility, thus paving the way for religion and all other alternative constructions of reality. That is, the specific structure of the ritual is insignificant when compared to the function of the ritual. Extrapolating from this general line of thought, we realize that people can gain the same personal and social profit from almost any system of reality transformation. In knowing this, we also realize that we should be able to incorporate beliefs and rituals that are favorable to us at a global level. Earlier I gave as an example the fervent belief that people could achieve a state of grace by doing their part to reduce the earth's population. But that potential religious creed was only mentioned in order to illustrate the type of belief that could be an aspect of a creative religion of the future. It would be arrogant and presumptuous of me to set out the full range of new religious beliefs needed at this point in time. Yet, if we ever do take such a step, it should be kept in mind that reality transcendence must be featured in any new beliefs that are eventually manufactured and marketed.

Eugene O'Neill touches on the all-important theme of reality transcendence in *Long Day's Journey into Night,* where the character Tyrone makes the statement that "when you deny God, you deny sanity."[68] The character Edmund has lost a transcendent god, but knows nonetheless that one must do whatever is necessary to make escape available to oneself. Edmund's general piece of advice to the world is "be drunken continually . . . with wine, with poetry, with virtue, as you will. But be drunken."[69] In Edmund, who seeks "drunkenness" in many godless ways, we see a perfect reflection of Western industrialized society today, where drunkenness is improvised and without a clearly pre-scribed pathway toward transcendence. Thus, if we move toward Becker's general science of society, it will again be necessary to add a distinct element of transcendence to the beliefs that are put forward.

A special difficulty arises as we attempt to introduce a reality-based belief system that is designed to propagate beliefs that are true, such as eupraxophy. In essence, we would be asking people to adopt reality-based beliefs (e.g., that it is imperative that we decrease the number of human beings), while also allowing that belief to break with reality. But this might not be as difficult as it seems. As one of many possibilities, the belief could be placed within a wider frame-work whereby people also believed that *supernatural* purposes were being served as they held and acted upon this-world beliefs. Also, the true beliefs could be given a necessary falsehood by *overriding* the content of any reality-based beliefs to the extent that they became transcendent from actual reality. Therefore, in answer to my earlier question about humankind's ability to tolerate true beliefs, I feel, in the end, that a well-conceived science of society could engineer beliefs that are true but also capable of distorting reality. Given our advanced state of communication and persuasion technology, we should be approaching a stage in our development wherein religion can be used to steer us in the directions in which we need to go for our survival without depriving believers of their necessary "drunkenness."

Endnotes

Chapter 1. The Problem of Reality

1. P. L. Berger and T. Luckmann, *The Social Construction of Reality: A Treatise in the Sociology of Knowledge* (Middlesex, England: Penguin, 1966).

2. Ibid., p. 149.

3. D. Heise, "Delusions and the Construction of Reality," in T. F. Oltmanns and B.A. Maher, eds., *Delusional Beliefs* (New York: John Wiley and Sons, 1988), pp. 259–72.

4. P. Kurtz, *The New Skepticism: Inquiry and Reliable Knowledge* (Buffalo, N.Y.: Prometheus Books, 1992), pp. 83–84.

5. Ibid., p. 92.

6. Berger and Luckman, *The Social Construction of Reality*, p. 65.

7. Ibid.

8. Kurtz, *The New Skepticism*, pp. 237–38, original italics.

9. Ibid., p. 249.

10. J. F. Schumaker, *Wings of Illusion: The Origin, Nature, and Future of Paranormal Belief* (Cambridge, England: Polity Press; Buffalo, N.Y.: Prometheus Books, 1990), pp. 14–37.

11. E. L. Rossi, "The Psychobiology of Dissociation and Identification," *Canadian Psychology* 28 (1987): 112–13.

12. E. Becker, *The Denial of Death* (New York: Free Press, 1973).

13. M. Jahoda, *Current Concepts of Positive Mental Health* (New York: Basic Books, 1958), p. 6, my italics.

14. H. A. Sackeim and R. C. Gur, "Self-Deception, Other-Deception, and Self-Reported Psychopathology," *Journal of Consulting and Clinical Psychology* 47 (1979): 213–15.

15. H. A. Sackeim, "Self-Deception, Self-Esteem, and Depression," in J. Masling, ed., *Empirical Studies of Psychoanalytic Theories* (Hillsdale, N.J.: Lawrence Erlbaum, 1983), p. 134.

16. S. Taylor, *Positive Illusions: Creative Self-Deception and the Healthy Mind* (New York: Basic Books, 1989).

17. A. Fenigstein, M. F. Scheier, and A. H. Buss, "Public and Private

Self-Consciousness: Assessment and Theory," *Journal of Consulting and Clinical Psychology* 43 (1975): 522–28.

18. Sackeim and Gur, "Self-Deception, Other-Deception, and Self-Reported Psychopathology," pp. 213–15.

19. D. L. Roth and R. E. Ingram, "Factors in the Self-Deception Questionnaire: Associations with Depression," *Journal of Personality and Social Psychology* 48 (1985): 243–51.

20. F. X. Gibbons, "Social Comparison and Depression: Company's Effect on Misery," *Journal of Personality and Social Psychology* 51 (1986): 140–49.

21. Taylor, *Positive Illusions*, p. 228.

22. Ibid., p. 237.

23. M. Maxwell, *Human Evolution: A Philosophical Anthropology* (New York: Columbia University Press, 1984).

24. E. O. Wilson, *On Human Nature* (Cambridge, Mass.: Harvard University Press, 1978), p. 175.

25. J. F. Schumaker, ed., *Religion and Mental Health* (New York and Oxford: Oxford University Press, 1992).

26. J. F. Schumaker, "The Mental Health Consequences of Irreligion," in *Religion and Mental Health*, pp. 54–69.

27. G. Santayana, "Interpretations of Poetry and Religion," in W. G. Holzberger and H. J. Saatkamp, eds. (Cambridge, Mass.: MIT Press, 1989).

28. See R. Ellmann, *Four Dubliners* (New York: George Braziller, 1987), p. 55.

29. See L. Sheaffer, *O'Neill: Son and Artist* (Boston: Little, Brown and Co., 1973), p. 605.

Chapter 2. The Mechanics of Dissociation and Suggestion

1. L. L. Whyte, *The Unconscious before Freud* (New York: Basic Books, 1960).

2. Ibid., p. 17.

3. M. Gazzaniga, *The Social Brain: Discovering the Networks of the Mind* (New York: Basic Books, 1985).

4. Whyte, *The Unconscious before Freud*, p. 188.

5. Schumaker, *Wings of Illusion*.

6. K. S. Bowers and D. Meichenbaum, *The Unconscious Reconsidered* (New York: Wiley, 1984).

7. J. F. Kihlstrom and I. P. Hoyt, "Hypnosis and the Psychology of Delusions," in T. F. Oltmanns and B. A. Maher, eds., *Delusional Beliefs* (New York: Wiley, 1988), p. 81.

8. Y. Dolan, *Resolving Sexual Abuse* (New York: W. W. Norton, 1991), p. 114.

9. L. E. Hinsie and R. J. Campbell, *Psychiatric Dictionary* (New York: Oxford University Press, 1970).

10. L. J. West, "Dissociative Reactions," in A. M. Freedman and H. I. Kaplan, eds., *Comprehensive Textbook of Psychiatry* (Baltimore: William and Wilkins, 1967), p. 890, original italics.

11. F. H. Frankel, "Hypnotizability and Dissociation," *American Journal of Psychiatry* 147 (1990): 828.

12. L. R. Frumkin, H. S. Ripley, and G. B. Cox, "Cerebral Hemispheric Lateralization with Hypnosis," *Biological Psychiatry* 13 (1978): 741–50.

13. Ibid., p. 748.

14. A. J. Mandell, "The Psychobiology of Transcendence," in J. M. Davidson and R. J. Davidson, eds., *The Psychobiology of Consciousness* (New York: Plenum Press, 1980), pp. 379–463.

15. P. Janet, *L'Automatisme psychologique* (Paris: Felix Alcan, 1889).

16. See N. M. Kravis, "James Braid's Psychophysiology: A Turning in the History of Dynamic Psychiatry," *American Journal of Psychiatry* 145 (1988): 1191–1206.

17. P. Janet, *The Major Symptoms of Hysteria* (New York: Macmillan, 1907).

18. P. Janet, *Les Stades de l'évolution psychologique* (Paris: Chaline-Maloine, 1926), pp. 185–86.

19. S. Freud, "Sketches for the 'Preliminary Communication' of 1893: A Letter to Josef Breuer," in *The Complete Psychological Works of Sigmund Freud*, ed. J. Strachey (London: Hogarth Press, 1966), vol. 1.

20. Ibid., p. 27.

21. S. Freud, *The Problem of Anxiety* (New York: Norton, 1936), p. 21.

22. K. S. Bowers, "Suggestion and Subtle Control," paper presented at the meeting of The American Psychological Association, Washington, D.C., 1982.

23. C. T. Tart, "A Systems Approach to Altered States of Consciousness," in J. M. Davidson and R. J. Davidson, eds., *The Psychobiology of Consciousness* (New York: Plenum Press, 1980), pp. 258–60.

24. Ibid., p. 255.

25. Ibid., p. 260.

26. Ibid., p. 266.

27. M. R. Haight, *A Study of Self-Deception* (Sussex: Harvester Press, 1980), p. 43.

28. J. P. Sartre, *Being and Nothingness* (New York: Washington Square Press, 1953).

29. E. R. Hilgard, *Divided Consciousness: Multiple Controls in Human Thought and Action* (New York: Wiley, 1977/1986).

30. E. R. Hilgard, "Neodissociation Theory of Multiple Cognitive Control Systems," in G. E. Schwartz and D. Shapiro, eds., *Consciousness and Self-Regulation* (New York: Plenum Press, 1976), pp. 137–71.

31. E. R. Hilgard, "Toward a Neodissociation Theory: Multiple Cognitive Controls in Human Functioning," *Perspectives in Biology and Medicine* 12 (1974): 301–16.

32. J. O. Beahrs, "Co-Consciousness: A Common Denominator in Hypnosis, Multiple Personality, and Normalcy," *American Journal of Clinical Hypnosis* 26 (1983): 100.

33. Ibid., p. 106.

34. Ibid., p. 111.

35. G. Schwartz, "Consciousness and the Brain Self-Regulation Para-dox," in *The Psychobiology of Consciousness*.

36. C. J. Lumsden and E. O. Wilson, *Genes, Mind, and Behavior: The Coevolutionary Process* (Cambridge, Mass.: Harvard University Press, 1981), pp. 107-8.

37. Bowers and Meichenbaum, *The Unconscious Reconsidered*, pp. 191–96.

38. Ibid., p. 191.

39. Ibid., p. 192.

40. R. E. Shor, "Hypnosis and the Concept of the Generalized Reality-Orientation," *American Journal of Psychotherapy* 13 (1959): 291.

41. W. E. Edmonston, "Conceptual Clarification of Hypnosis and Its Relation to Suggestibility," in V. A. Gheorghiu, P. Netter, H. J. Eysenck, and R. Rosenthal, eds., *Suggestion and Suggestibility: Theory and Research* (Berlin: Springer-Verlag, 1989).

42. Ibid., p. 69, my italics.

43. W. McDougall, *An Introduction to Social Psychology* (London: Methuen, 1908), p. 100, my italics.

44. H. J. Eysenck, W. J. Arnold, and R. Meili, *Encyclopedia of Psychology* (Bungay, Suffolk, England: Fontana, 1975), 2:1077, my italics.

45. G. W. Allport, *Pattern and Growth in Personality* (New York: Holt, Rinehart and Winston, 1961).

46. A. M. Ludwig, "The Psychobiological Functions of Dissociation," *American Journal of Clinical Hypnosis* 26 (1983): 93–99.

47. K. S. Masters, "Hypnotic Susceptibility, Cognitive Dissociation, and Runner's High in a Sample of Marathon Runners," *American Journal of Clinical Hypnosis* 34 (1992): 193–201.

Chapter 3. Hypnosis in Global Perspective

1. J. F. Kihlstrom, "Hypnosis and the Dissociation of Memory, with Special Reference to Posthypnotic Amnesia," *Research Communications in Psychology, Psychiatry, and Behavior* 7 (1982): 181.

2. Hilgard, *Divided Consciousness*.

3. Kihlstrom, "Hypnosis and the Dissociation of Memory," pp. 185–86.

4. R. E. Shor, "Hypnosis and the Concept of the Generalized Reality-Orientation," in R. E. Shor and M. T. Orne, eds., *The Nature of Hypnosis* (New York: Holt, Rinehart and Winston, 1965), p. 302.

5. E. Bliss, "Multiple Personalities, Related Disorders, and Hypnosis," *American Journal of Clinical Hypnosis* 26 (1983): 119.

6. Hilgard, *Divided Consciousness*, p. 71.

7. Shor, "Hypnosis and the Concept of the Generalized Reality-Orientation," p. 303.

8. F. Frankel, *Hypnosis: Trance as a Coping Mechanism* (New York: Plenum Press, 1976), p. 42.

9. E. R. Hilgard, *Hypnotic Susceptibility* (New York: Harcourt, Brace and World, 1965).

10. Hilgard, *Divided Consciousness*, p. 229.

11. B. J. Baars, "Momentary Forgetting as a Resetting of a Conscious Global Workspace Due to Competition between Incompatible Contexts," in M. J. Horowitz, ed., *Psychodynamics and Cognition* (Chicago: University of Chicago Press, 1988).

12. A. Tellegen and G. Atkinson, "Openness to Absorbing and Self-Altering Experiences ('Absorption'), a Trait Related to Hypnotic Susceptibility," *Journal of Abnormal Psychology* 83 (1974): 268–77.

13. E. Cardeña and D. Spiegel, "Suggestibility, Absorption, and Dissociation: An Integrative Model of Hypnosis," in J. F. Schumaker, ed., *Human Suggestibility: Advances in Theory, Research, and Application* (New York: Routledge, 1991), pp. 93–107.

14. B. Sidis, *The Psychology of Suggestion* (New York: D. Appleton and Company, 1898), p. 17.

15. E. L. Rossi, "Altered States of Consciousness in Everyday Life," in B. Wolman and M. Ullman, eds., *Handbook of States of Consciousness* (New York: Bantam Books, 1986), p. 97.

16. V. Barnouw, *Culture and Personality* (Homewood, Ill.: Dorsey Press, 1985), p. 393.

17. E. Bourguignon, "Introduction: A Framework for the Comparative Study of Altered States of Consciousness," in E. Bourguignon, ed., *Religion, Altered States of Consciousness and Social Change* (Columbus, Ohio: Ohio State University Press, 1973), pp. 3–35.

18. Barnouw, *Culture and Personality*, p. 390.

19. Ibid.

20. Ibid., p. 391.

21. A. Neher, "A Physiological Explanation of Unusual Behavior in Ceremonies Involving Drums," *Human Biology* 4 (1962): 151–60.

22. C. Ward and S. Kemp, "Religious Experiences, Altered States of Consciousness, and Suggestibility," in *Human Suggestibility: Advances in Theory, Research, and Application*, pp. 159–82.

23. Ibid., p. 168.

24. C. Ward, "Thaipusam in Malaysia: A Psycho-Anthropological Analysis of Ritual Trance, Ceremonial Possession and Self-Mortification Practices," *Ethos* 12 (1984): 315.

25. See Cardeña and Spiegel, "Suggestibility, Absorption, and Dissociation," p. 98.

Chapter 4. Religion: The Cultural Mask of Sanity

1. M. Argyle and B. Beit-Hallahmi, *The Social Psychology of Religion* (London: Routledge and Kegan Paul, 1975), pp. 97–99.

2. T. E. Long, "Some Early-Life Stimulus Correlates of Hypnotizability," *International Journal of Clinical and Experimental Hypnosis* 16 (1968): 61–67.

3. J. Hallaji, "Hypnotherapeutic Techniques in a Central Asian Community," in *The Nature of Hypnosis*, pp. 453–56.

4. P. Kurtz, *The Transcendental Temptation* (Buffalo, N.Y.: Prometheus Books, 1986).

5. A. F. C. Wallace, *Religion: An Anthropological View* (New York: Random House, 1966), p. 3.

6. Ibid., p. 65.

7. Ludwig, "The Psychobiological Functions of Dissociation," p. 96.

8. See J. E. Alcock, "Religion and Rationality," in *Religion and Mental Health*, pp. 122–31.

9. Wilson, *On Human Nature*, pp. 169–93.

10. H. Simon, "A Mechanism for Social Selection and Successful Altruism," *Science* 250 (1990): 1665.

11. Ibid., p. 1667.

12. M. L. Shames, "Hypnotic Susceptibility and Conformity: On the Mediational Mechanism of Suggestibility," *Psychological Reports* 49 (1981): 563–66.

13. E. Arbman, *Ecstasy or Religious Trance?* (Uppsala), 1: xv, 224, 478.

14. Wallace, *Religion: An Anthropological View*, p. 54.

15. Ibid., pp. 54–55.

16. G. Rouget, *Music and Trance: A Theory of the Relations between Music and Possession* (Chicago: The University of Chicago Press, 1985), p. xvii.

17. Ibid., p. xviii.

18. W. G. Jilek, "Brainwashing as a Therapeutic Technique in Contemporary Canadian Indian Spirit Dancing: A Case of Theory Building," in J. Westermeyer, ed., *Anthropology and Mental Health* (The Hague: Mouton Publishers, 1976).

19. R. Prince, "Can the EEG Be Used in the Study of Possession States?" in R. Prince, ed., *Trance and Possession States* (Montreal: R. M. Bucke Memorial Society, 1968), pp. 121–37.

20. A. Hultkrantz, "Ecological and Phenomenological Aspects of Shamanism," in V. Diószegi and M. Hoppál, eds., *Shamanism in Siberia* (Budapest: Akadémiai Kiadó, 1978), pp. 27–58.

21. Cited in Wilson, *On Human Nature*, pp. 183–84.

22. G. W. Williams, "Highway Hypnosis: A Hypothesis," in *The Nature of Hypnosis*, p. 483.

23. M. J. Herskovits, *The Myth of the Negro Past* (New York: Alfred Knopf, 1941), p. 215.

24. E. D. Adrian and B. H. Matthews, "The Berger Rhythm: Potential Changes from the Occipital Lobe in Man," *Brain* 57 (1934): 355–85.

25. J. Turner, *Without God, without Creed: The Origins of Unbelief in America* (Baltimore: The Johns Hopkins University Press, 1985).

26. See W. S. F. Pickering, *Durkheim on Religion* (London: Routledge and Kegan Paul), p. 341.

27. Rouget, *Music and Trance*, p. 316.

28. Wallace, *Religion: An Anthropological View*, p. 56.

29. Rouget, *Music and Trance*, pp. 291–92.

30. B. Bongartz, and W. Bongartz, " 'Nyangkap Semengat' or How

to Capture the Souls: Trance as Done by the Shamans of the Iban District in Northern Borneo," *Hypnos* 16 (1989): 108–11.

31. C. Grob and M. Dobkin de Rios, "Adolescent Drug Use in Cross-Cultural Perspective," *Journal of Drug Issues* 22 (1992): 121–38.

32. Ibid., p. 131.

33. Ibid.

34. Turner, *Without God, without Creed*, p. 267, my italics.

35. D. Berman, "Religion and Neurosis," *Free Inquiry* (Summer 1993): 16.

36. Schumaker, *Wings of Illusion*, chapter 2.

37. K. Dewhurst and A. W. Beard, "Sudden Religious Conversions in Temporal Lobe Epilepsy," *British Journal of Psychiatry* 117 (1970): 497–507.

38. W. James, *The Varieties of Religious Experience* (London: Longmans, 1902; rpt. 1952).

39. J. Frank, *Persuasion and Healing: A Comparative Study of Psychotherapy* (Baltimore and London: The Johns Hopkins University Press, 1973).

40. J. Westermeyer, "Some Cross-Cultural Aspects of Delusions," in T. F. Oltmanns and B. A. Maher, eds., *Delusional Beliefs* (New York: Wiley, 1988), pp. 212–29.

41. Rouget, *Music and Trance*, p. 320.

42. American Psychiatric Association, *Diagnostic and Statistical Manual of Mental Disorders*, 4th ed. (*DSM-IV*) (Washington, D.C.: Author, 1994), p. 765.

43. American Psychiatric Association, *Diagnostic and Statistical Manual of Mental Disorders*, 3rd ed. (*DSM-III*) (Washington, D.C.: Author, 1980), p. 356.

44. E. T. Higgins and M. M. Moretti, "Standard Utilization and the Social-Evaluative Process: Vulnerability to Types of Aberrant Beliefs," in *Delusional Beliefs*, p. 112, original italics.

45. B. M. Fagan, *The Aztecs* (New York: W. H. Freeman, 1984).

46. D. R. Heise, "Delusions and the Construction of Reality," in *Delusional Beliefs*, p. 270.

47. Ibid.

48. J. Strauss, "Hallucinations and Delusions as Points on Continua Function," *Archives of General Psychiatry* 21 (1969): 581–86.

49. American Psychiatric Association, *Diagnostic and Statistical Manual of Mental Disorders*, 3rd ed., rev. (*DSM-III-R*) (Washington, D.C.: Author, 1987), p. 395.

50. Ibid.

51. Ibid., p. 355.

52. Ibid., p. 401.

53. Ibid.

54. L. J. Chapman and J. P. Chapman, "The Genesis of Delusions," in *Delusional Beliefs*, p. 178.

55. Ibid.

56. See D. Meichenbaum, *Cognitive-Behavior Modification: An Integrative Approach* (New York: Plenum Press, 1977), p. 192.

57. R. Frétigny and A. Virel, *L'Imagerie mentale* (Geneva: Editions de Mont-Blanc, 1968).

58. *DSM-III-R*, p. 199.

59. Ibid., p. 200.

60. E. Becker, *Escape from Evil* (New York: Free Press, 1975), p. 159.

61. E. Durkheim, *The Elementary Forms of Religious Life* (London: Allen and Unwin, 1912; rpt. 1971), p. 52.

62. See Pickering, *Durkheim on Religion*, p. 106.

63. L. Raglan, *The Origins of Religion* (London: Watts and Co., 1949).

64. Ibid., p. 7, my italics.

65. J. Campbell, *Myths to Live By* (London: Souvenir Press, 1973), p. 97.

66. Ibid., p. 45.

67. J. Jacobs, "Religious Ritual and Mental Health," in *Religion and Mental Health*, pp. 291-99.

68. T. J. Scheff, *Catharsis in Healing, Ritual, and Drama* (Berkeley and Los Angeles: University of California Press, 1979) .

69. B. G. Myerhoff, "We Don't Wrap Herring in a Printed Page: Fusion, Fictions and Continuity in Secular Ritual," in S. F. Moore and B. G. Myerhoff, eds., *Secular Ritual* (Amsterdam: Van Gorcum, 1977), p. 214.

70. Ibid., p. 199.

71. S. J. Wolin and L. A. Bennett, "Family Rituals," *Family Process* 23 (1984): p. 401.

72. R. L. Grimes, "Ritual," in M. Eliade, ed., *The Encyclopedia of Religion* (New York: Macmillan, 1987), 11: 405.

73. K. H. Reich, "Rituals and Social Structure: The Moral Dimension," in H. Heimbrock and H. B. Boudewijnse, eds., *Current Studies on Ritual* (Amsterdam: Rodopi, 1990), p. 121.

74. Becker, *Escape from Evil*, p. 8.

75. E. d'Aquili, "Human Ceremonial Ritual and the Modulation of Aggression," *Zygon* 20 (1985): 22.

76. E. H. Erikson, "Ontogeny of Ritualization in Man," in R. M. Loewenstein et al., eds., *Psychoanalysis—A General Psychology. Essays in Honour of Heinz Hartman* (New York: International University Press, 1966).

77. V. Turner, "Myth and Symbol," *International Encyclopedia of the Social Sciences* (1968), 10: 567-82.

78. Frank, *Persuasion and Healing*, p. 100.

79. D'Aquili, "Human Ceremonial Ritual and the Modulation of Aggression," p. 29.

80. K. Lorenz, *On Aggression* (New York: Bantam Books, 1966), p. 72.

81. Myerhoff, "We Don't Wrap Herring in a Printed Page," p. 199.

82. C. Geertz, *The Interpretations of Culture* (New York: Basic Books, 1973), p. 90, my italics.

83. E. Cardeña, "Varieties of Possession Experience," *AASC Quarterly* 5 (1989): 14.

84. Wallace, *Religion: An Anthropological View*, p. 53.

85. J. Janssen, J. de Hart, and C. den Draak, "Praying as an Individualized Ritual," in *Current Studies on Ritual*, p. 83.

86. Ibid.

87. Ibid., p. 71.

88. Ibid., p. 84.

89. Ibid.

90. R. Stark, "Church and Sect," in P. E. Hammond, ed., *The Sacred in a Secular Age* (Berkeley and Los Angeles: University of California Press, 1985), pp. 134–49.

91. S. Freud, *The Future of an Illusion* (New York: Anchor Books, 1964; originally published 1927).

Chapter 5. Psychopathology: New Perspectives

1. Becker, *Escape from Evil*, p. 11.

2. A. J. Marsella and A. Dash-Scheuer, "Coping, Culture, and Healthy Human Development," in P. Dasen, J. Berry, and N. Sartorius, eds., *Health and Cross-Cultural Psychology* (London: Sage, 1988), p. 166.

3. E. Becker, *The Denial of Death* (New York: Free Press, 1974), pp. 189, 197.

4. G. Wijeyewardene, *Place and Emotion in Northern Thai Ritual Behavior* (Bangkok: Pandora, 1986), p. 246.

5. W. T. Hall, *Beyond Culture* (Garden City, N.Y.: Anchor Press/ Doubleday, 1976), p. 187.

6. Ibid.

7. Barnouw, *Culture and Personality*, pp. 361–62.

8. Campbell, *Myths to Live By*, p. 52.

9. E. Fromm, *The Sane Society* (London: Routledge and Kegan Paul, 1968).

10. Campbell, *Myths to Live By*.

11. H. Faber, "The Meaning of Ritual in the Liturgy," in *Current Studies on Rituals*, pp. 43–55.

12. Myerhoff, "We Don't Wrap Herring in a Printed Page," in *Secular Ritual*, p. 222.

13. V. W. Turner, "Liminal to Limnoid, in Play, Flow, and Ritual," *Rice University Studies* 60 (1974): 53–92.

14. H. Cox, *Feast of Fools: A Theological Essay on Festivity and Fantasy* (New York: Harper and Row, 1969), p. 67.

15. E. Bourguignon, "Possession and Trance in Cross-Cultural Studies of Mental Health," in W. L. Lebra, ed., *Culture-Bound Syndromes* (Honolulu: University of Hawaii Press, 1976), p. 50.

16. Durkheim, *The Elementary Forms of Religious Life*, p. 59.

17. D. G. Richards, "A Study of the Correlations between Subject Psychic Experiences and Dissociative Experiences," *Dissociation* 4 (1991): 83–91.

18. G. K. Ganaway, "Historical versus Narrative Truth: Clarifying the Role of Exogenous Trauma in the Etiology of MPD and Its Variants," *Dissociation* 2 (1989): 205–20.

19. J. W. Rhue and S. J. Lynn, "Fantasy Proneness, Hypnotizability, and Multiple Personality," in *Human Suggestibility: Advances in Theory, Research, and Application*, pp. 200–18.

20. J. Glicksohn, "Belief in the Paranormal and Subjective Paranormal Experience," *Personality and Individual Differences* 11 (1990): 675-83.

21. J. Durant and M. Bauer, "Who Believes in Astrology and Why?" *Skeptical Inquirer* 16 (1992): 347.

22. Ibid.

23. C. F. Emmons and J. Sobal, "Paranormal Beliefs: Functional Alternatives to Mainstream Religion?" *Review of Religious Research* 22 (1981): 301-12.

24. W. S. Bainbridge and R. Stark, "The Consciousness Reformation Reconsidered," *Journal for the Scientific Study of Religion* 20 (1981): 1-16; also W. S. Bainbridge and R. Stark, "Friendship, Religion, and the Occult," *Review of Religious Research* 22 (1981): 313-27.

25. M. Dobkin de Rios, *Hallucinogens: Cross-Cultural Perspective* (Bridport, England: Prism Press, 1990).

26. P. Cushman, "Why the Self Is Empty: Toward a Historically Situated Psychology," *American Psychologist* 45 (1990): 599-611.

27. L. Zoja, *Drugs, Addiction and Initiation: The Modern Search for Ritual* (Boston: Sigo Press, 1989).

28. Becker, *The Denial of Death*, p. 205.

29. Ibid., p. 199.

30. C. A. Ross, *Multiple Personality Disorder: Diagnosis, Clinical Features, and Treatment* (New York: Wiley, 1989).

31. E. M. Bernstein and F. Putnam, "Development, Reliability and Validity of a Dissociation Scale," *Journal of Nervous and Mental Disease* 174 (1986): 727-35.

32. A. Ludwig, "Altered States of Consciousness," in C. Tart, ed., *Altered States of Consciousness* (New York: Wiley, 1969), pp. 22-37.

33. M. A. Haberman, "Spontaneous Trance as a Possible Cause for Persistent Symptoms in the Medically Ill," *American Journal of Clinical Hypnosis* 29 (1987): 174.

34. E. L. Bliss, "Multiple Personalities, Related Disorders, and Hypnosis," *American Journal of Clinical Hypnosis* 26 (1983): 119.

35. Ibid., p. 115.

36. W. Abse, "Multiple Personality," in A. Roy, ed., *Hysteria* (New York: Wiley, 1982), p. 173.

37. C. A. Ross, "Comments on Garcia's 'The Concept of Dissociation and Conversion in the New ICD-10,' " *Dissociation* 3 (1990): 211.

38. Ross, *Multiple Personality Disorder*, pp. 310-11.

39. Ross, "Comments on Garcia's 'The Concept of Dissociation and Conversion in the New ICD-10,' " p. 211.

40. B. G. Braun, "The BASK (Behavior, Affect, Sensation, Knowledge) Model of Dissociation," *Dissociation* 1 (1988): 16-23.

41. R. A. Bryant and K. M. McConkey, "Hypnotic Blindness and the Relevance of Attention," *Australian Journal of Psychology* 42 (1990): 294.

42. Bliss, "Multiple Personalities, Related Disorders, and Hypnosis," pp. 114-23.

43. H. M. Pettinati, R. L. Horne, and J. M. Staats, "Hypnotizability in

Patients with Anorexia Nervosa and Bulimia," *Archives of General Psychiatry* 42 (1985): 1014–16.

44. J. Vanderlinden, W. Vandereycken, R. van Dyck, and O. Delacroix, "Hypnotizability and Dissociation in a Group of Fifty Eating Disorder Patients," in W. Bongartz, ed., *Hypnosis: 175 Years after Mesmer* (Konstanz: Universitäts Verlag, 1992), pp. 291–94.

45. S. Sanders, "The Perceptual Alteration Scale: A Scale Measuring Dissociation," *American Journal of Clinical Hypnosis* 29 (1986): 95–102.

46. P. J. V. Beumont and S. F. Abraham, "Episodes of Ravenous Over-eating or Bulimia: Their Occurrence in Patients with Anorexia Nervosa and with Other Forms of Disordered Eating," in P. L. Darby, P. E. Garfinkel, D. M. Garner, and D. V. Coscina, eds., *Anorexia Nervosa: Recent Developments in Research* (New York: Alan R. Liss, 1983), pp. 149–57.

47. J. F. Schumaker, W. G. Warren, G. Schreiber, and C. Jackson, "Dissociation in Anorexia Nervosa and Bulimia Nervosa," *Social Behavior and Personality* 22 (1994): 1–7.

48. L. Temoshok and C. C. Attkisson, "Epidemiology of Hysterical Phenomena: Evidence for a Psychosocial Theory," in M. J. Horowitz, ed., *Hysterical Personality* (New York: Jason Aronson, 1977).

49. M. Kaffman, "Inflexible Belief-Constructs in Families of Paranoid Patients," *International Journal of Family Psychiatry* 3 (1983): 487–500.

50. A. M. Ludwig, "Hysteria: A Neurobiological Theory," *Archives of General Psychiatry* 27 (1972): 771–78.

51. F. H. Frankel and M. T. Orne, "Hypnotizability and Phobic Behavior," *Archives of General Psychiatry* 33 (1976): 1259–61; also R. John, B. Hollander, and C. Perry, "Hypnotizability and Phobic Behavior: Further Supporting Data," *Journal of Abnormal Psychology* 92 (1983): 390–92.

52. D. Spiegel, T. Hunt, and M. D. Dondershine, "Dissociation and Hypnotizability in Posttraumatic Stress Disorder," *American Journal of Psychiatry* 145 (1988): 301–305.

53. Y. M. Dolan, *Resolving Sexual Abuse* (New York: W. W. Norton, 1991), p. 7.

54. B. A. van der Kolk and O. van der Hart, "Pierre Janet and the Breakdown of Adaptation in Psychological Trauma," *American Journal of Psychiatry* 146 (1989): 1530.

55. P. Janet, *Psychological Healing* (New York: Macmillan, 1925), p. 661.

56. E. R. Hilgard, "Neodissociation Theory of Multiple Cognitive Control Systems," in G. E. Schwartz and D. Shapiro, eds., *Consciousness and Self-Regulation: Advances in Research* (New York: Plenum Press, 1976), p. 143.

57. Ibid., p. 144, original italics.

58. Dolan, *Resolving Sexual Abuse.*

59. Ibid., pp. 7, 114.

60. A. M. Paley, "Growing Up in Chaos: The Dissociative Response," *American Journal of Psychoanalysis* 48 (1988): 77, 79.

61. F. W. Putnam, J. J. Guroff, and E. K. Silberman, "The Clinical

Phenomenology of Multiple Personality Disorder: 100 Recent Cases," *Journal of Clinical Psychiatry* 47 (1986): 285–89.

62. D. Spiegel, "Dissociation, Double Binds, and Posttraumatic Stress in Multiple Personality Disorder," in B. G. Braun, ed., *Treatment of Multiple Personality Disorder* (Washington, D.C.: American Psychiatric Press, 1986), pp. 65–66.

63. E. S. Bowman, "Understanding and Responding to Religious Material in the Therapy of Multiple Personality Disorder," *Dissociation* 2 (1989): 231–38.

64. Ibid., p. 232.

65. S. E. Finn, M. Hartman, G. R. Leon, and L. Larson, "Eating Disorders and Sexual Abuse: Lack of Confirmation for a Clinical Hypothesis," *International Journal of Eating Disorders* 5 (1986): 1051–59.

66. Bliss, "Multiple Personalities, Related Disorders, and Hypnosis," pp. 114–23.

67. D. P. Phillips, "Suicide, Motor Vehicle Fatalities, and the Mass Media: Evidence toward a Theory of Suggestion," *American Journal of Sociology* 84 (1979): 1150–74.

68. Ibid., p. 1168.

69. S. Kierkegaard, *Sickness unto Death*, trans. Walter Lowrie (Garden City, N.Y.: Doubleday, 1954; originally published 1849).

70. K. Lorenz, *The Waning of Humaneness* (Boston: Little, Brown and Co., 1987).

71. Spiegel et al., "Dissociation and Hypnotizability in Posttraumatic Stress Disorder," p. 301.

72. J. Braid, *The Power of the Mind over the Body* (London: John Churchill, 1846).

73. M. Kaffman, "Suggestion and Monoideistic Disorders: Anorexia Nervosa as a Paradigm," in *Human Suggestibility: Advances in Theory, Research, and Application*, pp. 289–308.

74. Hilgard, *Divided Consciousness*.

75. Ibid.

76. F. Frankel, *Hypnosis: Trance as a Coping Mechanism* (New York: Plenum Press, 1976), p. 37.

77. Frankel and Orne, "Hypnotizability and Phobic Behavior," pp. 1259–61.

78. J. Gerschman, G. D. Burrows, P. Reade, and G. Foenander, "Hypnotizability and the Treatment of Dental Phobic Illness," in G. D. Burrows, D. R. Collison, and L. Dennerstein, eds., *Hypnosis 1979* (Amsterdam: Elsevier/North Holland, 1979); also G. Foenander, G. D. Burrows, J. Gerschman, and D. J. Horne, "Phobic Behavior and Hypnotic Susceptibility," *Australian Journal of Clinical and Experimental Hypnosis* 3 (1980): 41–46.

79. Frankel, *Hypnosis: Trance as a Coping Mechanism*, p. 124.

80. Ibid., p. 125.

81. Bowers and Meichenbaum, *The Unconscious Reconsidered*, pp. 60–61.

82. Ibid.

83. Becker, *Escape from Evil*, pp. 23, 158.

84. Ludwig, "Hysteria: A Neurobiological Theory," p. 775.

85. Kaffman, "Inflexible Belief-Constructs in Families of Paranoid Patients," p. 494.

86. Ibid., p. 497.

87. J. Draguns, "Personality and Culture," in P. Dasen, J. Berry, and N. Sartorius, eds., *Health and Cross-Cultural Psychology* (London: Sage, 1988), p. 145.

88. A. Martínez-Taboas, "Multiple Personality Disorder as Seen from a Social Constructionist Viewpoint," *Dissociation* 4 (1991): 131.

89. N. Buhrich, "Frequency of Presentation of Anorexia Nervosa in Malaysia," *Australian and New Zealand Journal of Psychiatry* 15 (1981): 153–55; A. Yates, "Current Perspectives on Eating Disorders: History, Psychological and Biological Aspects," *Journal of the American Academy of Child and Adolescent Psychiatry* 28 (1989): 813–28.

90. R. A. Gordon, *Anorexia and Bulimia* (Oxford: Basil Blackwell, 1990), p. 11.

91. R. Brightman, "On Windigo Psychosis," *Current Anthropology* 24 (1983): 120–25.

92. Schumaker, *Wings of Illusion*, pp. 119–22.

93. R. Prince, "The Concept of Culture-Bound Syndromes: Anorexia Nervosa and Brain Fag," *Social Science and Medicine* 21 (1985): 197–203.

94. H. Geertz, "Latah in Java: A Theoretical Paradox," *Indonesia* 5 (1968): 93–104.

95. Ibid., pp. 101–102.

96. Ibid., p. 101.

97. R. Bell, *Holy Anorexia* (Chicago: University of Chicago Press, 1985).

98. C. G. Banks, "Culture in Culture-Bound Syndromes: The Case of Anorexia Nervosa," *Social Science and Medicine* 34 (1992): 867–84.

99. C. Wilbur and R. Colligan, "Psychologic and Behavioral Correlates of Anorexia Nervosa," *Journal of Developmental and Behavioral Pediatrics* 2 (1981): 89–92.

100. H. Bruch, *The Golden Cage: The Enigma of Anorexia Nervosa* (Cambridge, Mass.: Harvard University Press, 1978), p. 18.

Chapter 6. Treating the Individual and Society

1. A. Bergin, "Religiosity and Mental Health: A Critical Reevaluation and Meta-Analysis," *Professional Psychology: Research and Practice* 14 (1983): 170–84; also D. Larson, M. Pattison, D. Blazer, A. Omran, and B. Kaplan, "Systematic Analysis of Research on Religious Variables in Four Major Psychiatric Journals, 1978–1982," *American Journal of Psychiatry* 143 (1986): 329–34.

2. R. L. Moore, "Contemporary Psychotherapy as Ritual Process: An Initial Reconnaissance," *Zygon: Journal of Religion and Science* 18 (1983): 283–94.

3. S. Freud, "Obsessive Actions and Religious Practices," in *The Complete Psychological Works of Sigmund Freud*, 9:126–27.

4. P. Vandermeersch, "Psychotherapeutic and Religious Rituals: The Issue of Secularization," in *Current Studies on Rituals*, pp. 151–64.

5. E. Ouwehand, "Women's Rituals: Reflections on Developmental Theory," in *Current Studies on Rituals*, pp. 136–37.

6. Ibid., p. 136.

7. Ibid., p. 139.

8. Ibid., p. 136.

9. A. Giddens, *Sociology* (Cambridge: Polity Press, 1989).

10. J. Jacobs, "The Effects of Ritual Healing on Female Victims of Abuse: A Study of Empowerment and Transformation," *Sociological Analysis* 50 (1989): 265–79.

11. Ibid., p. 269–70.

12. J. H. Vespers, "The Use of Healing Ceremonies in the Treatment of Multiple Personality Disorder," *Dissociation* 4 (1991): 109–14.

13. Ibid., pp. 111–12.

14. Ibid., p. 113.

15. L. R. Propst, R. Ostrom, P. Watkins, T. Dean, and D. Mashburn, "Comparative Efficiency of Religious and Nonreligious Cognitive-Behavioral Therapy for the Treatment of Clinical Depression in Religious Individuals," *Journal of Consulting and Clinical Psychology* 60 (1992): 94–103.

16. A. Ellis and W. Dryden, *The Practice of Rational-Emotive Therapy* (New York: Springer, 1987).

17. A. Ellis, "The Case against Religion: A Psychotherapist's View," in B. Ard, ed., *Counseling and Psychotherapy: Classics on Theory and Issues* (Palo Alto, Calif.: Science and Behavior Books, 1975), p. 440.

18. L. R. Propst, "The Comparative Efficacy of Religious and Non-religious Imagery for the Treatment of Mild Depression Individuals," *Cognitive Therapy and Research* 4 (1980): 167–78.

19. Taylor, *Positive Illusions*.

20. Ross, *Multiple Personality Disorder*.

21. Kaffman, "Inflexible Belief-Constructs in Families of Paranoid Patients," p. 498.

22. Schumaker, *Wings of Illusion*, pp. 134–47.

23. W. G. Jilek, "Brainwashing as a Therapeutic Technique in Contemporary Canadian Indian Spirit Dancing: A Case of Theory Building," in *Anthropology and Mental Health*, pp. 201–13.

24. Ibid., p. 208.

25. Ibid., p. 209.

26. Ibid., p. 210.

27. M. Weber, "Economy and Society," in I. Roth and C. Wittich, eds., *Economy and Society: Outline of Interpretive Sociology* (Berkeley and Los Angeles: University of California Press, 1978), p. 242.

28. C. Lindholm, "Charisma, Crowd Psychology and Altered States of Consciousness," *Culture, Medicine, and Psychiatry* 16 (1992): 287–310.

29. R. Naroll, *The Moral Order* (London: Sage, 1983); also R. Naroll, "Cultural Determinants and the Concept of the Sick Society," in S. C. Plog

and R. B. Edgerton, eds., *Changing Perspectives in Mental Illness* (New York: Holt, Rinehart and Winston, 1969), pp. 128–55.

30. E. Fromm, *The Sane Society*, pp. 6, 11.

31. Ibid., p. 72.

32. E. Fromm, *To Have or To Be* (New York: Harper and Row, 1976), p. 360, original italics.

33. Kurtz, *The New Skepticism*, p. 264.

34. Wilson, *On Human Nature*, pp. 4–5.

35. Ibid.

36. Fromm, *The Sane Society*, p. 15.

37. Ibid., p. 352.

38. Ibid.

39. Ibid.

40. Wallace, *Religion: An Anthropological View*, p. 30.

41. Ibid.

42. Ibid., p. 32.

43. Ibid.

44. Becker, *Escape from Evil*, p. 122.

45. Becker, *The Denial of Death*, p. 186.

46. Becker, *Escape from Evil*, pp. 159–60, original italics.

47. Maxwell, *Human Evolution*, p. 208.

48. E. Becker, *The Revolution in Psychiatry* (London: Collier-Macmillan, 1964), p. 249.

49. Ibid., p. 234.

50. A. Gelb and B. Gelb, *O'Neill* (London: Jonathan Cape, 1962), p. 601.

51. Ibid.

52. T. Roszak, *Unfinished Animal* (London: Faber and Faber, 1975), p. 239.

53. Ibid., p. 158.

54. Ibid., p. 234.

55. Ibid., p. 248.

56. Ibid., p. 256.

57. P. Reiff, *The Triumph of the Therapeutic: Uses of Faith after Freud* (New York: Harper and Row, 1966), p. 65.

58. Cushman, "Why the Self Is Empty," 599–611.

59. Ibid., p. 601.

60. Ibid., p. 605–606.

61. P. Adams, *The Age* newspaper (Melbourne), March 25, 1989.

62. G. Greene, *The End of the Affair* (London: William Heinemann and The Bodley Head, 1951/1974), p. 87.

63. R. N. Bellah, "Toward a Definition of Unbelief," in R. Caporale and A. Grumelli, eds., *The Culture of Unbelief* (Berkeley and Los Angeles: The University of California Press, 1971), p. 155.

64. Kurtz, *The New Skepticism*, p. 194; also P. Kurtz, *Living without Religion: Eupraxophy* (Amherst, N.Y.: Prometheus Books, 1994).

65. Kurtz, *The New Skepticism*, p. 343.

66. B. F. Skinner, *Walden Two* (New York: Macmillan, 1962).

67. J. Conrad, *Victory* (London: J. M. Dent and Sons, 1915/1967), p. 219.

68. E. O'Neill, *Long Day's Journey into Night* (New Haven, Conn.: Yale University Press, 1955/1984), p. 132.

69. Ibid., pp. 132–34.

Bibliography

Abse, W. "Multiple Personality." In A. Roy, ed., *Hysteria*. New York: Wiley, 1982, p. 173.

Adrian, E. D., and Matthews, B. H. "The Berger Rhythm: Potential Changes from the Occipital Lobe in Man." *Brain*, 57 (1934): 355–85.

Alcock, J. E. "Religion and Rationality." In J. F. Schumaker, ed., *Religion and Mental Health*. New York: Oxford University Press, 1992, pp. 122–31.

Allport, G. W. *Pattern and Growth in Personality*. New York: Holt, Rinehart & Winston, 1961.

Argyle, M., and Beit-Hallahmi, B. *The Social Psychology of Religion*. London: Routledge & Kegan Paul, 1975.

Baars, B. J. "Momentary Forgetting as a Resetting of a Conscious Global Workspace Due to Competition between Incompatible Contexts." In M. J. Horowitz, ed., *Psychodynamics and Cognition*. Chicago: University of Chicago Press, 1988.

Bainbridge, W. S., and Stark, R. "The Consciousness Reformation Reconsidered." *Journal for the Scientific Study of Religion* 20 (1981): 1–16.

———. "Friendship, Religion, and the Occult." *Review of Religious Research* 22 (1981): 313–27.

Banks, C. G. "Culture in Culture-Bound Syndromes: The Case of Anorexia Nervosa." *Social Science and Medicine* 34 (1992): 867–84.

Barnouw, V. *Culture and Personality*. Homewood, Ill.: Dorsey Press, 1985.

Beahrs, J. O. "Co-Consciousness: A Common Denominator in Hypnosis, Multiple Personality, and Normalcy." *American Journal of Clinical Hypnosis* 26 (1983): 100–13.

Becker, E. *The Denial of Death*. New York: Free Press, 1973.

———. *Escape from Evil*. New York: Free Press, 1975.

———. *The Revolution in Psychiatry*. London: Collier-Macmillan, 1964.

Bell, R. *Holy Anorexia*. Chicago: University of Chicago Press, 1985.

Bellah, R. N. "Toward a Definition of Unbelief." In R. Caporale and A. Grumelli, eds., *The Culture of Unbelief*. Berkeley and Los Angeles: The University of California Press, 1971, p. 155.

Belzen, J. A. "The Psychopathology of Religion: European Historical

Perspectives." In J. F. Schumaker, ed., *Religion and Mental Health*. New York: Oxford University Press, 1992, pp. 33–42.

Berger, P. L., and Luckman, T. *The Social Construction of Reality: A Treatise in the Sociology of Knowledge*. Middlesex, England: Penguin, 1966.

Bergman, A. "Religiosity and Mental Health: A Critical Reevaluation and Meta-Analysis." *Professional Psychology: Research and Practice* 14 (1983): 170–84.

Berman, D. "Religion and Neurosis." *Free Inquiry* (Summer 1993): 16.

Bernstein, E. M., and Putnam, F. "Development, Reliability and Validity of a Dissociation Scale." *Journal of Nervous and Mental Disease* 174 (1986): 727–35.

Beumont, P. J. V., and Abraham, S. F. "Episodes of Ravenous Overeating or Bulimia: Their Occurrence in Patients with Anorexia Nervosa and with other Forms of Disordered Eating." In P. L. Darby, P. E. Garfinkel, D. M. Garner, and D. V. Coscina, eds., *Anorexia Nervosa: Recent Developments in Research*. New York: Alan R. Liss, 1983, pp. 149–57.

Bliss, E. "Multiple Personalities, Related Disorders, and Hypnosis." *American Journal of Clinical Hypnosis* 26 (1983): 114–23.

Bongartz, B., and Bongartz, W. " 'Nyangkap Semengat' or How to Capture the Souls: Trance as Done by the Shamans of the Iban District in Northern Borneo." *Hypnos* 16 (1989): 108–11.

Bourguignon, E. "Introduction: A Framework for the Comparative Study of Altered States of Consciousness." In E. Bourguignon, ed., *Religion, Altered States of Consciousness and Social Change*. Columbus, Ohio: Ohio State University Press, 1973, pp. 3–35.

———. "Possession and Trance in Cross-Cultural Studies of Mental Health." In W. L. Lebra, ed., *Culture-Bound Syndromes*. Honolulu: University of Hawaii Press, 1976, pp. 47–55.

Bowers, K. S., and Meichenbaum, D. *The Unconscious Reconsidered*. New York: Wiley, 1984.

Bowman, E. S. "Understanding and Responding to Religious Material in the Therapy of Multiple Personality Disorder." *Dissociation* 2 (1989): 231–38.

Braid, J. *The Power of the Mind over the Body*. London: John Churchill, 1846.

Braun, B. G. "The BASK (Behavior, Affect, Sensation, Knowledge) Model of Dissociation." *Dissociation* 1 (1988): 16–23.

Bridges, R. A., and Spilka, B. "Religion and the Mental Health of Women." In J. F. Schumaker, ed., *Religion and Mental Health*. New York: Oxford University Press, 1992, pp. 43–53.

Brightman, R. "On Windigo Psychosis." *Current Anthropology* 24 (1983): 120–25.

Bruch, H. *The Golden Cage: The Enigma of Anorexia Nervosa*. Cambridge, Mass.: Harvard University Press, 1978.

Bryant, R. A., and McConkey, K. M. "Hypnotic Blindness and the Relevance of Attention." *Australian Journal of Psychology* 42 (1990): 287–96.

Buhrich, N. "Frequency of Presentation of Anorexia Nervosa in Malaysia." *Australian and New Zealand Journal of Psychiatry* 15 (1981): 153–55.

Campbell, J. *Myths to Live by.* London: Souvenir Press, 1973.

Cardeña, E. "Varieties of Possession Experience." *AASC Quarterly* 5 (1989): 1–17.

Cardeña, E., and Spiegel, D. "Suggestibility, Absorption, and Dissociation: An Integrative Model of Hypnosis." In J. F. Schumaker, ed., *Human Suggestibility: Advances in Theory, Research, and Application.* New York: Routledge, 1991, pp. 93–107.

Chamberlain, K., and Zika, S. "Religiosity, Meaning in Life, and Psychological Well-Being." In J. F. Schumaker, ed., *Religion and Mental Health.* New York: Oxford University Press, 1992, pp. 138–48.

Chapman, L. J., and Chapman, J. P. "The Genesis of Delusions." In T. F. Oltmanns and B. A. Maher, eds., *Delusional Beliefs.* New York: Wiley, 1988, p. 178.

Cox, H. *Feast of Fools: A Theological Essay on Festivity and Fantasy.* New York: Harper & Row, 1969.

Cushman, P. "Why the Self Is Empty: Toward a Historically Situated Psychology." *American Psychologist* 45 (1990): 599–611.

D'Aquili, E. "Human Ceremonial Ritual and the Modulation of Aggression." *Zygon* 20 (1985): 21–30.

Dewhurst, K., and Beard, A. W. "Sudden Religious Conversions in Temporal Lobe Epilepsy." *British Journal of Psychiatry* 117 (1970): 497–507.

Dobkin de Rios, M. *Hallucinogens: Cross-Cultural Perspectives.* Bridport, England: Prism Press, 1990.

Dolan, Y. *Resolving Sexual Abuse.* New York: W. W. Norton, 1991.

Draguns, J. "Personality and Culture." In P. Dasen, J. Berry, and N. Sartorius, ed., *Health and Cross-Cultural Psychology.* London: Sage, 1988, pp. 141–61.

Durant, J., and Bauer, M. "Who Believes in Astrology and Why?" *Skeptical Inquirer* 16 (1992): 344–47.

Durkheim, E. *The Elementary Forms of Religious Life.* London: Allen & Unwin, 1912/1971.

Eaton, W. W. *The Sociology of Mental Disorders.* New York: Praeger, 1986.

Edmonston, W. E. "Conceptual Clarification of Hypnosis and Its Relation to Suggestibility." In V. A. Gheorghiu, P. Netter, H. J. Eysenck, and R. Rosenthal, eds., *Suggestion and Suggestibility: Theory and Research.* Berlin: Springer-Verlag, 1989.

Ellis, A. "The Case against Religion: A Psychotherapist's View." In B. Ard, ed., *Counseling and Psychotherapy: Classics on Theory and Issues.* Palo Alto, Calif.: Science and Behavior Books, 1975, p. 440.

———. "Suggestibility, Irrational Beliefs, and Emotional Disturbance." In J. F. Schumaker, ed., *Human Suggestibility: Advances in Theory, Research, and Application.* New York: Routledge, pp. 309–25.

Ellis, A., and Dryden, W. *The Practice of Rational-Emotive Therapy.* New York: Springer, 1987.

Emmons, C. F., and Sobal, J. "Paranormal Beliefs: Functional Alternatives to Mainstream Religion?" *Review of Religious Research* 22 (1981): 301–12.

Erickson, E. H. "Ontogeny of Ritualization in Man." In R. M. Loewenstein et al., eds., *Psychoanalysis—A General Psychology. Essays in Honour of Heinz Hartman*. New York: International University Press, 1966.

Eysenck, H. J.; Arnold, W. J.; and Meili, R. *Encyclopedia of Psychology*. Vol. 2. Bungay, Suffolk, England: Fontana, 1975.

Faber, H. "The Meaning of Ritual in the Liturgy." In H. Heimbrock and H. B. Boudewijnse, eds., *Current Studies on Rituals: Perspectives for the Psychology of Religion*. Amsterdam: Rodopi, 1990, pp. 43–55.

Fagan, B. M. *The Aztecs*. New York: W. H. Freeman, 1984.

Fenigstein, A.; Scheier, M. F.; and Buss, A. H. "Public and Private Self-Consciousness: Assessment and Theory." *Journal of Consulting and Clinical Psychology* 43 (1975): 522–28.

Finn, S. E.; Hartman, M.; Leon, G. R.; and Larson, L. "Eating Disorders and Sexual Abuse: Lack of Confirmation for a Clinical Hypothesis." *International Journal of Eating Disorders* 5 (1986): 1051–59.

Foenander, G.; Burrows, G. D.; Gerschman, J.; and Horne, D. J. "Phobic Behavior and Hypnotic Susceptibility." *Australian Journal of Clinical and Experimental Hypnosis* 3 (1980): 41–46.

Frank, J. *Persuasion and Healing: A Comparative Study of Psychotherapy*. Baltimore and London: The Johns Hopkins University Press, 1973.

Frankel, F. H. *Hypnosis: Trance as a Coping Mechanism*. New York: Plenum Press, 1976.

———. "Hypnotizability and Dissociation." *American Journal of Psychiatry* 147 (1990): 823–29.

Frankel, F. H., and Orne, M. T. "Hypnotizability and Phobic Behavior." *Archives of General Psychiatry* 33 (1976): 1259–61.

Frétigny, R., and Virel, A. *L'Imagerie mentale*. Geneva: Éditions de Mont-Blanc, 1968.

Freud, S. *The Future of an Illusion*. New York: Anchor Books, 1927/1964.

———. "Obsessive Actions and Religious Practices." In vol. 9 of *The Standard Edition of the Complete Psychological Works of Sigmund Freud*, edited by J. Strachey. London: Hogarth Press, 1907/1953.

———. *The Problem of Anxiety*. New York: Norton, 1936.

Fromm, E. *The Anatomy of Human Destructiveness*. New York: Holt, Rinehart and Winston, 1973.

———. *Beyond the Chains of Illusion*. New York: Simon and Shuster, 1962.

———. *The Sane Society*. London: Routledge & Kegan Paul, 1955.

———. *To Have or To Be*. New York: Harper & Row, 1976.

Frumkin, L. R.; Ripley, H. S.; and Cox, G. B. "Cerebral Hemispheric Lateralization with Hypnosis." *Biological Psychiatry* 13 (1978): 741–50.

Ganaway, G. K. "Historical versus Narrative Truth: Clarifying the Role of Exogenous Trauma in the Etiology of MPD and Its Variants." *Dissociation* 2 (1989): 205–20.

Gazzaniga, M. *The Social Brain: Discovering the Networks of the Mind*. New York: Basic Books, 1985.

Geertz, C. *The Interpretations of Culture*. New York: Basic Books, 1973.

Geertz, H. "Latah in Java: A Theoretical Paradox." *Indonesia* 5 (1968): 93–104.

Gerschman, J.; Burrows, G. D.; Reade, P.; and Foenander, G. "Hypnotizability and the Treatment of Dental Phobic Illness." In G. D. Burrows, D. R. Collison, and L. Dennerstein, eds., *Hypnosis 1979*. Amsterdam: Elsevier/North Holland, 1979.

Gheorghiu, V., and Kruse, P. "The Psychology of Suggestion: An Integrative Approach." In J. F. Schumaker, ed., *Human Suggestibility: Advances in Theory, Research, and Application*. New York: Routledge, pp. 59–75.

Gibbons, F. X. "Social Comparison and Depression: Company's Effect on Misery." *Journal of Personality and Social Psychology* 51 (1986): 140–49.

Gibbons, F. X., and McCoy, S. B. "Self-Perception and Self-Deception: The Role of Attention in Suggestibility Processes." In J. F. Schumaker, ed., *Human Suggestibility: Advances in Theory, Research, and Application*. New York: Routledge, pp. 185–99.

Giddens, A. *Sociology*. Cambridge: Polity Press, 1989.

Glicksohn, J. "Belief in the Paranormal and Subjective Paranormal Experience." *Personality and Individual Differences* 11 (1990): 675–83.

Gordon, R. A. *Anorexia and Bulimia*. Oxford: Basil Blackwell, 1990.

Gould, S. J. "Advertising and Hypnotic Suggestion: The Concept of Advertising Suggestion." In J. F. Schumaker, ed., *Human Suggestibility: Advances in Theory, Research, and Application*. New York: Routledge, 1991, pp. 341–57.

Grimes, R. L. "Ritual." In vol. 11 of M. Eliade, ed., *The Encyclopedia of Religion*. New York: Macmillan, 1987, pp. 405–25.

Grob, C., and Dobkin de Rios, M. "Adolescent Drug Use in Cross-Cultural Perspective." *Journal of Drug Issues* 22 (1992): 121–38.

Groth-Marnat, G. "Hypnotizability, Suggestibility, and Psychopathology: An Overview of Research." In J. F. Schumaker, ed., *Human Suggestibility: Advances in Theory, Research, and Application*. New York: Routledge, pp. 219–34.

Haberman, M. A. "Spontaneous Trance as a Possible Cause for Persistent Symptoms in the Medically Ill." *American Journal of Clinical Hypnosis* 29 (1987): 171–76.

Haight, M. R. *A Study of Self-Deception*. Sussex: Harvester Press, 1980.

Hall, W. T. *Beyond Culture*. Garden City, N.J.: Anchor Press/Doubleday, 1976.

Hallaji, J. "Hypnotherapeutic Techniques in a Central Asian Community." In R. E. Shor and M. T. Orne, eds., *The Nature of Hypnosis*. New York: Holt, Rinehart & Winston, 1965, pp. 453–56.

Heise, D. "Delusions and the Construction of Reality." In T. F. Oltmanns and B. A. Maher, eds., *Delusional Beliefs*. New York: Wiley & Sons, 1988, pp. 259–72.

Henry, J. *Culture Against Man*. New York: Vintage Books, 1965.

Herskovits, M. J. *The Myth of the Negro Past*. New York: Alfred Knopf, 1941.

Higgins, E. T., and Moretti, M. M. "Standard Utilization and the Social-Evaluative Process: Vulnerability to Types of Aberrant Beliefs." In T. F. Oltmanns and B. A. Maher, ed., *Delusional Beliefs*. New York: Wiley, 1988, p. 112.

Hilgard, E. R. *Divided Consciousness: Multiple Controls in Human Thought and Action.* New York: Wiley, 1977/1986.

——. *Hypnotic Susceptibility.* New York: Harcourt, Brace & World, 1965.

——. "Neodissociation Theory of Multiple Cognitive Control Systems." In G. E. Schwartz and D. Shapiro, eds., *Consciousness and Self-Regulation.* New York: Plenum Press, 1976, pp. 137–71.

——. "Suggestibility and Suggestions as Related to Hypnosis." In J. F. Schumaker, ed., *Human Suggestibility: Advances in Theory, Research, and Application.* New York: Routledge, 1991, pp. 37–58.

——. "Toward a Neodissociation Theory: Multiple Cognitive Controls in Human Functioning." *Perspectives in Biology and Medicine* 12 (1974): 301–16.

Hinsie, L. E., and Campbell, R. J. *Psychiatric Dictionary.* New York: Oxford University Press, 1970.

Hultkrantz, A. "Ecological and Phenomenological Aspects of Shamanism." In V. Dioszegi and M. Hoppal, eds., *Shamanism in Siberia.* Budapest: Akademiai Kiado, 1978, pp. 27–58.

Jacobs, J. "The Effects of Ritual Healing on Female Victims of Abuse: A Study of Empowerment and Transformation." *Sociological Analysis* 50 (1989): 265–79.

——. "Religious Ritual and Mental Health." In J. F. Schumaker, ed., *Religion and Mental Health.* New York and Oxford: Oxford University Press, 1992, pp. 291–99.

Jahoda, M. *Current Concepts of Positive Mental Health.* New York: Basic Books, 1958.

James, W. *The Varieties of Religious Experience.* London: Longmans, 1902/1952.

Janet, P. *L'Automatisme psychologique.* Paris: Felix Alcan, 1889.

——. *The Major Symptoms of Hysteria.* New York: Macmillan, 1907.

——. *Psychological Healing.* New York: Macmillan, 1925.

——. *Les Stades de l'évolution psychologique.* Paris: Chaline-Maloine, 1926.

Janssen, J.; de Hart, J.; and den Draak, C. "Praying as an Individualized Ritual." In H. Heimbrock and H. B. Boudewijnse, eds., *Current Studies on Ritual.* Amsterdam: Radopi, 1990, pp. 71–85.

Jilek, W. G. "Brainwashing as a Therapeutic Technique in Contemporary Canadian Indian Spirit Dancing: A Case of Theory Building." In J. Westermeyer, ed., *Anthropology and Mental Health.* The Hague, Netherlands: Mouton Publishers, 1976.

John, R.; Hollander, B.; and Perry, C. "Hypnotizability and Phobic Behavior: Further Supporting Data." *Journal of Abnormal Psychology* 92 (1983): 390–92.

Jordan, D. K., and Swartz, M. J., eds. *Personality and the Cultural Construction of Society.* Tuscaloosa and London: The University of Alabama Press, 1990.

Kaffman, M. "Inflexible Belief-Constructs in Families of Paranoid Patients." *International Journal of Family Psychiatry* 3 (1983): 487–500.

——. "Suggestion and Monoideistic Disorders: Anorexia Nervosa as a Paradigm." In J. F. Schumaker, ed., *Human Suggestibility: Advances in Theory, Research, and Application.* New York and London: Routledge, 1991, pp. 289–308.

Kierkegaard, S. *Sickness unto Death.* New York: Anchor Edition, 1849/1954.

Kihlstrom, J. F. "Hypnosis and the Dissociation of Memory, with Special Reference to Posthypnotic Amnesia." *Research Communications in Psychology, Psychiatry, and Behavior* 7 (1982): 181–97.

Kihlstrom, J. F., and Hoyt, I. P. "Hypnosis and the Psychology of Delusions." In T. F. Oltmanns and B. A. Maher, eds., *Delusional Beliefs.* New York: Wiley, 1988, p. 81.

Koenig, H. G. "Religion and Mental Health in Later Life." In J. F. Schumaker, ed., *Religion and Mental Health.* New York: Oxford University Press, 1992, pp. 177–88.

Kravis, N. M. "James Braid's Psychophysiology: A Turning in the History of Dynamic Psychiatry." *American Journal of Psychiatry* 145 (1988): 1191–1206.

Kurtz, P. *The New Skepticism.* Amherst, N.Y.: Prometheus Books, 1992.

———. *The Transcendental Temptation.* Amherst, N.Y.: Prometheus Books, 1986.

Larson, D.; Pattison, M.; Blazer, D.; Omran, A.; and Kaplan, B. "Systematic Analysis of Research on Religious Variables in Four Major Psychiatric Journals, 1978–1982." *American Journal of Psychiatry* 143 (1986): 329–34.

Lindholm, C. "Charisma, Crowd Psychology and Altered States of Consciousness." *Culture, Medicine, and Psychiatry* 16 (1992): 287–310.

Long, T. E. "Some Early-Life Stimulus Correlates of Hypnotizability." *International Journal of Clinical and Experimental Hypnosis* 16 (1968): 61–67.

Lorenz, K. *On Aggression.* New York: Bantam Books, 1966.

———. *The Waning of Humaneness.* Boston: Little, Brown & Co., 1987.

Ludwig, A. M. "Altered States of Consciousness." In C. Tart, ed., *Altered States of Consciousness.* New York: Wiley, 1969, pp. 22–37.

———. "Hysteria: A Neurobiological Theory." *Archives of General Psychiatry* 27 (1972): 771–78.

———. "The Psychobiological Functions of Dissociation." *American Journal of Clinical Hypnosis* 26 (1983): 93–99.

Lumsden, C. J., and Wilson, E. O. *Genes, Mind, and Behavior: The Coevolutionary Process.* Cambridge, Mass.: Harvard University Press, 1981.

McDougall, W. *An Introduction to Social Psychology.* London: Methuen, 1908.

Mandell, A. J. "The Psychobiology of Transcendence." In J. M. Davidson and R. J. Davidson, eds., *The Psychobiology of Consciousness.* New York: Plenum, 1980, pp. 379–463.

Marsella, A. J., and Dash-Scheuer, A. "Coping, Culture, and Healthy Human Development." In P. Dasen, J. Berry, and N. Sartorius, eds., *Health and Cross-Cultural Psychology.* London: Sage, 1988, pp. 162–78.

Martínez-Taboas, A. "Multiple Personality Disorder as Seen from a Social Constructionist Viewpoint." *Dissociation* 4 (1991): 129–33.

Masters, K. S. "Hypnotic Susceptibility, Cognitive Dissociation, and Runner's High in a Sample of Marathon Runners." *American Journal of Clinical Hypnosis* 34 (1992): 193–201.

Maturana, H. R. "Reality: The Search for Objectivity or the Quest for a Compelling Argument." *The Irish Journal of Psychology* 9 (1988): 25–82.

Maxwell, M. *Human Evolution: A Philosophical Anthropology.* New York: Columbia University Press, 1984.

Moore, R. L. "Contemporary Psychotherapy as Ritual Process: An Initial Reconnaissance." *Zygon: Journal of Religion and Science* 18 (1983): 283–94.

Myerhoff, B. G. "We Don't Wrap Herring in a Printed Page: Fusion, Fictions and Continuity in Secular Ritual." In S. F. Moore and B. G. Myerhoff, eds., *Secular Ritual.* Amsterdam: Van Gorcum, 1977, pp. 199–224.

Naroll, R. "Cultural Determinants and the Concept of the Sick Society." In S. C. Plog and R. B. Edgerton, eds., *Changing Perspectives in Mental Illness.* New York: Holt, Rinehart & Winston, 1969, pp. 128–55.

———. *The Moral Order.* London: Sage, 1983.

Neher, A. "A Physiological Explanation of Unusual Behavior in Ceremonies Involving Drums." *Human Biology* 4 (1962): 151–60.

Obeyesekere, G. "Culturally Constituted Defenses and the Theory of Collective Motivation." In D. K. Jordan and M. J. Swartz, eds., *Personality and the Cultural Construction of Society.* Tuscaloosa and London: The University of Alabama Press, 1990, pp. 80–97.

Ouwehand, E. "Women's Rituals: Reflections on Developmental Theory." In H. Heimbrock and H. B. Boudewijnse, eds., *Current Studies on Rituals: Perspectives for the Psychology of Religion.* Amsterdam: Rodopi, 1990, pp. 136–50.

Paley, A. M. "Growing up in Chaos: The Dissociative Response." *American Journal of Psychoanalysis* 48 (1988): 72–83.

Pettinati, H. M.; Horne, R. L.; and Staats, J. M. "Hypnotizability in Patients with Anorexia Nervosa and Bulimia." *Archives of General Psychiatry* 42 (1985): 1014–16.

Phillips, D. P. "Suicide, Motor Vehicle Fatalities, and the Mass Media: Evidence toward a Theory of Suggestion." *American Journal of Sociology* 84 (1979): 1150–74.

Pressman, P.; Lyons, J. S.; Larson, D. B.; and Gartner, J. "Religion, Anxiety, and Fear of Death." In J. F. Schumaker, ed., *Religion and Mental Health.* New York: Oxford University Press, 1992, pp. 98–109.

Prince, R. H. "Can the EEG Be Used in the Study of Possession States?" In R. Prince, ed., *Trance and Possession States.* Montreal: R. M. Bucke Memorial Society, 1968, pp. 121–37.

———. "The Concept of Culture-Bound Syndromes: Anorexia Nervosa and Brain Fag." *Social Science and Medicine* 21 (1985): 197–203.

———. "Religious Experience and Psychopathology: Cross-Cultural Perspectives." In J. F. Schumaker, ed., *Religion and Mental Health.* New York: Oxford University Press, 1992, pp. 281–90.

Propst, L. R. "The Comparative Efficacy of Religious and Nonreligious Imagery for the Treatment of Mild Depression Individuals." *Cognitive Therapy and Research* 4 (1980): 167–78.

Propst, L. R.; Ostrom, R.; Watkins, P.; Dean, T.; and Mashburn, D. "Comparative Efficiency of Religious and Nonreligious Cognitive-Behavioral Therapy for the Treatment of Clinical Depression in Religious Individuals." *Journal of Consulting and Clinical Psychology* 60 (1992): 94–103.

Putnam, F. W.; Guroff, J. J.; and Silberman, E. K. "The Clinical Phenomenology of Multiple Personality Disorder: 100 Recent Cases." *Journal of Clinical Psychiatry* 47 (1986): 285–89.

Raglan, L. *The Origins of Religion*. London: Watts & Co., 1949.

Reich, K. H. "Rituals and Social Structure: The Moral Dimension." In H. Heimbrock and H. B. Boudewijnse, eds., *Current Studies on Ritual*. Amsterdam: Rodopi, 1990, pp. 121–34.

Reiff, P. *The Triumph of the Therapeutic: Uses of Faith after Freud*. New York: Harper & Row, 1966.

Richards, D. G. "A Study of the Correlations between Subject Psychic Experiences and Dissociative Experiences." *Dissociation* 4 (1991): 83–91.

Rhue, J. W., and Lynn, S. J. "Fantasy Proneness, Hypnotizability, and Multiple Personality." In J. F. Schumaker, ed., *Human Suggestibility: Advances in Theory, Research, and Application*. New York: Routledge, 1991, pp. 200–18.

Ross, C. A. "Comments on Garcia's 'The Concept of Dissociation and Conversion in the New ICD–10.' " *Dissociation* 3 (1990): 211–13.

———. *Multiple Personality Disorder: Diagnosis, Clinical Features, and Treatment*. New York: Wiley, 1989.

Rossi, E. L. "Altered States of Consciousness in Everyday Life." In B. Wolman and M. Ullman, eds., *Handbook of States of Consciousness*. New York: Bantam Books, 1986, p. 97.

———. "The Psychobiology of Dissociation and Identification." *Canadian Psychology* 28 (1987): 112–13.

Roszak, T. *Unfinished Animal*. London: Faber & Faber, 1975.

Roth, D. L., and Ingram, R. E. "Factors in the Self-Deception Questionnaire: Associations with Depression." *Journal of Personality and Social Psychology* 48 (1985): 243–51.

Rouget, G. *Music and Trance: A Theory of the Relations between Music and Possession*. Chicago: The University of Chicago Press, 1985.

Sackeim, H. A. "Self-Deception, Self-Esteem, and Depression." In J. Masling, ed., *Empirical Studies of Psychoanalytic Theories*. Hillsdale, N.J.: Lawrence Erlbaum, 1983, p. 134.

Sackeim, H. A., and Gur, R. C. "Self-Deception, Other-Deception, and Self-Reported Psychopathology. *Journal of Consulting and Clinical Psychology* 47 (1979): 213–15.

Sanders, S. "The Perceptual Alteration Scale: A Scale Measuring Dissociation." *American Journal of Clinical Hypnosis* 29 (1986): 95–102.

Sartre, J. P. *Being and Nothingness*. New York: Washington Square Press, 1953.

Scheff, T. J. *Catharsis in Healing, Ritual, and Drama*. Berkeley and Los Angeles: University of California Press, 1979.

Schumaker, J. F. "The Mental Health Consequences of Irreligion." In J. F. Schumaker, ed., *Religion and Mental Health*. New York: Oxford University Press, 1992, pp. 54–69.

———. *Wings of Illusion: The Origin, Nature, and Future of Paranormal Belief*. Cambridge, England: Polity Press (also, Amherst, N.Y.: Prometheus Books), 1990.

Schumaker, J. F., ed. *Human Suggestibility: Advances in Theory, Research, and Application.* New York: Routledge, 1991.

———, ed. *Religion and Mental Health.* New York: Oxford University Press, 1992.

Schwab, J. J., and Schwab, M. E. *Sociological Roots of Mental Illness.* New York and London: Plenum, 1978.

Schwartz, G. "Consciousness and the Brain Self-Regulation Paradox." In J. M. Davidson and R. J. Davidson, eds., *The Psychobiology of Consciousness.* New York: Plenum Press, 1980.

Shafranske, E. P. "Religion and Mental Health in Early Life." In J. F. Schumaker, ed., *Religion and Mental Health.* New York: Oxford University Press, 1992, pp. 163–76.

Shames, M. L. "Hypnotic Susceptibility and Conformity: On the Mediational Mechanism of Suggestibility." *Psychological Reports* 49 (1981): 563–66.

Shea, J. D. "Suggestion, Placebo, and Expectation: Immune Effects and Other Bodily Change." In J. F. Schumaker, ed., *Human Suggestibility: Advances in Theory, Research, and Application.* New York: Routledge, pp. 253–76.

Shor, R. E. "Hypnosis and the Concept of the Generalized Reality-Orientation." *American Journal of Psychotherapy* 13 (1959): 582–602.

———. "Hypnosis and the Concept of the Generalized Reality-Orientation." In R. E. Shor and M. T. Orne, eds., *The Nature of Hypnosis.* New York: Holt, Rinehart & Winston, 1965.

Sidis, B. *The Psychology of Suggestion.* New York: D. Appleton & Co., 1898.

Simon, H. "A Mechanism for Social Selection and Successful Altruism." *Science* 250 (1990): 1665–68.

Skinner, B. F. *Walden Two.* New York: Macmillan, 1962.

Spiegel, D. "Dissociation, Double Binds, and Posttraumatic Stress in Multiple Personality Disorder." In B. G. Braun, ed., *Treatment of Multiple Personality Disorder.* Washington, D.C.: American Psychiatric Press, 1986, pp. 65–66.

Spiegel, D.; Hunt, T.; and Dondershine, M. D. "Dissociation and Hypnotizability in Posttraumatic Stress Disorder." *American Journal of Psychiatry* 145 (1988): 301–5.

Stark, R. "Church and Sect." In P. E. Hammond, ed., *The Sacred in a Secular Age.* Berkeley and Los Angeles: University of California Press, 1985, pp. 134–49.

Strauss, J. "Hallucinations and Delusions as Points on Continua Function." *Archives of General Psychiatry* 21 (1969): 581–86.

Tart, C. T. "A Systems Approach to Altered States of Consciousness." In J. M. Davidson and R. J. Davidson, eds., *The Psychobiology of Consciousness.* New York: Plenum Press, 1980, pp. 258–60.

Taylor, S. *Positive Illusions: Creative Self-Deception and the Healthy Mind.* New York: Basic Books, 1989.

Tellegen, A., and Atkinson, G. "Openness to Absorbing and Self-Altering Experiences, A Trait Related to Hypnotic Susceptibility." *Journal of Abnormal Psychology* 83 (1974): 268–77.

Temoshok, L., and Attkisson, C. C. "Epidemiology of Hysterical Phenomena:

Evidence for a Psychosocial Theory." In M. J. Horowitz, ed., *Hysterical Personality*. New York: Jason Aronson, 1977.

Turner, J. *Without God, without Creed: The Origins of Unbelief in America*. Baltimore: The Johns Hopkins University Press, 1985.

Turner, V. W. "Liminal to Limnoid, in Play, Flow, and Ritual." *Rice University Studies* 60 (1974): 53–92.

———. "Myth and Symbol." In vol. 10 of *International Encyclopedia of the Social Sciences* (1968), pp. 567–82.

Van der Kolk, B. A., and van der Hart, O. "Pierre Janet and the Breakdown of Adaptation in Psychological Trauma." *American Journal of Psychiatry* 146 (1989): 1530–40.

Vanderlinden, J.; Vandereycken, W.; van Dyck, R.; and Delacroix, O. "Hypnotizability and Dissociation in a Group of Fifty Eating Disorder Patients." In W. Bongartz, ed., *Hypnosis: 175 Years after Mesmer*. Konstanz: Universitäts Verlag, 1992, pp. 291–94.

Vandermeersch, P. "Psychotherapeutic and Religious Rituals: The Issue of Secularization." In H. Heimbrock and H. B. Boudewijnse, eds., *Current Studies on Rituals: Perspectives for the Psychology of Religion*. Amsterdam: Rodopi, 1990, pp. 151–64.

Vespers, J. H. "The Use of Healing Ceremonies in the Treatment of Multiple Personality Disorder." *Dissociation* 4 (1991): 109–14.

Wagstaff, G. F. "Suggestibility: A Social Psychological Approach. In J. F. Schumaker, ed., *Human Suggestibility: Advances in Theory, Research, and Application*. New York: Routledge, pp. 132–45.

Wallace, A. F. C. *Religion: An Anthropological View*. New York: Random House, 1966.

Ward, C. "Thaipusam in Malaysia: A Psycho-Anthropological Analysis of Ritual Trance, Ceremonial Possession and Self-Mortification Practices." *Ethos* 12 (1984): 307–34.

Ward, C., and Kemp, S. "Religious Experiences, Altered States of Consciousness, and Suggestibility." In J. F. Schumaker, ed., *Human Suggestibility: Advances in Theory, Research, and Application*. New York: Routledge, 1991, pp. 159–82.

Wedenoja, W. "Ritual Trance and Catharsis." In D. K. Jordan and M. J. Swartz, eds., *Personality and the Cultural Construction of Society*. Tuscaloosa and London: The University of Alabama Press, 1990, pp. 275–307.

West, L. J. "Dissociative Reactions." In A. M. Freedman and H. I. Kaplan, eds., *Comprehensive Textbook of Psychiatry*. Baltimore: William and Wilkins, 1967, p. 890.

Westermeyer, J. "Some Cross-Cultural Aspects of Delusions." In T. F. Oltmanns and B. A. Maher, eds., *Delusional Beliefs*. New York: Wiley, 1988, pp. 212–29.

Whyte, L. L. *The Unconscious before Freud*. New York: Basic Books, 1960.

Wijeyewardene, G. *Place and Emotion in Northern Thai Ritual Behavior*. Bangkok: Pandora, 1986.

Wilbur, C., and Colligan, R. "Psychologic and Behavioral Correlates of

Anorexia Nervosa." *Journal of Developmental and Behavioral Pediatrics* 2 (1981): 89–92.

Williams, G. W. "Highway Hypnosis: A Hypothesis." In R. E. Shor and M. T. Orne, eds., *The Nature of Hypnosis*. New York: Holt, Rinehart & Winston, 1965, pp. 482–90.

Wilson, E. O. *On Human Nature*. Cambridge, Mass.: Harvard University Press, 1978.

Wolin, S. J., and Bennett, L. A. "Family Rituals." *Family Process* 23 (1984): 401–20.

Yates, A. "Current Perspectives on Eating Disorders: History, Psychological and Biological Aspects." *Journal of the American Academy of Child and Adolescent Psychiatry* 28 (1989): 813–28.

Zoja, L. *Drugs, Addiction and Initiation: The Modern Search for Ritual*. Boston: Sigo Press, 1989.

Zollschan, G.; Schumaker, J. F.; and Walsh, G. *Exploring the Paranormal: Perspectives on Belief and Experience*. Bridport, England: Prism Press, 1990.

Index